Still Whispering
After All These Years

Still Whispering
After All These Years

My Autobiography

Bob Harris

Foreword by Robert Plant

Michael O'Mara Books Limited

For Trudie

And with heartfelt thanks and love to my family and friends, who have
made the events in this book so special

First published under the title *The Whispering Years* in 2001
This fully revised and updated edition first published in Great Britain in 2015 by
Michael O'Mara Books Limited
9 Lion Yard
Tremadoc Road
London SW4 7NQ

A CIP catalogue record for this book is available from the British Library.

Papers used by Michael O'Mara Books Limited are natural, recyclable products
made from wood grown in sustainable forests. The manufacturing processes
conform to the environmental regulations of the country of origin.

ISBN: 978-1-78243-360-6 in hardback print format
ISBN: 978-1-78243-361-3 in e-book format

1 2 3 4 5 6 7 8 9 10

www.mombooks.com

Cover design by Patrick Knowles

Designed and typeset by Design 23

Printed and bound by CPI Group (UK) Ltd, Croydon, CR0 4YY

Contents

Foreword to the 2015 Edition

THE ROCK'N'ROLL DOCTOR OF SEVENTIES MUSIC TV MOVES THROUGH the years with style and grace. His own excitement and love of music and his infectious enthusiasm to bring his audience the rhyme, reason and sounds of a new world is a work of heart.

He champions the unknown, the obscure and the legendary with equal zest and detail. He has stayed the distance – the good times and the others – with character and resilience, always digging deep and deeper.

ROBERT PLANT

Introduction

FOR AS LONG AS I CAN REMEMBER I'VE ALWAYS LOVED MUSIC, A passion that has largely defined my life. I'm extremely fortunate to be able to express that passion through my work. I've visited many of the major music centres in Europe and America, seen some of the great concerts and spent time with some of the biggest stars in the world. I've interviewed John Lennon in New York, Led Zeppelin and Bruce Springsteen in Los Angeles, The Rolling Stones in Munich, the Bee Gees in Miami, the top country stars in Nashville and found myself in situations most could only dream of. I've toured with T. Rex, David Bowie and Queen, compered at most of the major festivals. I've met royalty and an American president, produced records and presented on television and radio in what has sometimes seemed to be a cavalcade of once-in-a-lifetime experiences. But it hasn't all been good. My personal life has been through crisis, I've been so ill I nearly died. I've been threatened and derided. I've had to completely rebuild my career no less than four times. I've been a bankrupt. The following pages are the story of it all, beginning at a time when optimism was still a national characteristic.

ONE

A Passion for Music and Radio

HAVING BEEN ENCOURAGED TO MOVE TO THE SMOKE BY JON BIRD, a boyhood friend, I have to say, 1966 was a fantastic time to arrive in London. Jon and I met when my parents and I moved into the house next door to the Bird family when I was about 11 years old. Like our previous home, No. 63 Greenfield Road in Northampton was a police house. My Dad was in the local force, retiring in 1967 as an acting detective chief inspector, having spent most of his career in the CID. I'm an only child, so it was a great feeling to discover this terrific kid at No. 61.

Jon was a year older than me and was already a talented artist and sculptor. I remember a painting he did in the third year at school of horses pulling a plough across a field and away into the sunset, a typical country scene and the subject matter of many pictures before and since. But this painting was really memorable, particularly the use of colour. Jon was not afraid to take risks, and the gold, brown, burnt orange hue he'd created was particularly striking. He had a tremendous talent and soon qualified for the Central School of Art in Holborn, taking up his place there in 1965.

My own scholastic career ended rather less impressively. In the summer holiday between sixth form and my final year at Trinity High School, I was spotted by one of my teachers drinking a half of lemonade shandy at the bar of a local pub. The pub was on the outskirts of Northampton at Weston Favell, where I used to cycle to hang out with some local friends and go swimming in the lock near the mill house. I returned to school in September to find myself on report and summoned to the headmaster's office, where I found him red-faced in anger and brandishing his cane.

'Bend over, Harris,' is all he said. With all efforts at explanation summarily dismissed and in the knowledge that were this to happen I would be the first sixth-former in the school's history to get the cane, a sense of personal dignity and righteous indignation dictated my response. I turned tail, walked out of his office, cycled home, packed my saddle-bags with all the school books I could find, went back, dumped them on his desk and left. I hadn't enjoyed school anyway, except when I was on the sports field. I walked away from my education with two O levels, Art and English.

'Brilliant,' said Dad, who was waiting for me when I arrived home. 'What are you going to do now?' My father had been brought up in the depression-hit south Wales mining community of Pontardawe in the 20s and 30s, when a good education meant escape to university and a decent job, away from the pit closures and poverty of the valley. The punishing hours of a detective's life seemed a reasonable trade-in to a man schooled in the philosophy of hard work.

We spent many summers visiting relatives there when I was a child, although I always felt slightly claustrophobic, hemmed in by those tall, purple mountains. But the people were fantastic, a closely knit and truly supportive community. I spent a lot of time with Mair Jones, the girl who lived next door to my Mumgu and Dadcu in Edward Street, and with my cousin, Mary Hopkin, who lived higher up the valley in Altwen. Dad already knew how much I wanted to be on the radio, but a career in broadcasting seems a million miles away when you're 17, living in an East Midlands boot and shoe town, haven't got a job and have just walked out of school. Dad and I did a deal. He was very keen for me to follow in his footsteps. 'Have a go at it, Rob,' he said. 'Join the Police Cadets, have a look and see if you like the life. When you're 19, make the decision. If you're still determined to get into the music business and honestly decide you don't want to take up a police career, I'll back you one hundred per cent, but on one condition. You must give it everything for the next 18 months.' We shook on it. I joined the Northampton County Police Cadets, stationed at Wellingborough. And it wasn't too bad, particularly on the sports side.

I'd played in my school first XV at centre three-quarter, wearing the No. 13 shirt and modelling my game on that of Mike Weston, an England International of the time who, along with the great Richard

Sharp, was a massive hero. Rugby was a major part of my life in the Cadets and I was given a lot of time off for games, training and trials. In the winter it seemed as if I was spending more time on the rugby pitch than at the old-fashioned plugs and wires switchboard I was detailed to answer, which was fine by me. (My other major duty was making endless pots of tea for station officer PC Gray.) I even reached Midland Counties level, playing under floodlights in Stratford-on-Avon in front of six and a half thousand people, one of the few times in my life I've been genuinely nervous.

I completed my Duke of Edinburgh Award with an outward bound course in Eskdale, Cumberland (now Cumbria). Part of the course was an expedition that took us to the top of Scafell Pike, the highest mountain in England, which, to be honest, was a huge anti-climax. It's just a flat bit of shale with a plaque. We were shrouded in cloud, so I can't comment on the view. I just remember this ruddy New Zealander appearing out of the mist, wearing shorts and a short-sleeved shirt, sickeningly hearty while we stood shivering.

The other good thing about the Cadets was getting out in the cars on motor patrol, the big treat! The worst part was the monthly drill training and the fact that I had to keep my hair short to avoid the sergeant major screaming in my ear. But I can honestly say that I had a good time. I bought a Citroen Light 15, complete with running boards and three-speed dashboard gear change, from a bobby at the Wellingborough nick and have always been proud that it was my first car.

But I knew the life was not for me and although Dad was disappointed he was as good as his word and has backed me fully ever since. Bizarrely, his police work and the music industry had already overlapped. It was Dad who arrested P.J. Proby onstage at the Northampton ABC, during Proby's notorious trouser-splitting tour in 1965!

Proby was a Texan, brought to England by producer Jack Good in 1964 for a Beatles television special. A man of manic energy, Good's contribution to the development of British rock'n'roll was immense. He'd joined the BBC from Oxford University in 1956 as a trainee and, intrigued by rock'n'roll and the media's fear of it, devised *Six-Five Special,* the first British television pop music show. Having got the show on air by hoodwinking the Corporation into thinking it was to be a magazine show for young people, he moved across to ITV and unleashed the hysteria of *Oh Boy!* onto our screens in 1958. Recorded in front of a theatre audience of hundreds of screaming girls, the show helped launch the careers of Cliff Richard, Marty Wilde, Billy Fury, Adam Faith and a host of other UK Elvis-inspired lip curlers. The show was raw and fabulously exciting, showcasing some of the authentic American rock'n'rollers, among them Gene Vincent, who appeared clad in his customary black leather and wearing the leg iron that was a legacy from a teenage motorcycle accident. Good was the definitive opportunist and, as Vincent approached the microphone at the front of the stage and came into camera range, his Oxford accent could be heard clearly above the screaming girls, as he shouted his instructions to the afflicted singer. 'Limp, you bugger,' he implored. 'Limp!'

Following his appearance on *The Beatles Special,* P.J. Proby's career took off. Within a year he'd had five Top-20 hits and in early 1965 set off on a package tour of ABC theatres, with Cilla Black topping the bill. I found it hard to see his appeal. He had the voice of a pub singer, face contorted with sincerity as he wheeled out excruciatingly overblown versions of already melodramatic ballads, 'Somewhere' ('Thar's a per-lace foor wusss/some-a-where a per-lace foor wusss') and 'Maria' from *West Side Story.* But he had an image – ponytail and breeches. The problem was that the breeches kept splitting in the middle of his pelvis-swaying set and he didn't believe in wearing underwear. The first night he got a warning to cool it down or face being thrown off the tour. The second night he got massive press as public outrage, Eminem-style, was ignited. There were young children in the audience! The third night was the ABC Northampton and as Dad made his way across the stage, the curtains closed on the Proby career. Off the tour, he was a bankrupt three years later. Dad also arrested my future wife.

Sue Tilson was really cool. Everyone I knew seemed to know her name. She was three years older than me, had beautiful long, auburn hair, pale white skin and always dressed in a black rollneck sweater and jeans. She was a Beatnik and hung out with a whole crowd of arty, seemingly interesting people, some of whom were gay, all of whom dressed more or less the same as she did. They were mostly into John Coltrane and the Modern Jazz Quartet and read the Beat Poets, Jack Kerouac or J.D. Salinger's *Catcher In The Rye.* We met at a party, me stepping in when she was being hassled by some bloke she didn't want to know. She invited me to meet her and her friends at the Sunnyland Jazz Club, held weekly at one of the pubs near where she lived. She was a fantastic dancer and a wonderful person and I was drawn to her. She cared about people and talked passionately about her work with mentally handicapped children. She was politically aware and liked to discuss the issues of the day, most of which were beyond me. To start with, I was probably something of an embarrassment for her, this rather lovelorn police cadet hanging around in full view of all her cool friends. It took a bit of time to win her confidence, but we gradually began to see more of one another until finally I invited her home.

Like many of her friends, Sue had joined the Campaign for Nuclear Disarmament and had taken part in a major demonstration that had closed Mercer's Row and brought chaos to the centre of Northampton. 1963 was the time of the Aldermaston marches, and protests on both sides of the Atlantic about the Cold War America/Russia stand-off over Cuba. For a while we really did feel that there was a finger poised above that red button. Although it was all happening on what seemed like the other side of the world, we felt the implications and were aware of the potential consequences of the nuclear muscle-flexing that was part of the early-60s East/West political relationship. We were scared of it all and Sue had been one of the people sitting in the middle of Abingdon Street with the protesters, refusing to move even when Dad and other members of the Force arrested her and several of her friends. Blissfully unaware of all of this, I took her home to meet my parents. It was a very cold and difficult atmosphere when she and Dad finally stood face to face in the front room of our house! Still, despite everyone's initial reservations, she and my parents began to forge a friendship and affection that survived throughout the years. Sue and I got married in the summer of 1967.

Jon Bird had been regularly in touch, telling me how fantastic life was in London, that I must get up to town and visit him at his flat in Hampstead. 'The house is great, you'll absolutely love it,' he told me. And he was right.

Built in 1846, the building sits at an angle to the main road, taking up the entire corner of Rosslyn Hill and Hampstead Hill Gardens, which curves around and down at the back of the house. It was constructed across different levels, three stories at the front, four stories at the back, with a basement extension curving round into the small side garden. Inside, it seemed like a labyrinth, with little staircases and corridors linking the various sections of the house. The interior design was random, with lots of rooms of different sizes, some at opposite angles to one another, with big sash windows and loads of nooks and crannies.

The house was run by Hetta Empson, wife of author William Empson, famous for *Seven Types Of Ambiguity*, regarded as an important literary reference work at the time. I only met him once. He was a lecturer at Sheffield University and was away most of the time. Hetta lived on the ground floor and rented the rest of the house, a room here, a flat there, to students. The place always seemed to be packed with people, mostly from the London School of Economics (famously militant at the time). Jon shared a flat with a photography student called Roger Perry and the whole house had a vibrantly creative feeling. The atmosphere struck me as being totally amazing. I was desperate to move to London anyway and began regular visits to plug into the feeling.

Eventually one of the students vacated a small room on the first floor, just about big enough for a bed, a chair and my record player. I painted the walls purple, put up a couple of posters and moved in. It was £4 a week. I had no money at all, no real plans and certainly no prospects. But suddenly I was in London. I couldn't have felt more excited.

Recently I went to see the house again. I was looking up at the window of my old room when a woman strode purposefully across Hampstead Hill Gardens towards us, two teenage boys trailing behind. 'Why are you looking at that house?' she demanded.

'I lived there in the late 60s,' I explained. Her expression softened.

'Did you know Hetta?' she asked me.

'Yes, she was very kind,' I ventured, adding she would let me off the rent if I didn't have the money in return for doing a bit of cleaning in the hall and the stairwells.

'Hetta wouldn't like it here now,' she told me. 'The house has changed completely. It's all been renovated and split up into modern flats, something she never wanted to happen.' She went on to tell me more of the recent history, before introducing the two boys. 'These are Hetta's nephews,' she said. I asked her why they were there.

'Like you,' she said, 'we've just come to have a look.' It was a strange coincidence.

The memories came flooding back. Hampstead village was just a short walk up the hill and was so pretty to look at, with its narrow, cobbled streets and flower baskets. The residents looked colourful and interesting; the High Street buzzed with life. The wide open spaces of Hampstead Heath and Parliament Hill Fields were on the doorstep, the latter via South End Green, with its grocery shops, patisseries and pavement cafes, the former overlooked by Jack Straw's Castle, at the time one of the best pubs in London. There were galleries and bookshops selling the latest editions of new-generation publications like* *International Times* and *Oz*. And there was the Everyman cinema.

I didn't see it immediately as it was tucked back, just behind the main crossroads at the top of the High Street, but eventually I noticed the glass-fronted cabinet on the outside wall of the cinema, full of stills of the featured programme, a film by François Truffaut. I'd never heard of him before, but the pictures looked great and I wandered in – to be spellbound by *Jules et Jim* starring Jeanne Moreau. I'd never seen anything like it before, the story of a *ménage-à-trois*, and was fascinated by the style and gentle pace of the film. I wanted more of this, and with time on my hands, for a while I was able to see just about every new film that was featured in this beautiful, tiny cinema. I saw Fellini's *8½* and *La Dolce Vita*, discovered the Jean-Luc Godard movies *Alphaville* and *Masculin Féminin* and thought Jean-Paul Belmondo and Anna Karina were a sensational couple, radical, dangerous and cool. I couldn't believe what I was seeing on the screen. Sex, controversy, self-absorption, excess, revolution, existentialism. Previously I'd had no idea films like these existed. You certainly didn't see them at the Essoldo in Northampton, despite the row of double seats for the snoggers at the back of the balcony. The most exciting thing on screen had been the occasional naturist movie with an X certificate. But celluloid was the least of my culture shock.

I moved very few things to London with me, but I did take my record player and my record collection – all singles, dating back to 1957. Among them was 'Diana' by Paul Anka, my first record. I've kept that old 78, on the green Columbia label, 'the finest name on record', catalogue number DB3980. Still inside its original sleeve, it is now in a frame on my studio wall. My parents bought it for me when I was 11, along with a rather battered wind-up gramophone. My love affair with records had begun.

I first heard the sound of 'Diana' coming out of a jukebox as I was walking past a coffee bar in Cromer, on holiday with my parents. I stopped dead, went in, changed all my pocket money into threepenny bits and fed them into the jukebox, playing that record over and over until my money ran out. I couldn't wait to buy it and be part of the excitement that record represented to me. Buying records was the thing I wanted to do most. I started doing a paper round to fund my new obsession. While Mum did her shopping I'd be in the record department of our local Co-op, playing singles in the listening booths. I can still identify the ones I bought there because, for some reason, they used to cut off the top left-hand corner of the sleeves. Or I'd be down at John Leaver's record shop in Gold Street in the centre of Northampton. I'd cycle down there and just hang around, listening to the music they were playing in the shop, or waiting for the Decca delivery van to arrive with new releases on a Thursday evening at about 5.30. Decca had all the great labels at the time – London American, Coral, RCA, Brunswick. I could pick up the latest Elvis or Duane Eddy, Jerry Lee Lewis, Everly Brothers, Little Richard, Ricky Nelson or Buddy Holly single and have the thrill of feeling that I'd got this record a day before it was officially released!

John Leaver's even did imports, not that I could afford them. But I thought American records just looked so great, with the big jukebox holes in the middle. I finally got the money to invest in Del Shannon's 'From Me To You' in 1963, the first time a Lennon and McCartney song had made the American chart, on the pink Big Top label in a white and blue sleeve. It looked fabulous.

I was a big Del Shannon fan, and actually got to meet him on *Whistle Test* in 1974. He told me that he gave Max Crook a 50 per cent songwriting credit for creating the middle solo that makes 'Runaway' such a distinctive record. Not that either of them gained much financially, as they hardly received a penny in royalties. Despite having had 14 hit singles in the five years from 1961 to 1966 he was penniless by the end of the decade. It was particularly sad that, like Roy Orbison, he passed away just as a Tom Petty/Jeff Lynne-inspired revival was gathering momentum. There was even talk of him replacing the 'Big O' in The Wilburys. He recorded the album *Rock On*, which came out on Silvertone in 1991, with Lynne, Petty and Heartbreaker Mike Campbell, but died shortly before the album was released.

Music was the backdrop to my entire childhood. My Mum always loved the radio and I vividly remember my early years spent in the glow of the light from the radiogram, the biggest piece of furniture in our living room. I was born in 1946 and, like most other families, we didn't have a television in the house. The radio was our entertainment, our television of the mind. *Listen With Mother,* then Archie Andrews, and *Journey Into Space* were part of my daily routine. (I suffered scarlet fever when I was seven and radio was a big part of my recovery. Mum and I were in isolation in the house for more than two months. I can still remember the nightmare deliriums that came with a temperature of 105 degrees.) As I grew older I graduated to *The Goons,* started listening to the music shows on the Light Programme, and then discovered Radio Luxembourg, whooshing in on 208 metres medium wave.

Jack Jackson was the first DJ I really noticed and was the first, to my knowledge, to use a sound effect, a gag or some other device played in from tape to link from one record to the next. He'd tell jokes based on the lyrics of the song, or use the opening lyric line as the answer to a question he asked as he talked over the intro. He'd mess around. Compared to the very austere approach of most 'announcers' of the 50s, he sounded completely different. I didn't know it at the time, but this was the prototype developed so brilliantly by Kenny Everett in the 60s.

I also liked David Jacobs, mainly because he did *Pick Of The Pops* at 10.40 on Saturday nights on the Light Programme. I remember him playing 'There's A Moon Out Tonight' by The Capris when it made the charts, an absolutely fantastic record. He did a dedication for me on my 15th birthday, my first-ever mention on the radio, requested by my mother. She continued to write to him and it was nearly four decades later that he learned I was related to this person with whom he'd been exchanging listener/broadcaster correspondence. She didn't tell him she was Bob Harris's mother until I started doing programmes for Radio 2. I went along to his studio at Broadcasting House and 'came out'. He was taken aback, but was lovely about it and whenever I met him he would always smile and ask 'How's your mother?' Wogan always asks after Dad, but that's another story.

For my 12th birthday Mum and Dad bought me one of the original Dansette record players and I purchased my first two 45s – 'Problems' by the Everly Brothers and 'To Know Him Is To Love Him' by The

Teddy Bears, my introduction to Phil Spector. I was never a great fan of the 78s – big, heavy 10-inch chunks of breakable black shellac, with that tiny little label stuck there on the middle. By comparison, the new vinyl single looked sleek, beautiful and cool, a light, flexible seven-inch disc with the thin, shiny playing surface dominated by a huge, imposing label. I thought my two new singles were amazing and I took them to bed with me that night so that I could lie there and look at them. I propped them up against my bedside light and fell asleep gazing at the blue and white striped sleeves and the black London American label, with its triangular centre. I woke up the following morning to discover them distorted, warped and unplayable under the heat of the light.

I soon replaced my damaged copies and as I built up my singles collection I started recording reel-to-reel tapes on my newly acquired Grundig tape machine in Mum and Dad's back room. By now I'd replaced my Dansette with a Decca stereogram, my first and only autochange machine. I'd hold the microphone close to the speaker while the music played, then talk while the arm lifted and the little shelf on the spindle retracted to let the next record drop onto the turntable. The old Decca group 45s were all pressed with one groove, so as the needle touched the clear black vinyl at the edge of the record the groove would instantly hook the needle right to the front of the music. From the top of the fade to the beginning of the next track the whole process took approximately 14 seconds, enough time for me to back announce the record, talk about the music and introduce the next song. I got all my information about tours, new releases and gossip from the *New Musical Express* (NME) and I used to cut out the Top-30 singles chart each week and underline the records that I owned, compiling my own weekly Top-20 chart, which became the basis of the shows.

I loved rock'n'roll and feel very lucky that I caught most of it first hand – Eddie Cochran records in particular. He cut a lot of stuff that was fairly ordinary, but the good stuff was absolutely outstanding.

I still think 'Somethin' Else' and 'C'mon Everybody' are two of the best and most explosive records ever made. He was so good lyrically and in 'Summertime Blues' wrote one of the first pop songs to contain any kind of overt political message: 'I called my congressman and he said quote/I'd like to help you son but you're too young to vote.' Really great stuff.

I loved black music, blues and doo-wop. The stunning combination of strings and soul on The Drifters' 'There Goes My Baby' had absolutely blown my mind, a sound unique in 1959. Soon afterwards the group's lead singer, Ben E. King, released 'Stand By Me', still my all-time favourite single. The string phrases in the middle solo match any piece of classical music I've ever heard. Years later, I saw The Drifters performing on a retro-package tour in Great Yarmouth, of all places, and met Ben E. King backstage. I'd taken my original copy of the single with me (London Atlantic 45-HLK 9358) and he signed it, on one side, 'To Bob from Ben E. King, thanks for being a friend'.

The show mostly comprised sing-a-long, all-one-tempo medleys of greatest hits, one song merging seamlessly into the next. But midway through the set, as that familiar bass-lead introduction began, Ben E. King stepped forward to the main microphone and began to speak. 'I'd like to dedicate this song to a friend of mine who's in the audience tonight. Bob, this is for you.' I can't even begin to tell you how I felt. I never dreamed when I bought that record that, over 20 years later, the song would be dedicated to me from stage by the man who recorded it. He even recorded a special message to use whenever I played it on the radio!

I was avidly buying Sam Cooke singles and still marvel at his voice and the influence he had. I was gradually building up my Phil Spector collection, ('Then He Kissed Me' is my favourite single of his, although I think 'Baby I Love You' has the biggest 'wall of sound'). I was 17 when 'She Loves You' and 'I Want To Hold Your Hand' came out and I got them on the day of release. I even saw The Beatles live – at the *NME* poll-winners' concert at Wembley in 1966, their last UK appearance. It was pandemonium as everybody crushed forward trying to get to the stage. Two girls fainted onto me from the tier above. You couldn't hear a note above the screams. I thought it was totally intoxicating. I had no idea, of course, that seven years later I'd be up on that stage collecting my own award.

The music scene was absolutely buzzing at the time. Pirate radio was revolutionizing the airwaves, *Ready Steady Go* started the weekend, the British beat boom arrived in a sweep of energy from bands like The Kinks and The Who. The Animals released 'House Of The Rising Sun', the Stones put out 'Satisfaction'. The Byrds recorded 'Mr Tambourine

Man', and John Sebastian was beginning to produce the run of sunshine singles that characterized the sound of The Lovin' Spoonful. I arrived at Hampstead Hill Gardens with boxes full of them, along with other irreplaceable rock'n'roll stuff and priceless rarities. I thought it was a pretty good collection but I was quickly disillusioned.

My fellow inmates at Hampstead Hill Gardens were unimpressed by the teen side of Beatle-mania. *Revolver* got them interested, particularly 'Tomorrow Never Knows', but they weren't really into The Beatles, they were more into the Stones (few people, in those days, were into both). I'd been collecting chart singles while they were buying albums. I'd heard Bob Dylan's 'Rainy Day Women' and 'I Want You' as they had been played on the radio, but they were buying *Blonde On Blonde*. I loved The Yardbirds, but they'd discovered Cream, along with Davey Graham, John Martyn, Roy Harper and a whole load of people I'd never heard of before. For the first time I experienced the extraordinary guitar playing and hauntingly melancholy voice of English folk singer Bert Jansch. Paul Simon had recently lived in London, playing the folk clubs, and *Parsley, Sage, Rosemary and Thyme* was always on the turntable. They were passionate and knowledgeable about people I'd hardly even heard of. They liked acid rock while I was chewing bubble gum. 'Sue's Gonna Be Mine' by Del Shannon suddenly felt like a very uncool place to be.

I'd been in London less than a fortnight when I ditched two-thirds of my entire collection at one of the local second-hand record shops. I didn't care to start with as the money paid the rent. It took a while before it dawned on me what I'd actually done! I spent a lot of time during the next few years ferreting around in various junk shops, trying to find copies of some of the gems I'd so casually discarded.

Having no money was a problem and, outside of the house, I didn't know anybody in this big city. I spent a lot of time, as I always had done, with the radio. At last I could get good reception on Radio London, which was broadcasting, like the other pirate stations, from a boat anchored just outside Britain's three-mile coastal limit. I still think the Big L was one of the best radio stations I've ever heard. It opened my eyes to what music radio could do. The station generated a fantastic new energy, transmitted by a roster of new broadcasting talent – Dave Cash, Tony Blackburn, Dave Dennis (the Double D) – and through a package of fantastic jingles, a lot of them crafted by on board genius Kenny Everett. And, miraculously, starting at midnight, they had John Peel.

The Perfumed Garden was a revelation. The first time I heard it everything somehow fell into place. More than anything else before or since, listening to John ('broadcasting in my stoned solitude') sending out these programmes from the middle of the North Sea crystallized everything I'd ever felt I wanted to do with my life, that building up my record collection, spending all those hours and hours making tapes in the back room of my parents' house really could lead to something. I now knew that I wanted to be doing exactly what John was doing – turning people on to the most amazing music I could find. This was my plug-in moment. If I could've just pressed a button that very second and made it happen, I would have.

At that moment the passion I've always felt for music and the radio fused.

The music John was playing was sensational, a mix of progressive American rock, folk and UK psychedelia by people I'd mostly never heard of before. He was introducing Jefferson Airplane, The Misunderstood, The Creation, Love and The Doors mixed with tracks from *Revolver*, *Pet Sounds* by The Beach Boys and some of the 'Epistle To Dippy' stuff that Donovan was recording at the time. It was clear that he'd somehow managed to establish the freedom to play what he liked. I really wanted to meet this person.

I used to go to a club called Middle Earth in Covent Garden. Right through 1967 I was there almost every weekend. It was situated in a huge, dark cellar basement, illuminated by liquid light shows and black-and-white films projected onto the walls. They'd sometimes show Kenneth Anger movies and have naked girls wrestling in mud. There were magazine and clothing stalls and a lot of pot smoking. Alcohol was banned, live bands played all night. I saw sets from The Byrds, Pink Floyd, Brian Auger and Julie Driscoll, Traffic and, memorably, Captain Beefheart and his Magic Band, introduced by a tearful Peel, overcome that he was meeting his favourite band.

I saw Arthur Brown performing 'Fire' wearing a silver motorcycle helmet-like crown, which he had set alight in the middle of the number while he cavorted around the stage, flames dancing around the top of his head. The headband got so hot his hair started burning. For a few moments he carried on, trying to ignore the searing heat burning into his temples. But he eventually had to concede to the inevitable and with all semblance of cool discarded, wrestled the whole contraption off his head and hurled it to the back of the stage, where it landed in a firework display of sparks and flame, instantly igniting the back curtain. In the absence of any fire extinguishers or procedures, several burly roadies were seen stamping on the flames with their size 13s while Arthur Brown poured cold water over what remained of his hair.

Sometimes the club would move to the Roundhouse in Chalk Farm, a building that had previously been a maintenance bay/roundabout for steam engines, then a Gilby's gin warehouse before Arnold Wesker attempted to realize his dream to turn the place into an arts centre. In 1965 he moved in with his theatre project 'Centre 42' and opened the doors of the old building for the *International Times* Christmas party and for the 'happenings', drama, mixed-media events and concerts that followed. The Stones played there, so did Pink Floyd, Jefferson Airplane and The Doors. And I was there for a magical evening a few weeks before the release of The Beatles' *Sgt. Peppers Lonely Hearts Club Band* in the spring of 1967. I'd heard a rumour that there was to be a playback of some of the tracks from the album and was one of a few dozen people to turn up at the Roundhouse on the off-chance, not really knowing what to expect. We wandered into that dark, cavernous building, a few bare bulbs lighting the way, to discover DJ Jeff Dexter with a turntable he'd borrowed from Tiles club and a couple of 4 by 12 Marshall speaker columns. He was playing 'Fixing A Hole', 'Lovely Rita' and 'It's Getting Better' from an acetate given to him by Paul McCartney, and it was fabulous to sit and listen to those amazing songs echoing around that dark old dusty place – and exciting to think that we were the first people outside of the band to hear them.

Jeff was a central conduit in the underground music scene and he looked amazing – a little elf-like in figure, with long blond hair and rainbow clothes. He was the resident music man at Middle Earth and I still believe him to be the best DJ never to have broadcast. Occasionally, John Peel would be there to do a guest spot but I made no attempt to introduce myself and bridge that gap between icon and fan. At that time it just seemed to be too big a gap to jump. But the meeting was not as far away as I imagined.

I'd been buying a lot of the new magazines and university newspapers that were proliferating at the time, writing off to the editors, asking if there was anything I could do. I'd done a bit of writing (well, I'd had a letter published when I was 15 in the Northampton *Chronicle & Echo*!) and thought that maybe I could be some kind of London correspondent. I finally got a reply from *Circuit* magazine, published jointly by Queen's College, Cambridge and University College, London. They needed someone to distribute copies of the magazine around the newsagents and bookshops in central London. So I stacked a few hundred copies of *Circuit* into the back of my car and trundled them around the West End. I didn't care that it was menial. I could now say I was working for a magazine.

Soon after, a friend of Roger Perry's came to visit him at Hampstead Hill Gardens. His name was Tony Elliott and he was editor of the Keele University magazine, *Unit*. He told me he was looking for someone to feed stories and articles up from London into the magazine, a kind of London correspondent. It was perfect! He immediately commissioned me to write an article about an experimental mixed media group called The Exploding Galaxy, led by a kinetic sculptor called David Medalla, who were living in a commune in North London. I moved in and joined them for a while. Here's part of what I wrote. (Remember this is 1967, OK?!)

It is 3 a.m. at the Roundhouse in Chalk Farm, scene of London's UFO Club. Over a white circular screen that surrounds the central area, projected slides dribble a hundred magnified strobes of colour. Behind the screen it is dark except for a small circle of soft white light, around which, in the unfamiliar silence, sit nearly one thousand people. David Medalla announces the first dance and The Exploding Galaxy begin.

Four men and three women dance for almost 30 minutes. They wear a sash of flowers around their necks and tiny bells are attached to bands around their ankles. They dance barebreasted to the sound of bongos and a flute. The Exploding Galaxy are happy and people applaud and throw money. Someone says: 'Their dancing is like early morning with the sun rising and the mist and the wet yellow leaves falling in a gentle yellow sunlight.'

The Exploding Galaxy was formed only six months ago by David Medalla and Paul Keeler, but already it has expanded to contain almost 50 people. This, says Paul Keeler, is the significance behind the name.

'We hope the Galaxy will continue to expand until it contains one thousand, two thousand, even three thousand people. Then the audience as such will cease to exist.' But all attempts to define clearly how this will happen or what The Exploding Galaxy actually does or is are dismissed by them as being 'irrelevant' or 'of no real importance'. Almost the fact that they just 'be' is sufficient justification for what they are doing. 'The Exploding Galaxy does not have any specific aims,' says Paul Keeler. He speaks of the Galaxy as being 'a spirit of mind'.

Things happen in the moment they occur. The Exploding Galaxy experiment in almost every field of visual and verbal communication – ballet, poetry, kinetic drama, sculpture, painting, spontaneous happenings and films. Recent events include 'The Evolving Documents Show' at the Arts Lab, an open-air poetry reading by Michael Crawford and dancing by David Medalla and J. Henry Moore, watched by nearly 300 people; a five-hour ballet at the Roundhouse; and a people's show held at the Middle Earth club, Covent Garden, in which many of the audience joined in.

In addition, as reported in a July issue of *International Times*, 'The Exploding Galaxy gave a performance which must constitute London's most liberated theatrical performance in history. Arthur Brown, singing while wallowing on the floor with four Galaxy nudes, reached an all-time high in erectile music ... never have so many been so nude so early and for such good reason.'

The Exploding Galaxy have little or no money and this is one of its greatest problems. 'We are desperately trying to overcome the problems of poverty until it is not important,' says David Medalla.

While there is talk in the underground of a possible 'Underground Arts Council' which would help support The Exploding Galaxy and others like them, this idea is a long way from realization and for the present, at least, it seems the Galaxy must continue to live at poverty level.

They share a house where they have lived, without electricity, for the past five months. The house has been the subject of regular police raids and following an article which appeared in the *News Of The World* earlier this year, heavily criticizing both the people of the Galaxy and their activities, giving their North London address, they have received harassment from the police and general public. The *International Times,* however, was not slow to speak on their behalf. 'A secure and free place to live is what makes life possible for them. The police actions to deprive them of this constitutes state censorship of the lowest form – to deprive artists of their most basic needs in order to suppress what they have to say.'

Indeed, the police have been neither skilful nor tactful in their handling of The Exploding Galaxy in recent months, but this appears to have done little to suppress the extrovert and enigmatic personality of the group or the remarkable talent of some of its members.

It was odd to be writing all this, considering my background. The culture shock for me was total. Dad was none too pleased, reading about the raids in *News Of The World* and reading my criticism of the way the police had handled it all. I think he was most concerned that I might be getting into drugs. But despite the worries he had about the new life I was living, we didn't argue. Ultimately, I knew he trusted me.

Tony thought the article was fine and published it in the edition of *Unit* dated December 1967. He asked me if I'd like to do another piece and did I have any idea what I'd like to write about next. 'John Peel,' I said. 'I'd love to do an interview with him.' A couple of days later Tony phoned me to say John would do it and soon I met John at his place in Fulham. He was there with Marc Bolan, who was sitting cross-legged on the floor, strumming an acoustic guitar.

John went everywhere with Marc at the time. He was promoting the hell out of him and had it written into contracts that Tyrannosaurus Rex would appear with him at gigs and interviews. I began a close friendship with both of them that lasted through the next five years.

I liked Marc immediately. He was tiny and looked very pretty and mischievous, wearing his pastel-coloured silks, with his long, black corkscrew hair and elfin face. He had an incredibly cheeky grin

I found immediately endearing. But he was very focused. I got the impression of someone who knew exactly what he was doing and where he wanted to go. John was more resolute, world-weary. As I was setting up the tape machine, he told me that he'd been living in America and that the stacks of albums he'd brought back with him provided the soundtrack to his early Radio London shows.

The introduction to this interview was already written.

Pop music seems to be splitting in two. In one direction Engelbert and his mimics rush away with their adoring fans, whilst towards the other extreme, various groups and individuals led by The Beatles progress to a freer, improvised and distinctly creative sphere. Though most people seem content with the 'wallpaper' and fab-40 Radio 1, a freer and creative presentation is creeping in under the figurehead of disc-jockey John Peel.

John Peel, with his *Perfumed Garden* programme on Radio London, a mixture of records, poetry, letters and conversation, immediately satisfied a demand for intelligent listening and 'involvement' from the public. He will shortly have another *Perfumed Garden* on Radio 1 and at present is joint host of Sunday's *Top Gear*. In a conversation with Bob Harris he talks about the way pop music is evolving and about his career and attitude to pop resulting in his becoming Britain's first really creative DJ. Perhaps one day, when the oldish DJs at present monopolizing the network are eventually pensioned off, John Peel will be seen as a prototype for the future.

I switched on the machine and John began to talk.

I think it is unfortunate to have a concept of what pop music is because it is expanding so much now. It is difficult to say whether the principal writers at the moment are songwriters, poets or what they are. Groups are veering towards the theatre and all kinds of elements are being introduced into popular music, which I think can only result in the improvement of all of them.

I think eventually it'll all just become one; everything will become fused. Pop music will become television will become pop music will become theatre will become poetry will become whatever ... things are progressing in this direction. The theatre is becoming involved, for example the lightshow type ideas and the film clips groups are doing, and The Beatles' *Magical Mystery Tour.* Already pop music, poetry, films and TV are getting mingled in with one another until you won't be able to say where one begins and the other ends.

I only wish that when I was younger there was a *Perfumed Garden* scene, because I was so incredibly hung up and I'm sure it would've taken less time to get my ideas straightened out.

When I started to work for Radio London, I began by doing the 'fab 40' stuff and then I volunteered to do the late night show (12–2 a.m.), because no one else wanted to do it. After a time I began bending the format a little more each night until, by the time the attention of the station management had been drawn to it, it was already an established fact.

The other disc-jockeys reacted against it to begin with because this is something a disc-jockey has always wanted to do, to have this freedom thing, but the Radio London programme administrator, Alan Keen, was quite jazzed about the idea, so I started doing the whole *Perfumed Garden,* just bringing in more stuff as I thought of it, whatever happened to come up or whatever was suggested.

Letters played an important part in it. People would say: 'Hey, will you try to do this?' and I would try to do it. I think it is the way a radio programme should be, although not all radio programmes because obviously you have to have some of the wallpaper music that Radio 1 is providing so well at the moment.

But you also need, somewhere in your day or in your week, a programme where the people listening are not treated as though they are totally moronic. I don't know why I called the programme *The Perfumed Garden*. I didn't know about the book at the time, it was just a nice idea, wandering at night through a perfumed garden. As far as I was concerned, it was a state of mind.

I would like to think that it was more than just a pop record show because it did, I suppose, try to influence people into at least sitting up and thinking about the ideas that I believe are important. It doesn't mean that I thought everyone else had to believe in them, it was more a question of 'here you are – do what you like with them'.

But so many people became involved with it. I got incredibly involved myself and I think if you are doing that regardless of what it is you are doing, it communicates to other people. But you have to know that as you get involved in something, people are going to appreciate your involvement and perhaps try to become involved also and in this way the whole thing can just spill over.

I really think that it can have consequences beyond anyone's wildest hopes, because if people become really strongly involved in something and they really believe in it and can get other people involved as well, you've got the start of something very important.

You see, the people who were deeply involved with *The Perfumed Garden* weren't, in the main, people who were involved with the music scene. They were just very ordinary people living very ordinary lives in very ordinary places. The ideas behind it and the sense of involvement I felt may have communicated something new to them and they became involved. Something existed for them to become involved in, whereas previously nothing had.

Reading this again now, it strikes me how accurate John was with his 'pop will become television will become pop' theory. Yes, The Beatles had done *Magical Mystery Tour* and the surreal and wonderful film for 'Strawberry Fields Forever', which pioneered the idea of making a video to promote a new single. But no one could have predicted MTV (although Ronan O'Reilly, founder of Radio Caroline, did have a wacky scheme for a flying television station, pre-dating satellite) and the massive power of mainstream pop television.

As I packed the equipment to go, John passed me an album and asked if I'd heard it. I said I hadn't. 'Take it with you,' he said. 'I think you'll like it.' It was *Forever Changes* by Love on the Elektra label, one of the most brilliant and extraordinary records ever made. Even by today's standards it's a powerful album; surreal lyricism and biting, staccato guitar licks mixed with lush, romantic string arrangements in a kind of musical schizophrenia. I still love it, regularly play tracks on air.

My friendship with John and Marc grew over the next few months, during which I embarked on the only 'proper job' I've ever had. I'd worked in the dressing-gown department of Selfridges during Christmas 1966 to earn money and then, briefly, in a clothes-packing warehouse just off Petticoat Lane when I again fell behind with the rent at Hampstead Hill Gardens. But in spring 1967 I saw an advert for a job at Tiranti's, later known as the London Art Bookshop, in Charlotte Street and went for an interview. I didn't think I was really qualified but for some reason the Tiranti family seemed to take to me and offered me the job of assisting in the shop and looking after customers. It was one of the premier art bookshops in London and had the most serene and beautiful atmosphere, like a small private library. I couldn't believe how lucky I was, working in this beautiful place, with access to the best literature, meeting the artists, photographers, sculptors and designers who used to visit the shop from all over the world. I was like a sponge, soaking up all the new colours of my life.

Sue joined me in London later that year in my tiny bedsit, but we soon realized we needed more space and moved across Hampstead and into the top floor flat of 77 Platt's Lane. Sue had bought me a Philips portable record player and I would sit on the balcony overlooking the road, pretending I was playing music to a festival crowd. Little did I know that 25 years later I'd be back in Platt's Lane, fighting a legal battle with a fellow Radio 1 DJ that threatened the whole structure of my life.

Sue and I were at home one evening in the early summer of 1968 when we got a phone call from Tony Elliott saying he'd like to drop in and see us. He was on his way to France to take a year's sabbatical from university, but was planning to spend a couple of months in London. He had an idea for a one-off summer events magazine and asked if I wanted to help him get it published. It would be full time and I'd have to give up my job at Tiranti's. I was sad to leave, but I just couldn't deny this exciting new project.

The magazine consumed us from then on. I edited the music sections, Tony did movies and theatre, and all other editorial was shared. We made loads of phone calls to gather the information. Tony borrowed £70 from his aunt to fund a 5000 print run and Tony, his girlfriend Stephanie, Sue and I began laying out the first edition on the table in our kitchen, using Letraset and glue. The magazine was designed as a poster, to be pinned up on a wall or folded down and carried in the pocket. Cost was imperative and a magazine with staples was out of our price range. The name came last, but *Time Out* seemed the best two-word description of what the magazine would offer and we had the underground market to ourselves; there was nothing else like it. We were creating a magazine we wanted to read. The first edition cost one shilling and was published on 12 August 1968.

John Peel invited me onto his new BBC *Night Ride* programme to talk about it all. My first-ever broadcast, on a John Peel show! Marc Bolan was the first to react, sending me a most beautiful letter of congratulation.

We sold most of the copies of the first edition of *Time Out* to the queues at the Sunbury Jazz Festival and at the Hyde Park free concerts, such a glorious feature of the summers of the late 60s. So many great bands played there. I saw sets from Family, Fleetwood Mac, Pink Floyd, Roy Harper, Blind Faith and, memorably, The Rolling Stones with their new guitarist Mick Taylor and Mick Jagger dressed all in white, reading Shelley and releasing butterflies in memory of Brian Jones, who'd died a few days earlier. The money we made from the sale of those first copies financed edition two, for which Cream lyric writer Pete Brown wrote the editorial.

Much as I'd done with *Circuit*, I was filling the boot of my car with copies and driving all over London, trying to get the magazine into all the cool bookshops and other places I liked. I called in at Indica Books in Holborn, the Compendium Bookshop in Camden Town, the Arts Laboratory in Drury Lane, the Marquee in Wardour Street, Klooks Kleek Club in West Hampstead and the Country Club in Hampstead. I also stopped off at Musicland in Berwick Street, my favourite record shop, along with Simon's Stable in Portobello Road. Musicland always had loads of American imports and you could listen to them in the shop. I bought the new H.P. Lovecraft LP and asked the guy who was serving if he'd stick a dozen copies of *Time Out* on the counter for me, sale or return. He looked through the magazine for a few moments before agreeing to take a dozen copies if we reviewed his new album in our next edition. He handed me a copy of *Empty Sky*. The shop assistant was Elton John, earning a few bob on the side prior to the full-time launch of his career with the release of 'Lady Samantha' a few months later.

But it was the third edition of *Time Out* that really got us noticed. The cover was designed by one of my Tiranti customers, Alan Aldridge, a really hot name in graphic art at that time. It was a controversial cover, featuring a profile photograph of a woman's naked torso, onto which Alan had drawn an eye above the breast and a smiling mouth below it. By outlining the side of the breast to make it look like a nose, he created an image that looked at first glance like a face. It was a closer look that revealed it to be a nude woman.

With the combination of Alan Aldridge and naked female flesh, suddenly the media picked up on us. We got proper distribution, Eric Clapton was said to want to invest. We moved into the basement of 70 Princedale Road in Holland Park, underneath the offices of Blackhill Enterprises, the people who staged the Hyde Park festivals and managed Pink Floyd. Peter Jenner was one of the leading lights there, still one of the most intelligent and respected of music business figures. Keyboard player Rick Wright was around a lot, his wife Juliet was the receptionist. Vocalist Syd Barrett would often hang out, mostly motionless, staring into space. *Oz* magazine had their office a few doors away and Caroline Coon was on the same block, running the drug-advisory service 'Release' from No. 52. It felt like we had our own little underground community there.

Time Out's arrival at Princedale Road roughly coincided with Sue and I having to move from Platt's Lane. The owners of the house decided to sell and we had to go. On the recommendation of photographer Ray Stevenson we stayed briefly at Sandy Denny's house in Parson's Green, before moving into a ground floor flat in a large Victorian house in Blackheath on the other side of London. Initially we liked it, living on the edge of that big heath at the top of the hill, but we quickly realized we'd made a mistake. We were too far from the West End, at least an hour in the car most times. I'd previously been able to drive to Northampton in the time it was now taking me to get into central London.

Within only a few days of moving in we were burgled. Thankfully, he'd only just got in when I disturbed him and in his dash for the open window didn't have time to grab very much, but these things shake you up. A few days later we heard someone shouting from our front porch. As I opened the door a young guy fell into the hallway covered in blood. He'd been beaten up. It didn't bode well.

The one good thing about the house was the owner, Tim, who'd inherited it from his family. He was a medical student, ran the local college disco and kept all the equipment at home. He had a double deck unit, cassette, microphone, amplifier, speakers, all set up in the sitting room. The bass sound off that thing was fantastic. He said I could mess around with it as much as I wanted to and it was so great to be able to work with proper equipment at last. As my technique improved he took me out to do a set on one of his gigs. I took David Bowie with me.

I'd met David at a Tyrannosaurus Rex session at Trident Studios in Soho. He and Marc occasionally played on each other's records and both worked with producer Tony Visconti. The press later played up a rift between Marc and David but it wasn't like that at the time; they got on great. I still believe Marc's best piece of recorded guitar playing is his solo for 'The Prettiest Star', David's follow-up to 'Space Oddity'. Marc was a much better guitarist than people give him credit for, although he never had a great ear for tuning. Producer Tony Visconti was forever trying to devise diplomatic ways of telling him that the guitar was out. It became a big thing.

I loved those sessions, experiencing record production for the first time and the layering of the sound. It was fascinating what could be done and I was even able to contribute. Sue and I called into Trident one evening with Tony Woollcott, who eventually became a vice-president at Sony Music. David and Tony Visconti were recording the vocals for 'Memory Of A Free Festival' for the *David Bowie* album and needed to get some crowd atmosphere on the fade. Tony, Sue and I went into the studio, gathered round the microphone and began to sing. 'The sun machine is coming down, and we're gonna have a party, uh-huh-huh.'

We didn't have great voices, but it didn't matter. Having recorded the lines once, we recorded them again, then again and again, Tony Visconti gradually building up the voice tracks to resemble a festival crowd singing along with the song, adding some hearty whoops, yells, hollers, whistles and claps on the final fade. That first gig with David, however, had a completely different vibe.

It was a college end-of-term student celebration night in the East

End of London and subtlety was not part of the mix. My job was to fill the dance floor, and keep it filled, with Motown, Stax and heavy rock. About halfway through the evening I introduced David to a predominantly male crowd, already agitated that the dance records had suddenly stopped. He ambled out with his new girlfriend, Angie, who sat to David's right, her legs dangling over into the audience now packed up against the front of the stage. David switched on a small amplifier and plugged in a microphone and his guitar. He slid a tape into the cassette machine on the front, and as he pressed the start button, we heard the opening acoustic guitar chords of the backtrack to 'Space Oddity'.

Compared to the decibels I'd been blasting out, David's system sounded like a transistor radio. He hadn't even got to 'Major Tom to ground control ...' before the booing started. Wrong person, wrong night. Pints of beer started landing on the stage, glasses being smashed. By halfway through the song it was impossible for him to continue.

I suddenly found myself striding out into the middle of the stage in a red-faced state of righteous indignation. 'You mark my words,' I shouted, 'You'll remember the night you booed David Bowie off stage, you morons. More fool you. This man is going to be a big star!' I really did say that. Hasty exit left, grabbing record box en route.

Time Out was becoming a success. Sue and I managed to move back across the river, albeit into a small bedsitter in Hammersmith, and things were looking good. But I was getting uncomfortable with the way *Time Out* was going. Tony had a very specific agenda. He wanted to do a glossy, to be the editor of a successful, Nova-like commercial magazine, whereas I'd always thought of it as a conduit for the underground. It sounds very hippy-ish, but then that's what I was. Now we had an office and an expanding editorial board, office politics began to evolve. Tony began to realize I'd stopped enjoying this. I'd disappear for a couple of days, come back, make a few phone calls – my heart really wasn't in it any more. I arrived one morning to discover the locks had been changed and I couldn't get in. I'd been voted off the editorial board in my absence. Tony produced a letter, in which I relinquished any right to claim any ownership of any aspect of *Time Out* from then on, which I signed. I should have seen it coming, of course. I wasn't committed to the 'drive' ethos that was now propelling things along. Nor do I regret it. People have pointed out to me since what I might now be worth if I'd managed to maintain some kind of interest in *Time Out* (Tony Elliott is worth millions), but there you go. I just didn't like that office life. Now it was time to get myself on the radio.

TWO

'DJ Wanted ...'

SUE AND I, TOGETHER WITH OUR CAT MUMBLES, SPENT CHRISTMAS 1969 in a small stone cottage we'd rented next to the river in Bibury, in the middle of the Cotswolds. It was a really beautiful place, spoiled only by the ice-cream van that parked opposite every afternoon, and the constant influx of tourists. The place is a genuine English beauty spot and attracted hundreds of visitors each week. We regularly had people wandering into the garden and taking photographs through our windows.

With me out of work and Sue now at college we had absolutely no money. We were like Scratchet, throwing the odd lump of coal onto the fire, but as we listened to the church bell ringing in the New Year, I suddenly felt a tremendous sense of excitement and optimism. I had the strongest possible feeling that 1970 was going to be a good year.

Three days into January I got a call from Jonathan Green, editor of *Friends,* the UK equivalent of *Rolling Stone* magazine. He was planning to feature an article about Radio 1 and asked if I'd like to write and research it. Would I?! I jumped at the chance to plug in to where I wanted to be. I put the framework of the piece together and began to set up the interviews I wanted to do – DJs Jimmy Young, David Symonds and some of the programme producers. I asked John Peel who else I should talk to. 'Jeff Griffin,' he said. 'I think you and he will get on really well.'

Jeff invited me to meet him at Aeolian Hall, the home of the Light Entertainment and Popular Music Department for BBC Radio (full title!) in New Bond Street. I was surprised that this old building, in the West End of London, was so quiet and austere. Radio 1 was supposed to be a happening pop station and here were my long hair and loon pants being chided by middle-aged men in suits! But the atmosphere in

Jeff's office was great and, reassuringly, a track by Family was playing as I walked in.

Family were just about my favourite live band at that time. I must have seen them play dozens of times, at Klooks Kleek or the Marquee, or in Hyde Park at one of the free summer festivals. Roger Chapman is, without doubt, one of the all-time great lead vocalists and I'd never seen him give less than a hundred per cent. I was at the band's final concert, at the De Montford Hall in their home town of Leicester in 1974, to witness the ultimate Chappo high-energy assault. By mid-way through the set he'd worked himself into a frenzy, stomping and prowling around the stage, pounding the beat with every footstep. But as he bore down on the microphone he stumbled and fell. People rushed from the side of the stage to help him to his feet, as he crashed his foot right through the stage. He was stuck almost up to his waist and rescue wasn't easy. It took some time getting him out of there: the floorboards had splintered like a vice around his leg and it was clear he was in considerable pain. For a time he couldn't move at all, but it didn't stop him singing. He just carried on with the set while they got him free. What a trooper! The evening was completed by a wild end-of-term party at the Leicester Holiday Inn. Based around the pool and involving increasing nudity and general celebration, all was eventually brought to a halt by the hotel management at around 5.30 a.m., following many complaints.

Jeff's office was the definition of organized chaos – records piled up in stacks on the desks, seven-inch sleeves and LP covers scattered everywhere, shelves over-spilling with albums and interesting-looking 'A' label promotional singles. There were reference books, running orders, correspondence, cassettes and reel-to-reel tapes, rock posters on the walls. Half a dozen black BBC programme boxes were on the floor, labelled for different shows. Jeff introduced me to fellow producer Bernie Andrews, with whom he shared Room 421. There was a great banter going on between them and it was clear they also shared a massive enthusiasm for music and an absolute determination to get more of it into the system at Radio 1.

When the Labour government came up with the Marine Offences Bill and closed down the offshore pirate radio stations in 1967, the BBC was instructed to accommodate the new teenage audience the pirates had located and entertained so brilliantly. The resulting reorganization within the Corporation was radical, involving the updating (or re-branding, as we would now call it!) of the Light Programme, Third Programme and Home Service networks into Radios 2, 3 and 4 and the launch of a new pop music station.

Radio 1 was never going to be the same as the pirates. The BBC had draconian needle-time restrictions to adhere to and an old-school approach to shake off. At first, Radio 1 was only on air for 12 hours a day. (The 24-hour service was finally launched by my good self in 1991.) Some of the programmes were shared with Radio 2, most were packed with 'features' and live music sessions of one sort or another, often the equivalent of the Northern Dance Orchestra's version of 'Strawberry Fields Forever'. Jeff and Bernie saw this as a tremendous challenge – to make in-house recordings, with high-quality musicians, that sounded at least as good as their commercial counterparts, and feed that material onto the airwaves. They succeeded. A series of At The Beeb CDs by Fleetwood Mac, Led Zeppelin, Jimi Hendrix, David Bowie and others was released decades later, demonstrating the enduring quality of those recordings. Featuring fantastic live material and rarities from various BBC sessions in the late 60s and early 70s, they represent the best of BBC music heritage.

Jeff had joined the BBC in 1959 as a technical operator. He became a specialist tape editor and was part of the award-winning team, headed by producer Christopher Holme, that carried off the coveted Italia Prize for their production of Muriel Spark's The Ballad Of Peckham Rye in 1961. (All part of BBC 'training', as was a series with Mrs Mills and a stint as producer of the daily big-band programme Workers' Playtime, broadcast at mid-morning to coincide with factory tea-breaks.) He moved to the music department in 1964, producing shows for the Light Programme and for the World Service, where he launched a long-running series of blues and R&B shows, presented by Alexis Korner, a pivotal figure in the development of the UK blues–rock scene, the man who, in 1962, put The Rolling Stones together!

Jeff had just launched the weekly In Concert programme introduced by John Peel at the Paris Theatre, Lower Regent Street, another beautiful old BBC building. He was also producing the Radio 1 magazine show Scene And Heard presented by Johnny Moran. Bernie was working with Peel on the cutting-edge music show Top Gear.

We finished the interview and I started to talk about some of the ideas I had. I'd brought with me a running order I wanted Jeff to look at. The theme was to do with musicians expressing their feelings about the state of the world through their music and was based on a track list I'd been asked to put together the previous year for a show I hosted at the Royal College of Art:

1. FORD THEATRE:
   'Theme For The Masses'/'From A Back Door Window'
   LP: *Trilogy For The Masses*
2. THE BEATLES:
   'While My Guitar Gently Weeps'
   LP: *The Beatles/White Album*
3. AMERICAN AMBOY DUKES:
   'Shades Of Green And Grey'
   LP: *Migration*
4. SIMON & GARFUNKEL:
   'America'
   LP: *Bookends*
5. TOM RUSH
   'Child Song'
   LP: *Tom Rush*
6. CREAM
   'We're Going Wrong'
   LP: *Disraeli Gears*
7. THE ROLLING STONES:
   'Street Fighting Man'
   LP: *Beggars Banquet*
8. RICHIE HAVENS:
   'Oxford Town'
   LP: *Electric Havens*
9. THE DOORS:
   'The Soft Parade'
   LP: *The Soft Parade*
10. BLIND FAITH:
    'Presence Of The Lord'
    LP: *Blind Faith*

Jeff was impressed and liked the way I'd sequenced the tracks together and the work and the logic behind it. He suggested we do a pilot programme and said that if it sounded OK he'd submit it.

We recorded the pilot on 22nd April 1970 at Broadcasting House. I literally shivered with the thrill of walking into the place. I still do, despite all the changes that have taken place over the years. We went through the gold doors into the marbled reception hall and up to the first floor, where the continuity studios for all four national radio networks were clustered together next to the main technical area. The nerve centre.

Jeff dimmed the lights as I settled into Con C, one of the two main Radio 1 transmission studios. I got my albums and tapes out of the programme box and addressed the mixing desk in front of me. There was a row of rotational faders (volume controls) and switches, set back to allow room for paperwork – scripts, letters and running orders. Above the desk were three cartridge machines, used for playing in the station jingles and trails from eight-track tape. I had a microphone suspended in front of me, with two others on the opposite side of the desk for guests. There were three turntables, a record rack, a pair of funny, hard, shiny old black BBC headphones – and clocks. Clocks everywhere. One built into the desk, one on the wall ahead of me, one in each corner of the room, all of them illuminated. All I could hear in that silent, soundproofed room was the synchronized ticking of the passing seconds. There was a glass window on my left, through which I could see the control room, where an engineer was sitting, waiting to monitor the sound levels and record the show. I could hardly believe this was happening. I'd dreamed of this moment.

I made mistakes. We stopped and started a number of times during the recording as I mastered the pre-fade buttons (to listen to tracks off-air), the cueing of tracks, the layout of the faders and the general rhythm of it all. I've never found it particularly difficult to get my brain around the operation of broadcast desks. They look complicated, but you don't actually need a lot of that stuff. I just decide which faders and facilities I need and ignore the rest. It's like driving a car. You reach a point where you don't have to think about the mechanics of it.

The big problem I had to overcome was my reaction to my own voice. I'd never used headphones before and every time I spoke I kept putting myself off, distracted by how different I sounded from what I expected. You have to use headphones. Opening the microphone fader 'kills' the sound from the speakers, otherwise there would be feedback. For the first time in my life I was hearing myself as others heard me – and right in the middle of my head! That apart I didn't feel particularly intimidated by the occasion and things gradually began to go well. By the end of the evening we'd got a complete programme on tape.

Jeff called me a few days later to tell me that he'd passed the show to Radio 1 management as a DJ audition tape and that he'd let me know if and when he got some reaction. Needless to say, I couldn't wait. I called within a day or so, pestering him for news. He was irritated. 'Don't start phoning me the whole time. I said I'd call you.' I was going to have to be patient.

Marc Bolan's wife, June, had arrived unexpectedly at our flat a couple of hours before I was due to leave for the recording. 'I've been thinking about all this, Bob,' she said. 'You need advice from a good DJ.' We got into her car and headed across London to see Jeff Dexter.

'It's what you've always wanted. When you get to the BBC just smile, be nice and say yes to everything,' is what he told me. 'And get yourself some gigs. You need to get more experience.'

I started scanning the small ads under 'DJs Wanted' in the music papers and, along with about 50 others, I turned up for an audition on a wet Thursday evening at a dubious-looking, run-down pub near King's Cross station. The place was full of smoke, nicotine-brown paint was peeling everywhere and the facilities were basic, to say the least. Eight or nine regular pub tables had been pushed together to make a rudimentary stage, with three more tables placed on top, lined up to support the equipment. We were told to get up on the tables, play three records and do two links – about ten minutes in total. It was chaotic. The needle kept jumping across the records as the DJs teetered and tottered precariously on the tabletops, trying to keep their balance. Everyone got their feet stuck in the gaps between the tables. Somebody tripped, sending one of the decks crashing to the floor, so everything paused for a while for the necessary re-wiring and repair, hilarious entertainment as we all lined up to go on. I was near the back of the queue, just behind a guy called John Hall, who told me that he worked at the Birds Nest on the King's Road. We finally made it to the front after about an hour and a half and, despite the equipment, I thought he sounded great. He stuck around to hear my set, too. Thank God we didn't get the job. 'Come down and meet me this Saturday lunchtime,' he said before we left. 'I'll buy you a drink.'

King's Road was extremely fashionable at the time, with great shopping, particularly for records, clothes and expensive interior design. Trendy new restaurants, wine bars and boutiques were packed with bright young things. It was like a psychedelic promenade. In the middle of it all, the Birds Nest was probably the least hip place in the whole of Chelsea. A chicken-in-the-basket pub disco, very un-cool. But the equipment was superb. The DJ booth was right up against the edge of the small dance floor, and there were telephones on the surrounding tables so people could phone the DJ and ask for requests. The inside of the booth was like a mini radio studio. John taught me how to work the kit and said I could play a few records. It felt fantastic. I did about an hour, talking on the microphone, mixing in a few jingles, getting people onto the dance floor, taking a few requests in return for a couple of pints of beer and having a really good time. At the end of my set John introduced me to the manager. 'What are you doing this evening?' he asked me. 'We need someone to do a residency for us on Saturday and Tuesday nights.' This was just what I wanted.

I was on two shifts, 7.30 to 8.30, then 10 till 11. Kieran Travers did the show in between. I wonder what happened to Kieran. He had a great Kool & The Gang instrumental theme tune, which he'd jive-talk over to start his show, always in the same way. 'I've got some fingerpopping, hand-clapping, thigh-slapping, toe-tapping sweet soul music for you. Yeah!' Then straight into his first track. Great stuff.

The money wasn't good but I really didn't care. I'd been working there for only a week when a guy came up to the booth and said he'd like to talk to me at the end of my set. He told me that the Marquee was planning to launch a Saturday dance night and he was looking for a DJ. On the spot he offered me the gig and I started on 6th June 1970, beginning an association with that iconic rock venue that was to last for many years.

The facilities at the Marquee were pretty rudimentary. The equipment in the side-stage DJ booth was dangerous, more or less in bits, mostly covered by the gaffer-tape that was holding parts of it together. Every so often there'd be a crackle and you'd lose sound for a few seconds. The legendary, graffiti-scrawled dressing room behind that small black stage was about the size of a broom cupboard. It was always really hot and sweaty in the club, with a kind of gloop under your feet that seemed to glue your footwear to the floor.

I'd just got a copy of 'All Right Now' by Free and I played it at least half a dozen times that first night, along with 'American Woman' by The Guess Who, 'Whole Lotta Love' by Led Zeppelin and 'Vehicle' by the Ides of March. 'Spirit In The Sky' by Norman Greenbaum had just been at No. 1 and was a major floor-filler. I played 'The Green Manalishi' by Fleetwood Mac and 'In The Summertime' by Mungo Jerry, mixed in with some Stones and Creedence Clearwater Revival, a selection of Motown and Stax dance tracks, some James Brown, Aretha Franklin and the occasional burst of rock'n'roll. (Rule No. 1 on live gigs: you've got to know your audience!) The evening worked out great and the place got packed out every week. We started getting live bands in. Dream Police played on 18th July, Status Quo the following Saturday. I was beginning to earn a living!

Sue and I finally found a decent-sized flat that we could actually afford and moved to West Hampstead, about 15 minutes' drive from Broadcasting House through Regent's Park. We'd needed to find somewhere bigger because Sue was now expecting our first baby, due in November.

Jeff Griffin called at last. Radio 1 had recently launched *Sounds Of The 70s,* a new 'progressive' music programme strand, broadcast each weekday evening from 6 to 7 p.m., with a different presenter each night. David Symonds was on Monday, Mike Harding did a heavy metal show on Tuesday, the lovely, late Stuart Henry played mainly soft-rock and psychedelia on the Thursday programme and Alan Black was the jazz–rock man on Friday nights. Wednesday featured a repeat of the previous weekend's *In Concert* programme.

Jeff told me that John Peel was about to take a month's holiday (the last one I can remember him taking – he always said he didn't like being away from his show in case his stand-in did too well and replaced him). The plan was to re-broadcast a *Best Of In Concert* series while he was away but Jeff didn't want to repeat the repeat on the Wednesday evening, so instead he suggested that Radio 1 try someone fresh in that slot. On the basis of my pilot tape they agreed to give me a trial run, so he was phoning to offer me the four Wednesday programmes, beginning on 19th August.

'Hang on a second,' I thought, 'let me get this right. I'm going to be on Radio 1, sitting in for John Peel!' My first programmes ever, on national radio, deputizing for my great hero and mentor. I didn't think they wrote scripts like this.

'You'll only have 20 minutes needle-time each show,' Jeff interrupted. 'There'll be two sessions, recorded at the BBC, probably three/four numbers each. We'll use some stuff from the archives (Tyrannosaurus Rex, David Bowie, Graham Bond Organisation and Free), but we also need to get out and have a look at a few bands you'd like to have on.' Where to start?!

Jeff's call coincided exactly with the release of the *Elton John* album. Elton and I had kept in touch following our first meeting at Musicland and we immediately called him to book a session. He came in with a sharp new backing band called Hookfoot and within a couple of hours had recorded four songs for a combined session fee of £25!

I recommended a terrific little band I'd seen in Portsmouth called Aubrey Small, whose keyboard player, Rod Taylor, was the spitting image of Paul McCartney. I was a big fan of Argent, so we got them in as well. For a reason I can't remember, Family couldn't do it, so we needed one more new name for the first show. With that in mind, we went to see Wishbone Ash at the Marquee on 15th June. I thought they were absolutely stunning, with the two lead guitarists, Ted Turner and Andy Powell, à la The Yardbirds, in their Jeff Beck/Jimmy Page era, right out on the front of the stage, trading licks. Those guys really could play. At the end of the set we all crowded into that cramped dressing room and Jeff booked them on the spot. Their first-ever broadcast was on my first-ever show.

I also needed to top up my record collection. I did a systematic tour of London's import shops and we arranged appointments with the major record labels to raid those LP cupboards! I did an enormous amount of listening, and spent hours putting that first show together.

I arrived in the studio to discover a pile of telegrams wishing me luck, from Mike Hales at Elektra Records and Tessa Siddons at Transatlantic, from Tony Elliott at *Time Out*, David Bowie's office and Marc and June Bolan. And from Mum and Dad: 'Good luck this evening, every success in future'. The line-up on Radio 1 that day was Stevi Merike on *Breakfast*, Johnnie Walker at 9, Tony Blackburn at 10, then DLT with the *Radio 1 Roadshow* (from the Paris Theatre) at 12. Tony Brandon was on at 2, Dave Cash at 3 and Tommy Vance did the latest releases on *What's New* at 5.

As the programme began, I was amazed not to feel over-nervous. I just felt that this was where I'd always wanted to be – in a radio studio, doing a live show. To the point of over-confidence. Half an hour into the programme I was already congratulating myself on how well everything was going.

The first track was 'Cinnamon Girl' by Neil Young followed by 'Pavilions Of The Sun' by Tyrannosaurus Rex, Van Morrison's 'Into The Mystic', and the first Wishbone Ash song, 'Errors Of My Way'. Then came 'Silver And Gold' by Country Joe and The Fish, and some beautiful world music from *La Flute Indienne* by Los Calchakis, an album which has stayed with me ever since. I still play tracks from that old vinyl copy on air from time to time.

Everything felt great and I was on a roll as I pressed the button to fire the news jingle into the 6.30 headlines. I felt loose enough to talk over the music as I trailed the newsreader: '... and over to the newsroom we go, with Kingy Jimsbury.'

Jimmy Kingsbury was head of Radio Presentation at that time and was not amused. I think he sent upper management some formal bit of paper of complaint. My first lesson: don't even begin to take this thing for granted. Other than that, the programme went well. We got some correspondence and I felt I was already beginning to locate the core of what it was I wanted to do – to establish a real contact with the people who were listening, play them beautiful music and keep it simple.

Suddenly the pace of life increased. I got a call from the manager of T2, a new group just signed to Decca, inviting me to see them play at the Isle of Wight Festival. He took me down there in a small private jet and we buzzed the crowd! It was incredible flying over such a vast arena containing so many people. More than 450,000 people were there, many to see what was to be the last major live performance by Jimi Hendrix, who was appearing with his new group, Band Of Gypsys. We stayed for about three hours, enough time for me to walk up the bank and look out over the site in an attempt to take it all in. It was beautiful weather, the sun beating down from a clear blue sky, the ground dry enough for the crowd to stir up a cloud of dust that seemed to envelop the site in an orange haze.

I went backstage briefly and was introduced to Joan Baez, a woman of daunting intellect and strength. She paid me the huge compliment, following a *Whistle Test* interview a few years later, of thanking me for not asking her any 'dumb questions', which made a refreshing change from the '... so how long have you spent making this album?' kind of stuff I sometimes used to land the guests with!

As it turned out, T2 weren't actually playing at the main festival. They did a short set to about three dozen people, on a makeshift trailer stage which was tethered to the back of a lorry, just outside the perimeter fence. I thought they were pretty good. Then it was back to the plane, a final buzz of the site and home again by the middle of the evening. It felt surreal.

I was invited to compere for jazz group Centipede, formerly known as the Whole World (they'd changed their name to avoid a clash with Kevin Ayers's new group), who were doing a short tour of France and wanted me to introduce them on stage. I was thrilled. I'd never even been abroad before!

The group comprised 50 people, led by pianist Keith Tippett and his wife, Julie Driscoll, formerly the 'face of '68' and still idolized in France at that time. She was mobbed when we arrived at the airport. Zoot Money, Robert Wyatt and various members of the band that was to become Patto, lead vocalist Mike Patto and guitarist Ollie Halsall helped provide the rock 'spine', while the jazz collective improvised. I don't remember the venues, except that they were located deep in the French countryside. We stayed in a large manor house, where the bizarre after-gig, bar-room cabaret consisted of various male members of the ensemble, in the beam of a torch, contorting their genitalia into shapes silhouetted on the walls. The puppetry of the penis. 'Ducks In Flight' is a particular memory.

The frenetic pace lasted until the final programme of the series came to an end, then everything went quiet again. Jeff was away on holiday, my link with the BBC was severed and I felt a tremendous sense of anti-climax. The lull before the storm.

I'd got to know David Symonds quite well and really liked him. He'd been slotted into the BBC's Sunday morning schedule in 1966 as their main weapon against the runaway ratings success of the Radio London *Fab 40* chart show. In fact, Kenny Everett had opted to join him at the

Light Programme several months before the demise of Radio London, making jingles, doing sketches and creating various inserts for the show. The BBC promoted David heavily – he was their boy.

He was a good, if rather earnest broadcaster, very independent-minded, had a wry sense of humour, a resonant, very 'English' voice, and was completely dedicated to furthering the career of his protégé group, Fairfield Parlour, music made in the mould of his other great love, The Moody Blues. He'd helped fund Fairfield's recordings, part-mortgaging his house to cover the bills. Their main chance came with the release of a sweet single called 'Bordeaux Rose' in 1970, prior to the planned launch of their début album for the fashionable Vertigo label, recognizable by its distinctive, psychedelic 'bull's eye' label design. It just didn't happen for them, despite major television exposure including an appearance on *Top Of The Pops*, usually the key to chart success. At the crucial moment, the stock of the singles had dried up and by the time the feed line had been repaired the record had slipped out of chart contention. The band never recovered the lost ground, and David never recovered his investment. It happens all the time, unfortunately, but worse was to follow.

David had been battling with the BBC over the content of his new *Sounds Of The 70s* programme. They were at odds over the style. It came to a head when he arrived in the studio on 9th November in an apparent state of shambles for what proved to be his last show for Radio 1. I really felt for him, he had his heart in the right place. The following day I got a phone call from David's producer, John F. Muir, offering me the show until the end of the year to start with, then on from there, one six-week contract at a time. I broadcast my first *Monday Programme* on 16th November.

My daughter Mirelle was born exactly one week later, at the tiny cottage hospital in Hampstead. Sue and I had been to see Argent at the Roundhouse the night before, partly in the hope that the volume level would motivate some action from this baby, who was now a few days late. It worked, because early the following morning Sue went into labour. I didn't attend the birth, and wasn't really given the option. Pacing up and down the corridor outside is what expectant fathers were supposed to do in those days and I was still pacing a couple of hours before my radio show. Miri was born at 4.10, I had just enough time to see her and give her and her mum a hug before rushing to Broadcasting House and straight on air. Tommy Vance brought a celebratory bottle of champagne into the studio. Definition of happiness.

John Peel was incredibly supportive, talking about my show on air and promoting me in whatever way he could. Sue, Miri and I regularly stayed with him and his wife, Sheila (the Pig), at his house, Peel Acres, in Suffolk – visits he'd write about in his column in *Disc And Music Echo*. He'd become just about my best mate.

> The tiny pine tree is the halfway line. If the ball bounces before going into the ditch it's a point to the kicker. If the ball bounces on the paving before going into the flowerbed it's fair. Some of the rules of the complex football/tennis game Bob Harris and I played until we could hardly stand. We were out at the cottage and had spent two days dragging our ladies with us from junk shop to junk shop in search of bizarre old 78s [still looking for those singles I'd sold in Hampstead!]. The game evolved while Sue and the Pig (or Stig or Biggle) cooked the evening meal. In the end Bob won, but only just and I had a sore toe from the previous day. 'There's an incredible shop in Ipswich,' said Bob, so off we went. We finally parked about 30 minutes from a shop Bob assured us was 'really amazing ...'

Press coverage, generally, was starting to build up. It was complimentary and warm, in sharp contrast to the stick I was to get a few years later! *Record Mirror* published the first major Bob Harris profile article in January 1971. I did the sought-after 'Blind Date', a record review column for *Melody Maker*, and started figuring in DJ polls. Unexpectedly, I was becoming famous and life was getting excitingly hectic.

I left the good old Birds Nest in Chelsea and started doing rock club residencies, at the Tricorn in Portsmouth and the Country Club in Hampstead, often with a new band called America, managed by Jeff Dexter. Soon after we broadcast their first-ever sessions on my show, Jeff issued the following press release.

> Please don't tell anyone, but we hear from usually reliable sources that America is about to conquer Britain and eventually win over the rest of the world.

Already, America's invasion has taken place here very quietly. Severe brainwashing has been carried out. We can reveal that this took place in the unlikely area of Hampstead, in the very British-sounding Country Club.

The initial converts may have been few, but they include those with connections in high places. Whisper it to no one, but even the mighty British Broadcasting Corporation may not be immune. A certain producer, who would be unable to deny that his name is Bob Harris, was spotted at the very first of these meetings by the invaders of our shores. It has not gone unnoticed that on no less than four occasions this same Bob Harris has allowed no less than 50% of his *Sounds Of The 70s* programme to be taken over entirely by America.

It may have been by stealth in the UK, but America's impact in the States was meteoric. Less than a year later, in March 1972, they went to No. 1 in the *Billboard* chart with their début single 'Horse With No Name'. They went on to score 17 further hit singles, spanning 12 years, generating millions of dollars of income. But by then Jeff had lost them.

As the group began to develop, Jeff sought advice from an aspiring and already influential record company executive who was visiting London. David Geffen said he didn't like them, that they were 'a poor man's Crosby, Stills and Nash'. Nevertheless, Warner Brothers said they wanted to 'explore America's potential' and took them to Los Angeles, where the group found their careers put on temporary hold while the record company concentrated on another important project, the launching of The Eagles. Not that America minded this hiatus. They were ensconced in a house in Beverly Hills, with a pool, attendant female company and entertainment and were ecstatic to discover that this kind of stuff really did happen to guys in a band!

Shortly after they settled in California, Jeff received notification from the States that his management contract had been dissolved. In the legal battle that ensued, Jimmy Page referred Jeff to Led Zeppelin's management team, who helped Jeff to get some compensation but it barely covered his costs. He didn't even get a credit on the first album! The music industry is a tough business. America was just one of a number of guest bands to play live on my Radio 1 programme. Curved Air, Syd Barrett, Lindisfarne, Cat Stevens, The Faces and, at last, Family, all recorded sessions early in

1971. I was literally bombarding myself with sounds.

I saw Led Zeppelin at the Marquee. Bernie Taupin collected Sue and me in his new white Rolls Royce to see Elton's first big UK gig, at the Fairfield Hall in Croydon. I was there at the first-ever London gig by Thin Lizzy on 20th April, a showcase at the Speakeasy Club in Margaret Street (scene of later misadventures). I was mesmerized by bass player and vocalist Phil Lynott, the sheer intensity and power of his performance, the confidence he had. There weren't many black–Irish bass players around. He had a lot of bottle and he was making the most of it. The following day was a Loudon Wainwright showcase, totally destroyed by the heckling of a rampant Keith Moon, who kept complaining from the audience that Loudon's hair was too short! I even saw Grand Funk Railroad at the Albert Hall which, along with Blue Cheer at the Roundhouse a couple of years earlier, is one of the loudest concerts I've ever experienced.

Alan Black and I started a 'Sounds Of The 70s' night at the Marquee, with Argent headlining the first gig. But we weren't destined to be promoters. Maybe it was because we launched on 1st April. We made £6 that first night, the only really profitable gig of the whole three-month run, the low point of which was the no-show of Stone The Crows on a night we made just 63p.

Sue and I were spending an increasing amount of time with Marc and June Bolan, who were now living not far from us, in Little Venice, close to the canal. It was all happening for all of us, our careers seemed to be taking off at exactly the same time. 'Ride A White Swan' had gone into the charts three weeks before I started on Radio 1. Four months later we were at *Top Of The Pops* for the performance that marked 'Hot Love' hitting No. 1, the first T. Rex chart-topper, on 24th March 1971. We went out for a celebratory meal after the show.

Marc was absolutely ecstatic, talking about a forthcoming tour. He invited me to compere, saying that he'd like me to go out on stage for about 40 minutes, play music and chat while people arrived. There would then be a short break and I'd go back out to introduce the band. We did the first date at the Bournemouth Winter Gardens on 9th May. The crowd was excited but reasonably reserved. We really weren't prepared for what happened next. The following gig at the Portsmouth Guildhall on the 11th ended in total chaos.

The audience comprised mostly pubescent girls in a frenzy. You couldn't hear a note, the noise was so loud, and an all-pervasive smell began to envelop the auditorium as the band got into the set, the front row seat cushions filled with the urine of hormone hysteria. The girls were literally wetting themselves! I hadn't witnessed scenes like this since seeing The Beatles at Wembley in 1966.

We sat in the dressing room after the concert, reflecting on the madness we'd just experienced. We had a couple of beers, met a few people and chilled for a while. We could hear noises outside, but didn't know yet that almost the entire audience had emptied from the auditorium and reconvened outside the stage door, waiting for the group to show. It was pandemonium out there. By the time we were ready to leave, dozens of police were attempting to open up a corridor through the pressing crowd so that we could get to the cars – five big, gas-guzzling Vauxhall Crestas. The cars were already a mess. Everything that could be ripped off them had been. The number plates and windscreen wipers were missing, and one of the door handles was half hanging off.

The crowd surged forward as Marc appeared and we were immediately surrounded. It was frightening. Some of the girls were trying to get his jacket off as he struggled to get free. There were flashes of steel at exactly eye level, as a dozen pairs of scissors tried to cut locks from Marc's corkscrew hair. I really thought one of us might have an eye ripped out as people fell in the crush. Eventually we were bundled into the car and began to inch forward through the crowd. It was like being inside a tin can. People were on the bonnet, people were on the roof, faces pushed contorted against the glass of the windscreen. Someone was trying to smash a window to get in. Marc leaned back into his seat, snuggling down behind the feather boa he had round his neck, a big impish grin spreading across his face. He was absolutely loving it! Suddenly there was a grating crunch as the suspension collapsed under the weight of so many bodies. Three of those five cars were written off that night. We had to have a police escort back to the hotel.

It was exhilarating but genuinely scary. We clearly couldn't do things the same way again. From then on, even as the final note of the guitar was still resonating on stage, we were out of the venue, into the cars and gone. A headline in the *Glasgow Herald* on the 21st really summed things up. 'T Rextasy'. Simple. It was the first time I'd seen it referred to that way.

The other guys in the band were amused and bemused by the hysteria. Bass player Steve Curry and drummer Bill Legend were on a wage, while Mickey Finn had been around since Tyrannosaurus Rex had undergone its metamorphosis into T. Rex and gone electric. I didn't get to know him particularly well because Marc was the focus of it all. The other guys had to adapt to being in his shadow.

John Peel was getting increasingly agitated about the direction Marc had taken. He'd given lukewarm reviews to the previous singles, but could contain his disapproval no longer with the release of 'Get It On'. He slated it in his column, saying the only bit he liked was the '... meanwhile I'm still thinking' reference to Chuck Berry on the fade. Other than that, he felt Marc had abandoned his roots. Marc felt completely betrayed. To my knowledge, they never spoke again.

T. Rex records were also the cause of some consternation at Radio 1. Some of the daytime guys were complaining that Marc was giving me acetates and white labels, sometimes weeks in advance. They had a point, I suppose. Outside of Marc, I didn't play much chart stuff and they were being denied their 'exclusives', but Marc wanted to do it this way and I thought it was up to him.

I was having a fantastic time on the programme. Mark Wight, the network controller, seemed keen to promote me as a Radio 1 discovery. I hadn't joined from the pirates, or from Radio Luxembourg. I was all BBC.

Dad came up to London to sit in on one of the shows. I liked to get into the studio early, and usually arrived about 4.45, 15 minutes before the end of the *Terry Wogan Show*, which was broadcasting from Con C until 5. He and Dad hit it off immediately and sat chatting while I set up my show. 'What are the prospects like in the job?' Dad asked.

'Well, Mr Harris,' Wogan replied, 'it's very insecure. I'm on the fifth week of a 13-week contract and have no idea whether the BBC will give me another one.' That's been my position more or less ever since!

I've come to the conclusion that broadcasting is about as secure as coaching a football team, only in our case, results don't matter. You can have the best figures in the world, but if they want to take you off air – for realigning, repositioning, restructuring, refocusing – they will. Audience support, petitions, demonstrations – they really don't matter. If management don't want you, you're gone. Four times in my career I've been sitting on successful shows and lost them overnight. I'm not complaining about this, it's reality and you learn to be resilient.

Some years after that first meeting, Dad was waiting for me in Broadcasting House reception when Wogan came down the stairs. He walked over immediately, hand outstretched. 'Mr Harris! How good to see you again.' So warm. They were still chatting when I arrived and Dad was absolutely amazed he'd been remembered in this way. Good man, Wogan. It was only recently that we began to get to know each other, working together in Nashville covering the Country Music Association Awards for Radio 2. I'm a big fan.

Out of the blue I got a call from Roy Harper. I first saw him play in 1967 at one of the free concerts in Hyde Park and he hadn't changed, always completely uncompromising on stage, veering from angry rant to sweet melody. Stubborn, occasionally wild, but deeply kind-hearted, I warmed to Roy from day one.

He'd phoned to say that he'd got a leading part in a new movie and did I want to be in it. I thought he was joking. He told me that he was co-starring with Carol White, who'd played the lead in the groundbreaking and controversial television play *Cathy Come Home* five years earlier, that the film was called *Made* and he was playing the part of a rock star. Two of the scenes involved being interviewed by a television reporter, and he'd recommended me. They needed me in Brighton on 28th September to begin filming.

From the moment I arrived someone was assigned to stay with me, to make sure I didn't get injured or incapacitated in any way. Once you're committed to film you become expensive to replace. I was driven to the first location on the seafront, where we were to be filmed doing part of the interview in the back of a car – and what a car! – a white Rolls Royce convertible. Roy was sitting in the back seat, smoking a joint. 'This is the life,' he said and started to laugh his exaggerated, infectious laugh.

The front passenger seat had been removed and a camera bolted in. The lens was about three feet away from our faces, the cameraman squeezed in with his back pushed against the dashboard. For the next three hours, we drove up and down the promenade, Roy and I sitting in the back in the sunshine, talking about whatever came into our heads. None of it was scripted, most of it inane. They just asked us to 'improvise'. We couldn't stop giggling. It was pathetic!

The next day followed a similar pattern. We moved location to the pier, where Roy was holding a press conference and I was asking questions. We'd just embarked on the umpteenth take when a swooping seagull started cawing loudly above us. Roy leaned back, looked up at the bird and started laughing. 'There you go, man, far out.' He turned and addressed the camera. 'That's what it's all about, man.'

Cut. That was it.

'Thank you, Mr Harris. We won't need you again.' Amazingly, they left my scenes in. I saw it on television a few years ago; really dreadful film but fantastic fun to do. As it happened, those few hours in front of the camera would prove invaluable experience.

Sounds Of The 70s had become a poll-winning success. Towards the end of 1971 Radio 1 opened up a new slot, 10 p.m. to midnight, and for the first time broadcast the programmes in stereo, borrowing the Radio 2 transmitter. *The Monday Programme* was extended to two hours and I additionally began to do an album review show with Alan Black on Friday nights, produced by Aidan Day, who later moved on to the new London commercial station, Capital Radio. He was to become a central figure in my Sex Pistols experience a few years later.

After a very enjoyable year working in the relaxed atmosphere that surrounded John E. Muir, I was re-united with Jeff Griffin, who immediately imposed a stricter discipline on my routine, insisting that I attend his office at Egton House, the new home of Radio 1. He wanted me there every Monday morning at 11 o'clock sharp to go through the programme with me, to make sure my building was up to scratch. He also wanted me to improve my notoriously bad time-keeping. For every five minutes I was late he would take a track out of my running order and put in one of his own. It worked to start with, but then I began to slip. I lost one track, then three or four tracks the following week. A couple of weeks later I overslept. Oh my God! I arrived in the office in a fluster at about 1.15, to discover that Jeff had completely rebuilt the show. 'What's wrong with you, leaving me sitting here like this?' was one of the kinder things he said. He wouldn't budge, saying I'd forfeited the right of contribution. In all aspects, Jeff was teaching me the disciplines of programme building!

I was doing a lot of *Roundtable* programmes on Radio 1 with DJ Rosko 'the Yank who could crank', who was like a one-man force field, shouting into the microphone, careering around the studio. He had an amplification box for his headphones that generated awesome volume, like a pair of mini bass speakers strapped to his head. He'd get hot and sweaty and take off his shirt, then off would come his T-shirt in a swell of bare-chested ego. Nicky Horne was his assistant, soon to establish his own broadcasting career with *Your Mother Wouldn't Like It* on Radio Luxembourg.

The dynamics of this new DJ culture meeting the old-style BBC presentation was perfectly encapsulated on a handover midway through a *Roundtable* on which I was appearing with Alan Freeman. Rosko hit the jingle button as he introduced the bulletin, animated and insistent, sounding like a cross between a wrestling announcer and Wolfman Jack on double-speed. 'It's 5.30 on Radio 1, the station of the nation. Rosko's got the vibe, baby, and we got some newwwws you can uuuuse.' His voice lifted to a crescendo. 'It's yer main man, John Dunn!' There was a long pause, before we heard John deliberately clear his throat and begin the bulletin. 'With the news ... in English!' Absolutely priceless.

As 1972 began, I felt I was surfing the crest of a wave. I didn't feel particularly in control of events, but I was loving it all. *Melody Maker* published a most wonderful article I still treasure. Under the headline 'Bob Harris, just being himself', Michael Watts had written the following:

DJs are, essentially, extensions of their own private selves, or at least how they would like themselves to appear. And that's what makes Bob Harris so intriguing. Not only is he successful to the point of attaining the sort of following that Peel used to have, but his reason for being successful exactly reflects his own nature. To be a little banal, he's a thoroughly nice person, and he must be the foremost living proof within the pop world that you can make it on those terms.

Bob Harris is strictly a product of the English media. There's no fast American spiel; his voice is soft and intimate, his conversational approach low-key and aimed at the second-person pronoun. He's not an entertainer, as are, say, Tony Blackburn or Kenny Everett. His popularity, which is becoming considerable for his type of format, is based on the respect of his listeners for his musical taste: they know he's going to play what they will like. Some people would say he's John Peel's natural successor, in that he has cemented a firm relationship between himself and the audience with music as the primary justification. Of how many Radio 1 DJs can you say that?

Very complimentary and it meant a lot. But this was the Michael Watts who, in the same paper six years later, wrote the famous 'pen quills in the back' piece that demonstrated the extent to which press affection had turned to hostility. In fact, many things were to change during the next few years. My home life, my career, my sense of self. I had no idea, at this moment, how much television was about to shape my future.

THREE

Old Grey Whistle Test

LIKE MANY PEOPLE IN BRITAIN AT THE TIME, MY MUM AND DAD GOT our first television set to watch the Coronation in 1952, when I was six. Just as the Queen was being crowned our cat gave birth to kittens on the front room sofa – much the more momentous event for me at the time.

It seems to me that each decade since then has produced one outstanding television music show, a programme that featured the best music and successfully captured the spirit of the time. *Six-Five Special* was the first to bring rock'n'roll to British screens, in 1957. *Ready, Steady, Go!* was arguably the best of the lot and truly reflected the excitement of the Mersey Beat era and the club culture of the mid-60s. *The Tube* gloried in the anarchic mood of the post-punk 80s and *Later, With Jools Holland* reflects the wonderful diversity that characterizes modern-day, non-mainstream music.

In the 70s the No. 1 show was *Old Grey Whistle Test,* launched on 21st September 1971. By the end of that year I'd become a devoted fan. I thought there was something unique about the programme, an intimacy that made it special. The mix was great, with live performances, interviews, films and discussion, put across in an understated style that was new, honest and refreshing.

The show immediately featured people I liked. Family, Wishbone Ash and America were among the first bands to appear, along with The Who, Cat Stevens and Lindisfarne. Alice Cooper, catsuit open to the navel, swaggered onto my television screen, looking the epitome of sleaze, his pet snake wrapping itself around the microphone as he sang 'Under My Wheels'. Frank Zappa came on, talking about being banned from the Royal Albert Hall, and showing clips from his new film *200 Motels.* Muddy Waters was featured in a profile interview.

Stevie Wonder previewed his new album. There was vintage film of Hendrix, The Doors and the Stones. Poco played 'Just For Me And You'. It was clear that this was a programme that really knew what it was doing. Where else on British television could you get to see all of this stuff?

The man who made it happen was producer Michael Appleton. Like Jeff Griffin, Mike joined the BBC in 1958, as a studio manager in Bristol. It could be really good fun, working in the regions. In London, TV and radio were located in different areas of the city, with consequent impact on flow between them. In contrast, in Bristol, both radio and TV were housed in the same buildings in Whiteladies Road, so there was plenty of overlap between the two.

Mike's first job was to provide sound effects for radio drama productions using various devices found in the corners of the studios – slamming the miniature door, or stepping through the little gravel pit, for crunchy footsteps. Gradually, he began to get opportunities to put down the coconuts and other contraptions in the sound booth and take up the faders in the vision-mixing gallery, feeding material into the prime-time current affairs programme *Tonight*. It was Mike's ambition to eventually join the *Tonight* production team but, by the time he made it to London, the show had been taken off. Nevertheless, it was a good time to land at Television Centre and Mike found himself in the presentation department, working on pilot programmes, in the lead-up to the launch of the Corporation's second national television channel – BBC2.

Mike was the producer of a new arts programme called *Late Night Line Up*, fronted by Joan Bakewell. Broadcast seven nights a week, *Line Up* featured news and reviews from the whole arts spectrum, from television output and the new film releases to the latest exhibitions and gallery showings.

There was a freedom at the BBC that allowed programme makers to express themselves. Outside of the Light Entertainment department there was little in the way of a budget, but the upside was that Mike was left to get on with producing his shows with very little interference from management. He took full advantage, increasingly filtering popular music features into *Line Up*, before launching a new, dedicated album music show in 1968, timed to reflect the recent introduction of colour television to the UK.

Colour Me Pop began as a short series of 25-minute programmes, each devoted to one LP. The first featured The Small Faces, playing live versions of tracks from their new album, *Ogdens' Nut Gone Flake*. Audience reaction was reasonably good and Mike began to refine the prototype, founding a series called *Disco 2* in 1969 (it wasn't a disco show, the word had a different meaning in those days) a new release showcase that incorporated some vintage film and studio material and was introduced, briefly, by Tommy Vance. The format wasn't quite right, so Mike began to experiment with different presentation devices, including the amazing telestrator, with which he handwrote details of the music onto the screen while the act was actually performing. A particular memory as a viewer is of Nico, sitting flame-haired and solemn as she droned at her harmonium, gradually disappearing behind the handwriting filling the screen, as Mike put lines through several attempts to telestrate her Velvet Underground connections, like a teacher crossing out with chalk on a blackboard.

But the defining moment came away from the studio, with the arrival of James Taylor's *Sweet Baby James*. It was the atmosphere of this album, the tone and feel of the music, that set the agenda for a final programme re-launch. Mike was getting closer and closer to the format he envisaged: what he needed now was a name for this creative new show, something that reflected the strength of the centrepiece of the whole concept – the song.

The Beatles had revolutionized the pop scene in ways more profound than just record-breaking singles sales. Specifically, they wrote their own material, almost unheard of when the band first emerged in 1962. Reinforced by the later popularity of Bob Dylan, they proved you could do it yourself. Until then, many of the successful hit makers performed material fed to them from music publishers.

The 50s and early 60s had been the halcyon days for the great songwriting factories, the Brill Building in New York being the most famous. Situated on Broadway, it contained an amazing array of solid gold talent. From their tiny cubicles, young writers such as Carole King, Gerry Goffin, Doc Pomus, Mort Shuman, Neil Sedaka, Barry Mann, Cynthia Weill, Jeff Barry, Ellie Greenwich and Leiber and Stoller were pumping out songs on a 9 to 5 conveyor belt of Top-10 hits. Some of the greatest records of all time come from that magical era of Tin Pan Alley. Mainstream Nashville still works in the same way.

The Brill Building had its own designated doormen, cleaners and ancillary workers, known as the Old Greys. At the end of the working week, all were invited into a playback room to listen to a selection of the new songs (a process now known as auditorium testing). The mantra was the 'hook'. If the Old Greys could hum or whistle along to the chorus of a song having heard it only once, it proved the song was catchy, had a good hook and was likely to be a hit. In other words, it passed the 'Old Grey Whistle Test'. That's how the programme got its name. It was the title Mike had been looking for.

Whistle Test began in Presentation B, a tiny studio usually used for the weather forecast, tucked behind a lift shaft on the fourth floor of Television Centre. In terms of size, facilities and access it was hardly Abbey Road. The black walls were hung with wires and all kinds of electrical paraphernalia, the mixing desk had only six faders, with a total of eight microphone points, just about enough for the average drum kit. The studio wasn't even properly soundproof. Turn up the volume and the beat could clearly be heard in main reception, on the other side of that huge, circular building, and bands began to bring in their own sub-mixers to fuel the level. Edgar Winter's performance of 'Frankenstein' was so loud it was impossible for the cameramen to hear directions. One of them was so affected by the impact of the bass beats that he was physically sick.

The choice of studio was a needs-must. Incredibly, the budget for the first series was only £500 a show. Everything had to come out of that, including appearance money, payments for rights clearances for music and film, design (in-house designer Roger Ferrin came up with the opening sequence and the star-kicker logo), hospitality, facilities and even the presenter's fee of £40 per programme!

Presentation was the lynch pin. Mike wanted a journalist who was able to broadcast, someone to whom he could delegate full responsibility for scripts and research. He auditioned a few people and finally settled on a double header of *Melody Maker* writer Richard Williams and author/singer Ian Whitcomb. Ian was a hit-maker in the States, making the Top 10 in 1965 with 'You Turn Me On (The Turn On Song)'. The follow-up single was called 'N-E-R-V-O-U-S!', a song he'd written to describe his frustration at his own tendency to stutter when under pressure, a condition about which Mike was unaware.

Mike had already resigned himself to losing Richard for the first two shows (his wedding coincided with the beginning of the series and he was away on honeymoon!) and had decided to use Ian in the main anchor role. Unfortunately, the closer it came to transmission, the more Ian began to struggle. Despite his assurances that once the show was underway he'd be all right, Mike felt he couldn't take the risk and rebuilt the entire programme minutes before transmission, voicing the links himself from a nearby sound booth.

Things didn't quite gel with Richard. His preference was for jazz and he just didn't feel right about some of the music featured on the show. 'There were some great moments on that first series,' he told me. 'Curtis Mayfield played live, Dr John sat at the piano giving me a 10-minute potted history of New Orleans music, John Martyn came in with his Echoplex. And I interviewed Captain Beefheart, a great moment for me. But I didn't like progressive rock or heavy metal and didn't feel comfortable introducing them on air.' Nor did he enjoy the television experience.

'I couldn't stand being recognized,' he explained. 'I hated being accosted in the supermarket by people berating me because Jeff Beck or someone hadn't been on the show.'

It was also difficult for Richard, juggling between the programme and his full-time work on *Melody Maker*. 'I'd arrive at Television Centre at 8 o'clock on Tuesday morning, write the script, then go on to work at the newspaper,' he recalled. 'I'd work through my day, get back to the studio by about 7.30 that evening in time for a couple of run-throughs, then the programme would go on air. I never really plugged in, didn't particularly want to be on television and eventually couldn't wait to get back to the rest of my life. I think I got out just in time, to be honest, before I became too identified with it.'

Apart from a three-year diversion to head the A&R department at Island Records, Richard has been working for newspapers since: as editor of *Time Out* magazine, features editor at *The Times,* editor of the *Independent Sunday Review* and later as a writer with the *Guardian* on Sport and Editorial Features. 'The best part about the experience was Mike Appleton, a real gentleman,' he concluded. 'The fact that the music was his taste didn't make it bad taste.'

By the middle of the first series Mike was beginning to look for Richard's successor. He had plenty of time. *Whistle Test* ran for 42 weeks a year.

Mike phoned and invited me onto the show to chair a live discussion about the Night Assemblies Bill, draconian measures being proposed in Parliament at the time. The rock fraternity was up in arms because they were convinced that implementation would mean the end of music festivals and other events where people gathered overnight.

Although I didn't know it, this was my audition. Soon after, Mike asked me if I'd like to present the programme full-time, beginning at the start of the second series, in September 1972. I didn't really think about it too much. I'd never particularly wanted to be on television, it wasn't an ambition. I've always felt completely satisfied by radio. But I certainly wanted to be a part of a programme that was putting out so much good music.

I arrived for my first day at the office with my shoulder bag stuffed with albums, tapes and ideas. Mike convened a production meeting and handed me a piece of paper. 'It's the running order,' he announced, before turning to talk technicalities with the rest of the team – production assistant Jenny Carson, researcher Alma Player and director Colin Strong.

'The running order?!' I'd expected things to be like they were at Radio 1, with me doing all the building. 'What if I have to introduce people I don't like?'

'Ah ... then that's the challenge,' replied Mike, smiling in his urbane way. This was all something of a shock.

'Er ... maybe we should've talked more about this before I said yes ...'

But Mike was unshakeable and it took me a while to get my brain around the way this was going to work. Eventually I realized that the best tactic was to bombard Mike with loads of stuff, then wait for some of it to filter into the programme. I'd play him tracks, recommend live bands, cajole, persuade and then be patient. Nagging was counterproductive. Some weeks the programme would be full of things I liked, other weeks not. It took time and a few arguments, but gradually we built up a deeply felt trust in one another, and a belief that it was the programme that was important, above spats over personal taste.

I was still adjusting to the implications of all this the following evening, as the opening title sequence began to roll at the beginning of my first-ever show. As the drumbeat kicked in on 'Stone Fox Chase' by Area Code 615, the programme's theme tune, I suddenly felt incredibly nervous. I'd transferred my script onto the autocue machine, a device that reflected my words up into the lens of the camera that faced me a few feet away and I'd read through the links a million times that day. We'd done two run-throughs and one complete dress rehearsal. What could possibly go wrong? But this was the real thing and it hit me that in a few seconds' time I would be appearing live on television sets across Britain. Mum and Dad would be watching, Sue, my little daughter Miri, all my friends ... just like I'd watched the first series. I had this massive panic that I'd just go completely speechless and let everyone down. As the floor manager began to count down the last 10 seconds, my eyes flashed to the gallery next door. I could see the bank of screens through the darkened glass, Colin Strong poised, finger raised, ready to shout 'Cue studio'. I started to shake.

This was very different from radio, where I built my shows, drove my own equipment and felt completely in control. Sitting in the harsh glare of the key light, in the middle of that bare, black studio, I felt vulnerable and alone. As my face appeared on the monitor set, I turned to the camera and automatically began to read as the autocue rolled through my script. It was my voice coming out, but not as I knew it. I was speaking at roughly half my normal volume and twice my normal speed, trembling round the edges. I introduced a film of 'Just Like A Woman' performed by Bob Dylan onstage with George Harrison and Leon Russell. The Everly Brothers played live in the studio and I interviewed American Spring, talking with Marilyn Wilson about her husband, Brian, and playing 'Good Time' from the new American Spring album, illustrated by a clip of film, edited to the music.

There were no videos then. The new technology wouldn't be making an impact for another four or five years, so the film clips compensated for an almost total lack of available promotional material. The films came from the collection of Philip Jenkinson, one of the *Line Up* presenters, who'd listen to the tracks Mike gave him and trawl through his library to find an appropriate visual, often to stunning effect. The cartoon express train that accompanied 'Keep Yourself Alive' by Queen, and the vintage black-and-white footage of Alpine skiers that provided such an appropriate setting for Mike Oldfield's *Tubular Bells* are particularly memorable. Phil Carson, UK label manager of Atlantic Records (and future husband of Mike's assistant, Jenny) was in the control room when the *Tubular Bells* sequence was transmitted. Massively impressed, he recommended the album to his opposite number in New York. Atlantic rush-released it in America, where it hit the Top 3, went gold and spent nearly six months on the 'Billboard' chart, success that underpinned the expansion of Richard Branson's Virgin empire.

By the end of that first show I'd begun to conquer my nerves and had actually begun to enjoy myself. There were no major hitches and I was further amazed by the extent of the adrenaline rush I felt afterwards. Live television was a buzz.

Four months later, the 1972 *Melody Maker* readers' poll was published. *Whistle Test* was voted the No. 1 television show, *Sounds Of The 70s* was the No. 1 radio show and I was voted No. 2 in the DJ poll, second to John Peel (Noel Edmunds was third, Kid Jensen fourth and Pete Drummond fifth). The *NME* results were the same, and as Mike and I walked out to collect the award at the Poll Winners' Concert at Wembley I couldn't have felt more proud and happy. Only a few years earlier I'd been in that audience, watching as The Beatles received the accolades. Now I was on that very same stage, holding the trophy aloft like I'd won the World Cup.

'Nobody at Wembley could dispute the unsurpassed supremacy of BBC2's *Old Grey Whistle Test*, voted Britain's top TV show,' read the photo caption in *NME*. 'A deafening ovation greeted host Bob Harris and producer Michael Appleton when they came on stage to receive the award.' To this day, I can still recall the way I felt at that very moment.

It was clear that *Whistle Test* was beginning to make an impact. Following the appearance of Focus on the programme early in 1973, the reaction was so great that for the next 10 days their record company had to concentrate the entire resource of their pressing plant on fulfilling demand for their two available albums.

As well as *Whistle Test* and my two shows on Radio 1, I was piloting an American radio programme (*Hands Across The Water*), writing for several music magazines, rushing around seeing bands, and introducing gigs. I compered the five-day London Music Festival with Argent, Nazareth and Ten Years After. I introduced Genesis at the Reading Festival and Elton John at the Sundown in Edmonton, following which Elton launched his Rocket Record label at a party aboard the 'Sloop John D' on the River Thames, described by the *Melody Maker* as 'the biggest name-dropping rave-up of recent times'.

The report read as follows:

> Through your Raver telescope, we spied Rod Stewart, clad in leopard skin jacket and sipping expensive brandy, the rest of The Faces circumnavigating the deck. Ahoy, who's that in the sunglasses? Cat Stevens, hiding behind naval beard, and gracious, who's that chappie in the sporty white hat – it's Paul Simon, looking diminutive and rather lost. Avast, the heavies – Ringo in Battle of Jutland beard, and Harry Nilsson demonstrating a pocket tape recorder, the size of a Swan Vesta. Elton cut his cake with the aid of June Bolan and Bob Harris sat cross-legged in the corner, pretending not to notice the stripper removing what little remained of her clothing.

I introduced Terry Reid, Family and all-girl band Fanny at Lincoln Rock, a nasty experience, as it turned out, when we discovered the promoter had left town before paying anyone. Everyone was up all night, sitting in the lobby of the hotel – a bunch of angry, ragged rock'n'rollers furious at having lost their money and resentful at being interviewed by the local police. I travelled to Germany to see The Rolling Stones play the Olympic Stadium in the middle of their 1973 European tour, and filmed an interview with Mick Jagger in the City of Munich Restaurant. I went to David Bowie's party at Haddon Hall and out to dinner with Bernie Taupin. I was at Morgan studios in Willesden, north London with Marc Bolan, for a crazy night of filming for Ringo Starr's T. Rex documentary *Born To Boogie*. Rod Stewart and Harry Nilsson were among those who contributed to the creation of a new record at the studio – the highest ever bar-bill in a single session. I was on the guest list, having a really good time. I was a married man living a single man's life. It was beginning to mix badly with commitments at home. I was rolling in late too many nights.

Sue had little respect for the music business and thought it was shallow. Nor was she impressed by fame, or the material benefits that came with it. She loved the radio and believed in my programmes, but television had now added a whole new dimension to our life together. She had deep reservations that I was becoming intoxicated by it all.

Our second daughter, Emily, was born on 2nd February 1973, two months premature. I was in Northampton, visiting Mum and Dad, when I got the call telling me Sue had been taken to hospital. I rushed back to London and arrived as Emily was born soon after 8 o'clock that evening. She was such a little thing, all scrawny in her incubator. We weren't allowed to touch or hold her while she fought for her life for the next 10 days – agonizing, when that's all you want to do. But she's a strong one, our Ems, and soon she recovered and was home with us.

I began to realize how much I was losing touch with the rhythm of my family, but what could I do? I'd signed contracts, made commitments. My work was taking me away, but this is what I'd always dreamed of. I couldn't understand why Sue felt so unhappy, when things were going so well and it's clear to me now that my thoughts were selfish. I loved the girls with all my heart, but I wasn't spending enough time with them, and Sue and I were finding it harder and harder to talk.

John Peel began to express his disapproval of my apparent disregard. He was very fond of Sue and thought she was getting a raw deal. Soon after I started on *Whistle Test* he stopped talking to me altogether. We were walking towards each other along the third-floor corridor at Egton House, home of Radio 1. He walked straight past me. I caught him up and pulled him by the arm into the nearest empty office. He wouldn't look at me, staring at the floor, impassive as I tried to get him to tell me what I'd done wrong. Eventually I just had to let him walk out of there, our friendship in ruins. I never discovered the full reason and the silence lasted nearly 20 years.

Family life was about to be stretched even further by the arrival of a new group in my life. I first saw Wally at a *Melody Maker* band competition final at the Roundhouse, in June 1973. They were from Harrogate in Yorkshire, and had an unusual sound for a British band, comprising drums, bass, guitar, keyboards, violin, pedal steel and vocals, melded together in swirling, extended jams. They didn't win the competition but I thought they were fantastic, and immediately got them in to do a session on *The Monday Programme* and recommended them to Phil Carson at Atlantic Records. Unbeknown to me, Rick Wakeman had seen them too, at their London 'warm-up' gig a few days earlier, at the Greyhound in Fulham, and had also given Atlantic a glowing report. Along with Led Zeppelin, Rick's group Yes was the label's biggest seller and Phil signed them straight away, asking Yes's manager Brian Laine to look after them and commissioning Rick and me to co-produce their first LP, starting immediately. The band couldn't believe it and neither could I. Everything was happening so fast for all of us.

Atlantic brought the band down to London to begin rehearsing for the sessions. I spent a lot of time with them in pre-production mode, familiarizing myself with their songs and going through the arrangements. Vocalist Roy Webber was the main inspiration, with influences similar to mine – David Crosby, Neil Young, Jackson Browne, West Coast and country rock. We immediately forged a friendship that thrives to this day. He is a wonderful person – bright, creative, charismatic, generous, humorous and kind. And he's a red, my contact for tickets to Old Trafford. Red Webber.

The band began to hang out at our flat, often sleeping over. Roy, guitarist Pete Cosker and steel player Paul Middleton were the most frequent visitors, and their runner, Dennis. Occasionally, all seven of them would be crashed out in sleeping bags on the floor in my music room, or on the front room sofa. Miri thought the chaos was fantastic, particularly all the instruments everywhere and the jam sessions.

I'd never done any production work in my life, so I was relying heavily on Rick to give me a beginner's guide, but it didn't happen. I arrived at Morgan studios to discover that he was in America with Yes. I'd had no idea he was going to be away and stood staring blankly at the state-of-the-art, 72-channel mixing desk that shimmered in the middle of the control room in front of me, wondering what the hell I was going to do. It looked like the control panel of a *Star Trek* space ship. Rick's engineer, Paul Tregurtha, waited for me to give him some instructions. 'Where do we start?' was about as much as I could manage.

'Sorry, mate, can't hear a thing,' he said and laughed. My heart sank. 'No, seriously. The first thing we do is get a drum sound.'

We began work on a song called 'Your Own Way', and I immediately enjoyed the process – creating the right sound for each of the instruments and placing them into the overall sound picture, of balancing each instrument with the others and the decision-making involved. What to put in and what to leave out. I've always thought of production as creating the right setting to highlight the songs, as opposed to being a featured device in its own right. It's all too easy to use all the available technology and 'swamp' the recording.

I really liked the idea of what I call 'corner chords' – putting in a rich guitar chord every four or eight bars to bind everything together and create dramatic impact. (The Bee Gees have often used corner chords on their productions, to great effect. Think of 'Heartbreaker' by Dionne Warwick, for example.) It's a kind of 'signature' that crops up on most of the things I've recorded. Roy called it the 'Harris Strum', from which came my nickname with the group – Harry Strum.

Apart from a string section on the fade that Rick arranged for us later (I hummed a riff to him, which he notated), we'd all but finished 'Your Own Way' by the end of that first day. It was a wonderful and emotional experience – hearing our work take shape in those huge speakers.

The album had an open-ended production budget, and Atlantic additionally set up a tab for us on the bar with unlimited access to free food and alcohol. The temptation was just too much. Within hours of the band's violinist, Pete Sage, making a couple of phone calls, friends began to arrive from Harrogate. It seemed like coach loads turned up, putting stuff on the tab, shrouding the place in a cloud of dope smoke. By the start of our fourth session they'd been joined by the guys from Black Sabbath, who were recording across the road, and the bar-bill record that had stood since that crazy night with Marc Bolan and Ringo Starr was consigned to history. Pete told me he'd taken a few Polaroids of the ensuing madness and sent them to Phil Carson, so he could see how the work was coming along. The following day Brian Laine arrived at the studio to impose some discipline and, within minutes, everybody but the band and Dennis were heading back up to Yorkshire.

Brian was getting the band a lot of work. They would frequently break off from the sessions to go out on the road, first with Leo Sayer, then with Lindisfarne. They supported Yes at Alexandra Palace and turned up at festival gigs throughout the summer. The album was released to a four-star 'spotlight' review in *Billboard*. They came into *Whistle Test* and then embarked with me on a college-tour 'Whistle Stop

Roadshow', taking us all over the country in a three-and-a-half-hour package that also featured an acoustic performer, an audience question-and-answer session and a selection of films from the programme. I took Marc Bolan's top road manager, Pete Walmsley, out with me to help with the organization.

The support act was singer/songwriter John Golding, who'd sent me a copy of a most beautiful LP called *Discarded Verse*, which he'd recorded in a little studio in Daventry, in my home county of Northamptonshire. I was so impressed by what I heard that I immediately called up the number on the letter he'd stapled to the album sleeve. It rang for ages. I was just about to put the phone down when a voice grudgingly responded.

'Do you know what time it is?' he said. I must admit I didn't. I'd been listening to music for hours, picking tracks for my radio programmes. 'It's 2 o'clock in the bloody morning!' he told me. I apologized and explained that this was Bob Harris from Radio 1 and that I'd like him to come into *The Monday Programme* to do a session – news that did nothing to lighten his mood. 'Whoever you are, will you please stop phoning and leave me alone!' With that, he hung up.

I didn't know that he'd also sent the album to John Peel. John's reaction had been exactly the same as mine, and he too had called to talk about an appearance on his show. Having already taken some persuading that this really was John Peel, my call an hour later convinced John Golding that someone was playing a practical joke. All became clear when we spoke again the following day.

I passed *Discarded Verse* across to Atlantic Records and they signed him on the spot. When we finished the first Wally album I went back into Morgan studios to make a record with John called *Photographs*, using the same production team as before – Paul Tregurtha, tape engineer George Nicholson and Rick Wakeman. Unfortunately, Rick was in poor health at the time and suffered a mild heart attack soon after we started. But he was brilliant, composing the arrangements from tapes I sent him in hospital and in the middle of it all discharging himself for a day, to come into the studio to supervise the 57-piece orchestra he'd booked to play on 'All My Words Were Taken Away', which closed the first side of the LP. It was a spectacular moment but the title of the song somehow summed up John's attitude to it all. He resented the production process, sitting around while all this stuff was being added to his songs. He felt that they were being 'stolen' from him, which I can understand. Nevertheless, there are some wonderful tracks on that album. 'Loner' on side two is my favourite, with Wally featured as backing musicians.

The band was really great to be around; funny, gentle, creative people I really cared for a lot. They were also totally chaotic, seemingly unaware of the concept of taking responsibility. Important meetings to shape their future came and went without them, publicists would set up top-line magazine and newspaper interviews they couldn't see the value of turning up to. Trying to keep them organized on tour was exhausting. I'd introduce them onstage to discover that half of them were still in the bar. Even when I did a head count before going on, they'd still somehow manage to disappear between then and the end of my introduction, off somewhere, maybe in the dressing room area, in a haze, blissfully ignoring the concern around them that they were beginning to blow it.

Atlantic continued to pump in money. Wally briefly visited America's West Coast and toured Japan with Yes. Roy was increasingly, if reluctantly, taking on the role of spokesman, particularly during the Japanese trip. 'Who does your lighting?' asked a local journalist at the gig in Tokyo.

'We don't have our own lights,' replied Roy. 'We use the Yes rig.'

'No, you don't understand. Your lighting. Who does your lighting?'

'Well, as I say, Yes let us use theirs.'

The journalist was getting frustrated. 'I'm not asking you about that. I want to know about the songs!'

Roy laughed as the penny dropped. 'Oh ... our *writing*. It's me. I do our writing!'

There was something different about them when they got back, somehow. Some of the spirit seemed to have gone out of them, replaced by an unsettling world-weariness. Pete Cosker was becoming particularly affected by the tantalizing possibility of graduating to the successful rock star lifestyle he was already attempting to live, and was finding normal routines more and more difficult to adjust to. At the same time, Atlantic were doing some totting up, to discover that they'd so far underwritten the band to the tune of £87,000. The guys were told this was make-or-break time and that the pressure was now on.

Having started the second album at Morgan, we were relocated to Chris Squire's home studio in Virginia Waters, where it seemed to do nothing but rain. We recorded the sound of a particularly heavy downpour, which we used as a backing track for a song called 'The Mood I'm In', during which Pete wound out a guitar solo that literally cried with pain. He was standing under a spotlight, his skin a kind of porcelain-yellow colour, bathed in the unhealthy sweat of the alcohol and amphetamines that had kept him awake for the previous three days.

The album got great and much appreciated support from Johnnie Walker, who made the single 'Nez Percé' his record of the week on Radio 1. I'm still really proud of that track, recorded during our last weekend at Morgan. Roy had arrived at the studio with the song as a work in progress, having been inspired by a book he'd been reading about Elizabeth Wilson, wife of the chief of the Nez Percé Native American tribe. For the next two days we worked on the arrangement, beginning with a lone piano introduction up to Roy's vocals, adding more voices on the first chorus. As other instruments come in one by one, the track gradually builds through Pete Sage's beautiful violin section to a glorious, swirling steel guitar solo by Paul Middleton, arriving at the final chorus before the instruments pull back Phil Spector-style, re-building again on the fade. By the end of the second afternoon the track was mixed and finished. I thought it sounded absolutely wonderful, but Roy had reservations.

'It needs something on the fade,' he ruminated as we walked across to the bar. 'You know the vocal on 'Dark Side of the Moon'? We need something like that.' We walked into the bar and couldn't believe our luck when we found Madeline Bell, taking a break from her session, relaxing with a cup of coffee and a newspaper. As well as having been a big hit maker with Blue Mink, she was among the most sought-after session singers in London. 'Perfect!' said Roy. 'Go and ask her if she'll do it.' She said she only had a few minutes but agreed to come and listen to the track.

'I'll only do it if I like it,' she announced. We waited apprehensively as she put on the headphones and stood under the light facing the microphone, waiting for the music. 'Just play the bit you want me to sing,' she instructed. We played her the tape and took a quick voice level while she was humming along for pitch. After a few seconds she stopped and told us to do a take. George put the machine in record, and for the next 30 seconds we sat spellbound as she instinctively melded with the music, her voice soaring effortlessly around the top notes, mixing perfectly with the texture of the track. Roy was right, it was the consummate finishing touch. 'Was that all right?' she asked us, looking at her watch. 'I've got to get to my session.' She didn't even have time to hear a playback, but it was wonderful, Madeline. You made the track.

Despite our best efforts, Atlantic declined to give the *Valley Gardens* album much support. They were reluctant to add much to their already heavy investment and soon pulled the plug altogether. Roy started getting calls from Dave Dee, the new Atlantic label boss, demanding the return of all their equipment. Simultaneously, Brian Laine told them he was no longer representing them. No record company, no gigs, no gear. After struggling on for a while with some equipment they'd borrowed from Manfred Mann's Earthband, the guys were faced with the reality that the band was finished. It's a tough business.

For Pete Cosker, the loss of the band was catastrophic. Saddled with a chronic drug problem and with no money, he returned to Yorkshire, drifting through a few gigs, a few jobs, then gradually into homelessness. The other guys tried to help, but Pete became increasingly resentful, occasionally threatening and abusive. Over the next few years his life collapsed completely and he eventually died a truly horrible death in a Harrogate squat. Following a massive overdose, he was found slumped on top of the faulty electric fire that provided his only heating, the front of his body so badly charred that he was hardly recognizable. It nearly breaks my heart, just thinking about it. It's so tragic that the life of the sensitive, smiling, baby-faced lad who spent so many happy hours with us in those long-ago days in West Hampstead, mesmerizing us all with his beautiful guitar playing, should have changed so much as to end like that.

I was getting increasingly desperate to talk to someone about everything, to get advice on how to handle what was happening in my life. Pete Walmsley said I needed proper management and introduced me to Philip Roberge, a New Yorker working in London, looking after the UK affairs of Dee Anthony, who managed Peter Frampton and Gary Wright. Rod Stewart's ex-girlfriend Dee Harrington was his secretary, Judy Garland his idol. Philip also represented jazz–rock group Back Door, British blues maestro Duster Bennett and the incomparable Alexis Korner.

I'd met Alexis through Jeff Griffin a few years earlier and, as our friendship grew, I increasingly turned to him for advice. He'd done it all, having first worked for the BBC soon after the Second World War, before founding the Blues and Barrelhouse Club with Cyril Davies in the early 50s, a venue that soon became a famous stopping-off place for visiting American blues exponents. When Chris Barber began to include blues into his otherwise traditional jazz set, he called in Cyril on harmonica and Alexis on guitar, to augment his live band and accompany singer Ottilie Patterson. It was a learning curve for both of them, and they soon broke away to form Blues Incorporated in 1961 and set up the Ealing Rhythm and Blues Club in a basement underneath the local ABC bakery.

Blues Incorporated variously included musicians drawn to the Ealing Club from all over Britain. Young hopefuls such as Long John Baldry, Jack Bruce, Ginger Baker, Eric Burdon, Graham Bond, Charlie Watts, Brian Jones and, briefly, Mick Jagger were part of the ever-changing line-up of the group. The encouragement and on-going support and enthusiasm Alexis so willingly offered were proving crucial to the development of a whole new generation of young British talent, his protégés going on to find later success with bands such as Cream, The Animals and The Rolling Stones. Later, he was the guiding influence in the formation of Free and in the early career of Robert Plant, as well as having hit singles of his own as a part of the band CCS, whose version of 'Whole Lotta Love' opened *Top Of The Pops* for many years.

After hosting programmes with Jeff for BBC World Service, he took his unique musical approach to Radio 1, where his idiosyncratic mix of 'any music with soul', effortless knowledge and rich, chocolate voice proved an irresistible magnet to this young broadcaster.

I loved hanging out with Alexis, particularly going to gigs. I learned so much. He took Sue and me to see Bob Marley, at the famous 'Live At The Lyceum' concert, in the summer of 1975. The music was fantastic but it turned out to be a nightmare experience. Midway through the evening I began to feel really weird. I couldn't understand what on earth was happening, everything seemed to be turning to liquid in front of my eyes. I felt an uncontrollable urge to dive into the pool of people around me. I couldn't understand why I couldn't find Sue, who reappeared to tell me she'd been sick and urgently suggested that we leave. Someone offered to run us home, and we piled into a Mini, the sunroof open on that hot June night. As we drove through the West End of London, the buildings seemed to be bending over and coming in through the gap in the roof, ejecting a thick liquid into the car that I really thought was going to drown us. Sue tried to restrain me as, consumed by terror, I desperately tried to haul us out of the car.

Somehow we made it home, but the problem of getting me up the 67 stairs of our mansion block was immense. I was violently sick as I fell in through our front door, feeling gruesomely unwell. Sue dialled 999.

It was LSD. Someone must have spiked our drinks. We'd put our glasses down onto the floor for a few moments to light a cigarette. It must have happened then. It was the only explanation we could come up with. What I knew for sure was that I didn't want to experience anything like it again and that Sue's resilience was getting stretched to the absolute limit. Rock'n'roll was completely taking over my life and, on top of everything else, I'd begun to see another woman.

I first saw Jackie at the Speakeasy Club. She was sitting with a group of friends in the restaurant. Having just been on holiday she had a deep brown tan, shown to good effect by a loose white top, which had fallen off her shoulder. She got up to dance and I followed her through the club. I thought she looked amazing, with her long black hair and the way she moved when she danced. I went over to her table and we sat and talked for a while. She gave me her telephone number. On the way home I resolved not to call her. About ten days later a postcard arrived at Jeff's office from the States, addressed to me. 'Noo Yoik, just like I pictured it. Love Jack.' That was it. I suddenly really wanted to see her again.

She'd modelled in the late 60s, then started her own clothes business, working with record companies and promoters to design merchandizing for tours and album launches. She really loved rock'n'roll, knew loads of people, seemed to understand the industry, and had clear ambitions for my role in it, which was more than could be said for me at the time. I was more aware of being in the whirl of becoming famous, an experience I was struggling to come to grips with.

Loads of work was coming in, people I'd never met before were telling me how great I was. Everybody seemed to want me to do something for them, with big smiles on their faces. Press coverage was extensive and complimentary (among my awards in 1973 was one from *NME* for 'talking soft and saying little'). Doors opened everywhere.

I began to believe all this stuff. I could feel my radar going haywire and I didn't like it. I just couldn't work out who was sincere any more, a confusion I even tried explaining to the press. 'It seems to be automatic that immediately you get a television programme, people expect you to get all big-time,' I wrote in 1973 in *Sounds* magazine. 'And they don't just expect, they accept the fact that you already have done. It's been really disappointing to see people who previously I was close to get like this. You know, suddenly I'm not just Bob, someone they could maybe come round and listen to a few albums with. Suddenly I've become "Bob Harris". But I don't think I've changed.' I needed somebody to help and support me and Jackie offered wise council and protection, with not a hint of disapproval.

The resulting devastation on my home life was total and I began to do damage. One day I was staying with Sue, the next I'd be with Jackie. Miri was hysterical with fear, throwing herself to the floor and gripping my ankle with all her might, in an attempt to stop me from walking out the door. She and Em heard constantly raised voices and witnessed their mother's deep unhappiness. Sue told me years later that she'd felt completely trapped. Her priority was the girls, yet not even the maternal instinct was completely clear-cut in those new-found days of strident feminism.

'Do you remember how many couples around us at the time were breaking up?' she asked me. 'The pressure was on young women to break out and express their own identity. I felt it too, but you don't necessarily want to if you have kids. You want to be with them.' Sue didn't particularly want to be out at the concerts and parties with me, the music industry just didn't impress her. But neither did she want to spend so many evenings on her own, stuck in the flat, looking after the girls and, for the first time, everything wasn't 'really great' any more. America was my escape.

FOUR

The States, the President and Punk

I LEFT THE SLEET AND RAIN OF A STRIKE-TORN, POWER-CUT BRITAIN on 8th February 1974 and headed for the sunshine of California, to record material for the six-part *The Beach Boys Story* for Radio 1. Sitting there on that 11-hour journey, I couldn't believe my luck. Here was a chance to give my brain a break, enjoy a new experience and spend time with one of my all-time favourite bands.

Jeff Griffin was already there. He'd spent a couple of weeks in Los Angeles with Bill Fowler, head of the Warner Brothers UK Promotion Department, talking to people, getting background information and setting up interviews. They met me at the airport and took me to our hotel, The Beverly Rodeo, on Rodeo Drive in Beverly Hills, right in the heart of one of the best shopping streets in the world, enveloped by palm trees, and a short drive from Sunset Strip. The weather was glorious, with a cloudless blue sky. Overnight I'd flown from winter weather into summer sunshine, a first-time experience for me.

The freeway system was incredible, with anything from three to seven lanes, all packed with traffic. The fumes were so bad they made our eyes smart. Exits and entrances fed cars in and out on both sides, tailgating was the norm, despite all the 'Keep Your Distance' decals. With a speed limit of 55mph, everyone just cruised their 5.5-litre engines in the nine-miles-per-gallon sunshine, filling the LA basin with a smog so thick you could photograph it. I was in the front of the car, dialling across the radio stations, looking for 93KHJ. The Love Unlimited Orchestra was No. 1 with Barry White's 'Love's Theme', soon to give way to 'Seasons In The Sun' by Terry Jacks. Al Wilson was in the Top 3 with 'Show And Tell', such a great record.

Los Angeles sprawls across an area more than 60 miles from top to toe, in straight lines and rectangles. You can see across the whole city from the Hollywood Hills, an incredible sight, particularly at night. A poolside view is best of all and we soon realized that getting anything done in Los Angeles was a *mañana* affair. 'The weather's great and the vibe's laid-back. Let's do it tomorrow, man.'

Before we met the Boys, we decided we had to see the beach – specifically Venice Beach, with its writers and actors, and all those browned-skinned Californian girls in their bikinis, roller-skating past the murals and the street entertainers on the promenade, while the guys worked out at the beach gymnasiums. The music seemed to pump at us from everywhere, from the brightly coloured psychedelic clothes shops and cafes that edged the sand, or from a hundred ghetto blasters that provided the accompaniment to the hand-ball games. Serious research, of course, exploring the culture of The Beach Boys' music.

Many of the most exciting late-night activity centres were situated close together, on or near Sunset Strip. Three great music clubs, the Roxy, the Whisky-A-Go-Go and the Troubadour, where Elton John made his American début, were within a few blocks of each other, all within walking distance of the famous Continental Hyatt House Hotel, where most of the main bands stayed when they were in town, complete with its ABC cinema-style awning, announcing their arrival. In the centre of it all was the main social centre, a disco called the Rainbow Bar and Grill, and there was even a Tower Records store at the end of the block. Add the X-rated clubs and cinemas and it seemed to me that these few hundred yards offered a greater concentration of rock'n'roll lifestyle than anywhere else in the world. Alice Cooper, having just joined us from the local golf course and the unlikely pleasure of a couple of rounds with Johnny Mathis, offered to take us out for a night on the town.

The Rainbow Bar and Grill struck me as being the Los Angeles version of the Speakeasy and was full of Brits. Hamish Stuart and Robbie McIntosh were there, celebrating the completion of the new Average White Band album, featuring their American No. 1 single 'Pick Up The Pieces'. Frankie Miller had a table, Phil Lynott was holding court. We bumped into Iain Matthews, then Gerry Beckley from America, who told us that there was a party at Danny Hutton's house in the hills, if we wanted to go. (Mama told me not to, but we did call in.) Alice introduced me to Al Kooper. Wow, this was amazing.

With some other people from Warner Brothers, we finished up at a little studio off the Strip, meeting Frank Zappa for an early-hours playback of some new stuff he'd just recorded. Having had virtually no sleep since I'd arrived in town, I sank down gratefully into a beanbag in the middle of the control room and, as someone pressed the playback button and manic Zappa improvisation filled the speakers at a million decibels, I fell asleep. I woke to an embarrassed silence, everybody looking at me. The man was not best pleased.

By the following morning I'd completely lost my voice. The combination of the smog, Marlboro cigarettes, late nights and loud conversation meant that I arrived at Carl Wilson's house to record our first interview with a throat so sore I could hardly speak.

Arrangements with The Beach Boys were best described as 'loose'. They were supposed to be gathering for rehearsals for a big tour, due to start in ten days' time, but so far none of them had turned up. Al Jardine was expected 'sometime soon', Mike Love was at a transcendental meditation centre in Switzerland, Dennis Wilson was – God only knows where. Carl was planning to rehearse the backing musicians with the help of drummer Ricky Fataar from The Flame, who'd joined the group with Blondie Chaplin and Daryl Dragon to replace the missing Bruce Johnston and Brian Wilson, but Ricky didn't seem to be in town either. Meanwhile, the rehearsal studios stayed empty, apart from a few roadies and a couple of prospective back-up guys, just hanging out and jamming.

The Beach Boys were enjoying a remarkable renaissance at that time. Having been America's answer to The Beatles in the mid-60s, producing records described as having 'changed the face of American music for the next 30 years', they'd drifted dramatically into decline. Brian Wilson, the main creative inspiration, took to his bed, brother Dennis took up with Charles Manson. Their record sales collapsed as new psychedelic bands dominated the charts. They just weren't cool any longer and when they left Capitol Records in 1969 in a blaze of litigation, it seemed their time had gone.

But the release of the glorious *Surf's Up* album in 1971 not only revived their musical and commercial viability, but in songs like 'Don't Go Near The Water' and 'Student Demonstration Time' they demonstrated an ecological and political awareness hitherto unsuspected. Carl Wilson had taken the production reins in the absence of his brother Brian, and had brought a more cerebral, mellow approach to the music.

I liked Carl a lot. He was friendly and helpful, a very warm, peaceful person, but with a melancholy air about him, I thought. His house was situated in Coldwater Canyon, at the end of a long tarmac drive, enclosed by the hills. We started recording our interview in his 'meditation room', before the combined interruptions of young son and telephone calls caused us to postpone further conversation until a couple of days later, at the group's studio in Santa Monica. It was a truly magnificent complex, converted from an old cinema, with state-of-the-art equipment, stained glass windows, kids' rooms, chill-out areas and creature comforts, situated a few miles from the beach. The band had recently transported most of the main equipment to Baambrugge, in the Netherlands, where it had been reassembled for the recording of their 1973 *Holland* album, broken back down and returned to Santa Monica, an eight-month project that had cost the group almost a million dollars.

I called Mike Appleton to alert him to the possibility of a television interview, excuse enough for him to get on a plane and join us (hobbling on a stick as he'd hurt his back) in time to record a separate piece at the studio with Carl for *Whistle Test*. After several attempts, Jeff had also managed to pin down Al Jardine for a couple of hours, so we now had material in the can. Predictably, Dennis failed to turn up the following day, so while we waited outside we recorded an impromptu interview with Ricky Fataar, in the back of his station wagon.

Jeff had tried all kinds of ways to get in touch with Brian Wilson, but with no success. He hadn't given any interviews for several years and we knew that just talking to him would be a major coup. Carl told us that Brian didn't even come out of his room these days, that he didn't want to see us, and that we should plan to finish off without him. But we persevered, phoning the record company, contacting his manager, trying to break down the wall of people protecting him. It was probably people like us, and the weight of expectation, that sent him to his room in the first place.

We explained the problems to Brian's co-writer, Van Dyke Parks, while he sat crunching celery on the corner of my bed, following an interview in my room at the Beverly Rodeo Hotel the following day. He picked up the phone and dialled a local number. 'Hi, Brian. Yeah, fine. I'm with some guys from the BBC. They want to come over and talk to you. I'll tell them to be there at 8.' After all our frustrating attempts to get through, we couldn't believe it was that easy!

One of the nicest moments of the whole trip was an interview that afternoon with Dory Previn, an intelligent and controversial woman, formerly married to orchestra leader André Previn. We sat in the rustic kitchen of her home in Hollywood Hills as she performed 'Coldwater Canyon' and 'Brando', two songs from her new LP. She told us that she liked to drive out into the desert and primal scream to relieve her inner stress. I kept thinking of Brian Wilson.

Two hours later we checked in at the security post on the perimeter of the exclusive Bel-Air estate as the guard phoned ahead to get clearance from the Wilson family to open up the electronic gates and let us through. Brian's wife, Marilyn, was waiting for us at the house and took us through a thick, oak doorway, down a short staircase and into a long, high-ceilinged, wood-panelled room, empty except for two leather sofas, a mahogany coffee table and a white piano. As Jeff set up the recording equipment we could hear what sounded like electronic music, thumps and odd wailing noises coming from somewhere in the building but Marilyn seemed unconcerned. She and I had met before, on my first-ever *Whistle Test* and she was friendly, relaxed and happy to talk. We'd been recording for 10 or 15 minutes when suddenly the door burst open and there at the top of the staircase, hands in pockets, stood Brian Wilson. He looked dishevelled and uncertain, transferring his considerable weight uncomfortably from one foot to another, staring at the polished wood floor.

Marilyn explained why we were there and, after standing for a while making up his mind what to do, he slowly came down into the room towards us, staring intently at the stereo microphones Jeff had placed in stands on the table. 'What is that?' was the tentative, straight-faced enquiry, as he circled the table to look at the microphones more closely. 'Is that a submarine?' Jeff and I looked at one another, not really knowing what to say. This was a serious question. Brian stood for a minute or so in the silence, examining the microphones. Finally, he looked up and around the room, then walked over to the piano. 'I tell you what, you guys, I'll play you a song.'

This was an incredible moment, more than we'd ever hoped for. Here we were, in Brian Wilson's piano room, about to hear an exclusive preview of a brand new song. The feeling was electric. Jeff clicked the tape machine into record mode as Brian lifted the piano lid and prepared to play. He paused for a moment, then wrung his hands and looked across at Marilyn. 'Er ... honey, what's wrong with the piano?'

'Oh, Brian, don't you remember?' She smiled sympathetically. 'It's being fixed. You know ... they've taken some of the keys with them.'

My heart sank as I saw the gap under that piano lid, looking like a huge open mouth without any teeth. Brian sat for a moment, thinking. Then, without another word, he slowly got to his feet, stuffed his hands back into his pockets, and ambled reflectively out of the room. A few moments later, the electronic music started again. We thanked and cursed our luck in equal measure.

The Beach Boys' schedule meant that we couldn't do any more recording until the first gig of their tour, when Mike Love and Dennis Wilson were due to arrive. So we took up an offer to spend a couple of days filming and recording with Jesse Colin Young, one of my favourite artists at that time. Originally from New York, he gained great success on the West Coast, writing the hippie anthem 'Get Together', a Top-5 single, recorded with his group, The Youngbloods. The resulting residuals and royalties had funded the building of a dream – a remote house, situated 15 minutes off the nearest highway, close to the ridge top in a hillside forest near Point Reyes, northern California, about 30 miles from San Francisco. The view was absolutely breathtaking, stretching 15 or 20 miles through the trees across to the Pacific Ocean, sparkling in the distance. He'd added a log-cabin studio below the house and put a glass roof on it, so that he and his family could see each other while he was working. The studio was also the focal point of the Racoon record label, with Michael Hurley the most prominent and eccentric of the roster of local roots-based artists the label featured. It was such a beautiful, organic place I didn't want to leave. The close family feeling that existed there touched a chord with me, and the visit triggered a friendship that lasted several years. Jesse and his wife, Suzi, came over to London a few months later, when Jesse supported Crosby, Stills and Nash at Wembley on 14th September, on a bill that also included The Band, Joni Mitchell and Tom Scott. My wife, Sue, had a particularly strong affinity with Suzi and felt that, as a couple, they'd found a way to successfully integrate the pull of the music industry with the demands of family life.

Jeff and I briefly returned to Los Angeles before flying on to Colorado Springs to complete our final recordings with The Beach Boys. We met Mike Love and his girlfriend at the airport and drove them to the Airforce Academy, the rather austere opening venue of the tour. No one seemed to be approaching the gig with any enthusiasm. In contrast to the temperature on the West Coast it was freezing cold under a threatening grey sky. The building had an icy chill, as we echoed our way through the corridors to the dressing room, where we found Dennis Wilson having a shower. 'I'll only do the interview if we record it now,' he told us through the steam. 'You're gonna have to come in and join me.' Jeff suspended a microphone above the water and I tried shouting questions at him from outside the cubicle. Eventually, Carl persuaded him to relent and come out so we could finally get about 15 minutes of his undivided attention.

The gig wasn't good. The band played in a huge gymnasium inside the Academy building and the sound was awful, echoing back off the walls. The guys seemed to be doing little more than going through the motions, mechanically playing their 'greatest hits' medleys. The atmosphere remained flat throughout. But I got to meet Jim Stafford, who was supporting them on the tour, a really nice guy. I still play 'Spiders & Snakes' on the radio from time to time.

We left the venue immediately after the show and got to the hotel just as it started to snow. It was already past midnight, yet we still had to record the interview with Mike Love, a matter of some urgency since we were leaving at 6.30 that morning to catch a plane. Mike, Jeff and I sat up all that night, talking. Carl joined us, then Al Jardine. It was like a gathering of old friends and provided all the remaining material we needed. We lost time completely and by the time I finally opened the curtains and looked out, four or five inches of snow had fallen.

It was just getting light as we slithered towards the airport in our hired car. I still have no idea how Jeff managed to find the way in that blizzard. Every road sign was a white-out – and this was way before satnav. After a 90-minute delay while ice was removed from the wings of the plane, we finally took off, heading for New York, where we arrived exhausted, late that afternoon. After California it looked disgusting. The city was almost bankrupt at the time and it showed. There were piles of rubbish everywhere, the roads were badly potholed. The springs were poking up through the back seat of the yellow cab as we careered into Manhattan, the bullet-shielded driver hurling us past what seemed like endless blocks of boarded-up, graffiti-covered building fronts, burnt-out cars and people sleeping rough. There was a tangible atmosphere of menace on the streets. After the sunshine and glamour of Hollywood, with all those manicured lawns and movie star houses, the contrast was dramatic. I wasn't to know then, but each time I've been back to New York I've liked it more and more. Over 20 visits, spanning more than 25 years, I've watched as the place has gradually been transformed from the ugly neglect of the mid-70s into one of the safest and cleanest big cities in America.

Yes were playing at Madison Square Garden that evening and, despite feeling flat and sleepy, Jeff and I joined up with Mike Appleton again and made it to the gig. It was a spectacular triumph, one of the high spots of the band's entire career. They were in commanding form, sharp and structured, the audience lapping up the spectacular stage presentation to the extent of three encores. I recorded a conversation with Steve Howe and Rick Wakeman the following day, before going over to Atlantic Records to film interviews with Aretha Franklin and her legendary producer, Jerry Wexler, a great hero of mine.

We then embarked on a celebratory evening on the town with Dave Cousins and a couple of the guys from the Strawbs, Bill Fowler and Rick, who set us up at the table of a local bar with a pack of cards, for a game of Jacks. 'The rules are simple,' he explained. 'When the cards are dealt, the first person who gets a Jack nominates a drink. The second person nominates a mixer. The third person pays for it. The fourth person drinks it. If it's some vile combination like sherry and tomato juice you can drink something of your own choice, except you've got to have a double.'

We all agreed it sounded fair enough except, for some reason, I kept getting the fourth Jack. Surrounded by glasses, I remember very little of the rest of the evening, except that we finished up at CBGB's Club at about 2 o'clock in the morning where I probably fell over.

We sat on the plane home the following day feeling absolutely exhausted, in my case hung over, but thrilled and excited by our American experience. We had loads of good material in the can and we now knew we could make this work, picking up local crews and planning as we went along. It was the trip that paved the way for many future visits.

When we got back we went straight from Heathrow Airport to Television Centre to broadcast that week's *Whistle Test*. As well as a live Babe Ruth session and concert footage of Loggins and Messina, the programme featured the Yes interview, already rush-edited from the conversation we'd recorded in New York 36 hours earlier. When I finally got home, I slept for two days solid.

The Beach Boys Story was broadcast on Radio 1 at the end of 1974, after my *Monday Programme* had teamed up with *Whistle Test* for a concert by Van Morrison and the Caledonia Orchestra, live from the Rainbow Theatre, on 21st May that year. It was the first time BBC radio and television merged for a stereo rock simulcast. I left a long track running in the studio at Broadcasting House, jumped into a fast car, pelted down the Westway and arrived at Television Centre in time to back announce the track and introduce the concert. You couldn't do that today. You'd be gridlocked for about an album and a half.

I didn't know it then but the first part of my Radio 1 career was coming to a close. Derek Chinnery, who'd taken over from Mark Wight as Network Controller, didn't much like the kind of music we were featuring on *Sounds Of The 70s*, and took all the programmes off the air early in 1975. It was the first time I'd ever lost a programme and the last time I appeared on Radio 1 for more than 14 years.

I immediately joined Radio Luxembourg, recording two shows a week at their studios in Mayfair, central London. I didn't really enjoy the experience, to be honest. Despite the fact that Alexis Korner came in with me a few times, my heart wasn't in it and I've always preferred to do programmes live. But with the rest of my life so busy, it didn't seem overly important. It would be a couple of years before I really locked back into radio again.

The Van Morrison concert was part of a new expansion of *Whistle Test* output. More facilities had been made available to the programme with a move to TC5, a huge, hanger-like studio on the ground floor of Television Centre, also used for *Top Of The Pops*. The extra space meant that we could now accommodate two full band line-ups, all live. War came in to play 'Baby Brother', Bob Marley and the Wailers performed a brilliant version of 'Stir It Up'. The late Jim Croce and Bill Withers, two of the nice guys of the music industry, came in to perform, Tim Buckley did 'Dolphins' and 'Honey Man', Captain Beefheart larged his way through 'This Is The Day'. We broadcast The Rolling Stones and Stevie Wonder specials, concert footage of Steely Dan and a Joni Mitchell concert at the New Victoria Theatre. Supertramp and Manfred Mann's Earthband did excellent studio sets and we regularly featured Queen, with whom we had, by now, become good friends.

We began to stage the occasional concert at the Shepherd's Bush Theatre, with Jackson Browne, Eric Clapton, Bonnie Raitt and, famously, Dr Hook, changing out of their mock Bay City Rollers outfits behind a thin screen, which did little to cover their modesty. Mike Appleton and Jeff Griffin additionally extended their collaboration with the introduction of *Sight and Sound In Concert* and *Rock Goes To College*.

Whistle Test also forged a particularly strong association with Led Zeppelin. Their manager, Peter Grant, was otherwise keen to keep them off the small screen. They didn't put out singles, so they didn't do *Top Of The Pops* and they refused invitations onto the big American TV shows that had traditionally been an important part of the circuit. They wouldn't normally do television interviews but they really liked our show, so whenever they had anything to say, they said it to us. I interviewed them in all sorts of places, from American hotel rooms to a boat on the River Thames, mostly talking to Robert Plant.

Led Zeppelin had recently launched their Swan Song record label and threw a huge Halloween Party 'on the night of the full moon of 31st October 1974', to mark the UK release of the label's first album, *Silk Torpedo* by The Pretty Things. Coaches ferried us to Chislehurst Caves in Kent for one of the most bizarre events I've ever attended. It was like being at a medieval orgy. Flames from huge torches flickered light across the dark, dank recesses of the caves, while a crowd of maybe 200 people watched George Melly perform jazz tunes and bawdy songs in a nun's habit, naked girls wrestling in jelly in open coffins at his feet. Some people were covered in fake blood, others were wearing Dracula outfits or bondage gear. Horror films were projected onto the walls while theatre groups enacted torture plays and executions. In all, it was a strange and disturbing night, one of many Led Zeppelin experiences through the years.

Whistle Test ended 1974 with the now traditional 'best of the year' selection on New Year's Eve, preceded by an 'Elton John Special', live from the Hammersmith Odeon, and simulcast on Radio 1. It was a wonderful night, with Elton at his happiest and best. Looking out from the side of the stage, it felt so good to see so many smiling faces expressing their deep affection for Elton, arms waving, joining in with every lyric of every song.

I bumped into Elton again a few weeks later at a Labelle reception in Kensington to mark the release of 'Lady Marmalade'. He was leaving as I arrived, rushing off to Heathrow Airport to catch a plane to the States. He told me he was playing at Madison Square Garden in a few days' time and planned to invite John Lennon to the concert. It was an appearance that proved to be a high point in Elton's American career, with John Lennon joining him onstage for a triumphant performance of 'Whatever Gets You Through The Night', after which John was quoted as saying, 'Yeah, I enjoyed it. But I wouldn't want to do it for a living.'

I'd asked Elton to tell John how much we wanted to talk to him and a few days later Mike and I were in the office when John Lennon called from New York. He told us that he would love to do something around the release of the *Rock 'N' Roll* album, that he was missing England, and that this would be a perfect opportunity to send his son, Julian, a postcard from America. He talked about possible times and dates, and Mike asked him if he'd like the fee sent out immediately. 'I don't want a fee,' he retorted at the suggestion.

'This is the BBC, John,' explained Mike. 'There are systems. We have to draw up a contract and pay you a fee, otherwise you're not a credited contributor and we won't be able to use the piece on the programme.'

'How much is it?' asked John.

'Fifteen pounds,' replied Mike.

'You're not serious?' I could hear John's laughter from the other side of the room. 'Well, I'll tell you what to do,' he suggested. 'Bring me £15-worth of chocolate olivers. I can't get them over here.'

With the handwritten rider clause added to the contract, we delivered the chocolate olivers (a version of Bath Oliver biscuits, covered in dark chocolate) when we met, at the beginning of April 1975, at the BBC offices in the Rockefeller Center on 5th Avenue.

John had recently returned to Yoko in New York, following his 18-month 'lost weekend' in Los Angeles with his new love, Yoko's assistant, May Pang, working with Phil Spector on the *Rock 'N' Roll* album, a period of 'avoiding reality', as he put it. 'I was sick of that thing where "John Lennon writes new song ... is it about Paul or is it about himself?",' he explained. 'I told Phil I just wanted to be [his wife] Ronnie on this one. It was the first time since the early days of The Beatles that I'd let an album get out of my control. I'll never do it again. The sessions got really crazy. There'd be 27 people there and 15 of them would be out of their minds. Phil Spector works in strange ways, his woodwork to perform.'

While he was in Los Angeles, John had also been working on the production of the new Harry Nilsson album. 'We had some fun. There was Harry, Keith Moon, me and Ringo, all living in the same house, and we had some moments, folks.' John laughed. 'But it got a little near the knuckle. Harry was encouraging me. Usually there's someone there saying "shut up, Lennon", but there was nobody there and it all got totally ridiculous. That's when I straightened out, then suddenly I was the straight one in the middle of all these mad, mad people.'

We talked a lot about his fight for a green card, without which he wouldn't leave America, fearing immigration would never let him back in. During protracted legal wrangling and court appearances he'd met opposition from the Nixon administration and the right wing, the same kind of people who burnt Beatles records after his famous 'we're bigger than Jesus' quote in 1966.

'It keeps the Conservatives happy that they're doing something about me and what I represent,' he told me. 'But it also keeps the Liberals happy that I haven't been thrown out yet.' He went on to tell me about being followed and having his phone tapped. 'At that time it was pre-Watergate, so you can imagine ... John Lennon says his phone's being tapped, men following in car. I think they wanted to scare me, and I was. I was scared paranoid. People thought I was crazy ... well, they do anyway. You know, "Lennon, you big-headed maniac, what do they want to follow you around for?" And that's what I'm saying. What do they want? I'm not going to cause them any problems.'

He'd been told that Elvis Presley regarded him as subversive and had colluded with President Nixon to compile evidence of extreme political activity and possible drug use. Lennon and Presley met once, in a Los Angeles hotel room in 1965, and had taken an immediate dislike to one another. 'The whole thing was affecting my work,' he reflected. 'I tried to pretend that it wasn't happening to me, that it was water off the back, or whatever that thing is. But when I got right down to it, and I got down to it, folks, I realized that it was a constant thing, non-stop, like a toothache that wouldn't go away. I think I've come to terms with it a bit, but it was interfering with everything. It was affecting my whole life, actually.'

'I go through these troughs every few years,' he went on. 'It was less noticeable in The Beatles because the image of The Beatles would carry you through it. I was in the middle of a trough when we were doing *Help!* but you can't really see it. I'm singing *Help!* for a kick-off. But it was less noticeable, because you were protected by the image and the power of The Beatles. Now, when it happens, I'm on my own, so it's easier to get sniped. So, I've been in a trough and now I'm coming out of it. Whoopee! I'll be around for the rest of my life in this business and I just don't take it too seriously any more.'

I asked him if he regretted writing 'How Do You Sleep?', a stinging condemnation of Paul McCartney. 'No,' was the reply. 'Somebody said the other day it was about me.'

He thought for a moment. 'Two things I regretted,' he said. 'There was so much talk about Paul that people missed the track. It was a good track. And I should've kept my mouth shut. It could've been about anybody and I regret the association. But ... why do you wanna regret? He lived through it, and the thing that matters is how he and I feel about it. Him and me are OK, so I don't care what writers or commentators say about it, I go through my thing. You know, "Lennon Blasts Hollies", that kind of thing.' We laughed.

'I've always been that. Our first national press was about me beating up a disc jockey at Paul's 21st birthday party. That was the first Beatles national press and we got the back page of the *Mirror*. I've always been a little loose. I hope it'll change, because I'm fed up with waking up in the papers. But if it doesn't, my friends are my friends, whatever way.'

Personally, I've always really liked McCartney. We first met outside Broadcasting House, soon after I started doing *Whistle Test*. Jeff Griffin and I had got out of my car and I was just locking the door when I felt a tap on my shoulder. 'Are you Bob Harris?' enquired a familiar, smiling figure. I nodded, completely taken aback. 'Good one. Keep up the good work.' He gave me a thumbs-up sign. 'Sorry, can't stop. Just wanted to say hello.' And with that, he ran back to a waiting taxi. We stood transfixed, watching as the cab headed into the traffic and on towards Oxford Circus. A double thumbs-up from the back window and the car was gone. I turned to Jeff.

'Err ... that wasn't who I thought it was ... was it?'

'Nah,' said Jeff. 'Couldn't have been.'

After contemplating the event for a few moments, I was inclined to agree. By the time we reached Jeff's office in Egton House, We'd convinced ourselves that it must have been someone else.

Eighteen months later I met Paul formally for the first time, to record an interview with him about Buddy Holly. He'd recently acquired the publishing rights for the Holly song catalogue and was promoting 'Buddy Holly Week'. 'Yeah, 'course it was me. I'm a fan,' he told me.

We met again for an interview when the *Wings Over America* album was released in 1976. Linda invited me to the MPL offices in

Soho Square and took me down to where Paul was working on some new music. I was amazed to discover that he'd entirely recreated the EMI Studio 2 control room in the basement of the building, complete with the analogue equipment, tape machines and mixing desk The Beatles had used on the *Sgt. Pepper* album. The real Abbey Road control room has a window through which you can look down, as from a television gallery, into the cavernous studio below. In an attempt to re-produce this sense of space in such a small basement, Linda had taken a photograph of the studio through the control room window, blown it up to full size and put it on the appropriate wall. They'd built in a false door where the real door should have been and even put a battery behind the tiny clock on the wall, so it said the right time. It was a perfect recreation of the famous control room that had housed so many Beatles memories, built with meticulous and affectionate attention to detail.

Watching the John Lennon interview again, I was struck by how informal it was. No publicists rushing around saying 'You can't say that.' Thirty minutes, one camera – you don't see television like that any more. Yet the relaxed atmosphere promoted the intimacy that led to John being extraordinarily open about his thinking. I was able to learn a lot about him as a person by giving him the space to talk. So it was with Mick Jagger, Robert Plant and others. A mutual level of trust existed, which led to people feeling comfortable and willing to open up about themselves.

John called us when we got back to the UK to say that he'd really enjoyed the experience and that he planned to record a couple of songs for us with his band Elephant's Memory, especially for the show. We were still waiting for the film a few hours before the programme went out, but it arrived just in time, with 'Stand By Me' and 'Slippin' And Slidin'' the two featured songs.

Live television can be a hazardous experience. I was intrigued that Lou Reed needed to have a minder on each shoulder when he joined me in the studio. Then I noticed that those two huge guys were literally supporting him, one under each arm, the toes of his black boots dragging across the floor as they dumped him into the chair beside me. I looked at him as he sat there motionless, his eyes closed, with 20 seconds to go before we went live. I did the introduction and asked him the first question. The few seconds of subsequent silence felt like a lifetime but gradually, from deep in his throat came a kind of growl, developing into an approximation of speech. It was as if someone had slowly begun to turn a key in his back, as he gradually wound himself up enough to give me some kind of answer, and go on through the rest of the interview.

Soon after, Keith Richards arrived in the gallery, swigging from a bottle of Jack Daniels, half-empty by the time he ambled through to join me. By the end of the interview the bottle was finished, yet he was completely unaffected. The myth was reality. Keith really could take it, an impression confirmed by an after-programme visit to one of the top Knightsbridge restaurants, where a centre table had been reserved for our party of 14. Keith moved crockery and cutlery aside, casually pulled a foolscap envelope out of his pocket, and emptied several thousand pounds-worth of cocaine onto the middle of the table, oblivious to the reaction of people sitting nearby.

Yet, this kind of moment was and is not exceptional. Drugs and rock'n'roll have always had a close relationship, often more overt in the bomb-proof world of superstardom. Personally, I've acquired a strong aversion to hard drugs in general, cocaine in particular. It's a very insidious, persuasive addiction, fooling users by making them feel indestructible, while stripping away their health, their self-respect and their bank account. Unless you've got the constitution of a Keef and the spending power of a global multinational, stay clear.

If you ever thought that getting into drugs was a good idea, the appearance of Paul Kossoff on *Whistle Test* in 1975, a few months before his death, must surely have changed your mind. Totally disorientated and incapable of cohesive speech, he should never have been wheeled out into the studio in front of live television cameras. After struggling for a minute or so to disguise the obvious, I called on the help of Leo Sayer, who was standing behind me ready to begin his live set, who immediately joined me, sitting on the edge of my little rostrum as he talked about Paul's career and expressed his sincere admiration for the musician he once was.

Rolling Stone critic Jon Landau had, by now, famously identified the future of rock'n'roll. Summed up in two words it was ... Bruce Springsteen. The *Born To Run* album had just been released to fantastic critical acclaim, an album that still has impact today as recording of high energy, magnificent intensity, great musicianship and potent lyrical imagery. With its songs about jobs, cars, girlfriends and escape, it touched a chord with a whole generation of young American working-class kids, accurately voicing their aspirations, frustrations and fears. The album and subsequent record-breaking tour became the biggest music event for years, and we decided that the next major *Whistle Test* project would be to explore the possibility of screening Bruce's one-off UK show at the Hammersmith Odeon in the autumn of 1975. To discuss the various plans involved, his manager Mike Appel invited Mike Appleton and me over to Los Angeles for an end-of-tour showcase gig at the Roxy Club, on Sunset, on 17th October 1975. It was the week Bruce made the front cover of both *Time* and *Newsweek* magazines, a unique feat at the time. All the billboards on the Strip were saying the same thing, a big Columbia-funded advertising campaign reading 'Is The World Ready For ...?' Expectation had been set at stratospheric level and everyone was wondering if he could live up to the hype.

As I looked around the club, people were sitting back in their chairs waiting, arms folded, with 'OK, kid, let's see how good you really are' expressions on their faces. George Harrison was there, and The Carpenters. Jimmy Connors was at a table with some friends, all the big music business people were doing hospitality. Bruce Springsteen could easily have died that night, but instead he was sensational. After the first number we were all on our feet, people at the back were up on the tables for a better view. The atmosphere was incredible, the onstage camaraderie within the E Street Band spilling into the audience and adding to the vibe of warmth and excitement. They did six encores, including a memorable acoustic version of 'Pretty Flamingo', Bruce sweating in his denim shirt, bathed in a thin shaft of smoky blue light as he lived those lyrics. It was a fabulous 'right place, right time' experience. Now we knew what all the fuss was about, and why people have always said that to really 'get' Bruce Springsteen, you HAVE to see him live. While he, Mike Appleton and Mike Appel had their meeting the next day I got to play handball with the guys in the band on Santa Monica Beach.

I saw many wonderful concerts over the next couple of years. I introduced Queen in Hyde Park to a crowd of more than 150,000 people in September 1976, and the Knebworth Festival that same summer. Elton John took me to see The Eagles at Wembley and I saw Paul McCartney's triumphant Wings concert there in 1976. I compèred at the Whisky-A-Go-Go for Tom Petty and The Heartbreakers, then again in Los Angeles the following year at the Roxy, when we filmed The Cars. Rory Gallagher, Hall and Oates, and Lynyrd Skynyrd were among those who performed outstanding concerts for *Whistle Test* at the Shepherd's Bush Theatre. Above all those fabulous nights, however, that magic performance by Bruce Springsteen was the best I'd ever seen.

As it happened, we weren't able to reach an agreement to televise the Shepherd's Bush gig, which is probably just as well, as he was strangely muted that night. Not so when we saw him next, in New Haven late in 1978. Without doubt, this is my all-time favourite concert, even better than that night at the Roxy, and this time we had the television cameras with us.

The venue was about the size of the Hammersmith Odeon, so it was big enough to generate a real atmosphere, but not too big that the performer was a distant dot on the stage. Bruce was absolutely electric, strutting around the stage like he owned it, coming down into the audience time after time, to be completely engulfed by mesmerized, dancing fans. We filmed a section of the set and put out 'Rosalita' on the programme a few weeks later.

It was a four-hour show, beginning at 8 o'clock, with just a short break midway through. He looked exhausted when I met him as he came off stage at the end of the final encore. 'When do you want to do the interview?' I asked, expecting him to tell us to wait while he chilled out for a while and recovered.

'Let's do it right now,' he said. We'd already set up the lights and the camera in his dressing room, so we just sat down and started to talk. He was eloquent, interesting and convincing, as he sat wiping away the sweat with the towel he'd draped round his neck, regularly thumbing his nose like a boxer. He talked passionately about his music, about the friendships within the band and about the frustrations of the two-and-a-half-year hiatus forced on his career by the litigation between himself and his now ex-manager, Mike Appel.

We finished filming about 2.15 in the morning. 'Do you wanna come and see some music with me?' he asked us.

There was a local band playing at a club called Toad's Place, about five blocks away. A couple of the guys from the E Street Band came with us, along with Mike Appleton and our crew. It was an odd feeling, walking down the sidewalk on that frosty night, Bruce Springsteen in the middle of a whole crowd of us, like mates out on the town. My final memory is of Bruce, working his way to the front of the audience in that little club, getting the lead singer's attention and asking if it was OK for him to join the band on stage. The guys just couldn't believe it. (I never did find out who they were. Bruce didn't know, he'd just heard they were good.) After a short consultation, he took the microphone. Mike and I were leaving the club to collect our car and head back to New York just as they started into 'Pretty Flamingo'.

We were gradually spending more and more time in America compiling material for the show, particularly during the summer breaks when we would generally spend three or four weeks following leads wherever they took us. We might be in Los Angeles for a few days, then fly to Miami or San Francisco, picking up local crews as we went along. We tended to leave New York to the end of the trip, for a shorter hop home and the summer of 1976 began in Macon, Georgia, and the Capricorn Record Label picnic, held at a magnificent 180-acre lakeside park on the edge of the town, owned by company boss Phil Walden.

Phil had previously managed Otis Redding, and told me about the problems of a white guy managing a black guy in a segregated town. He showed us the 'white only' 'black only' signs that still disfigured the main street. 'There were clubs I couldn't go into,' he explained. 'A white guy wouldn't be safe in there. I could only hear Otis if they were carrying the show on one of the local radio stations. So I'd be a few blocks away, sitting in the car, listening to make sure the show went OK. There were a lot of places Otis couldn't play. It was hard in those days.'

The Capricorn picnic was a three-day event, showcasing members of the Allman Brothers Band, Wet Willie, the Marshall Tucker Band and other label favourites and involving venues all over town. Music-business people were invited from all over America to party. It was expected that presidential nominee Jimmy Carter would be attending, as he did every year, to thank those involved in the record company for the profits that pumped money into his political fund. We were told that he would be happy to meet the BBC, and we arranged to record an interview with him at the lakeside, in an open pavilion overlooking the water.

My day began at 6.30 in the morning with a visit by two secret service men who burst into, then took apart, my hotel room, luggage and belongings. Having vigorously established that I meant the future president no harm, they stayed, one on each shoulder, throughout the day to prevent the possibility of a last-minute change of mind, even accompanying me to the toilet, until the interview had been recorded. A few hours earlier, incumbent President Ford had declared his intention to run in the forthcoming presidential race, and the media attention surrounding Democratic candidate Carter that day was intense to say the least. But he'd agreed to do only one interview, and that was with us.

As Mike and I stood in the pavilion, waiting for him to arrive, I tried to take in the extraordinary scene being played out around me in the hot summer sunshine. We were in a cordoned-off area, surrounded by security men, looking out over the lake and the grounds. The band Stillwater were playing on a makeshift stage, close to the water's edge, partly obscured from where we were by the smoke of a huge barbeque cooking sizzling southern food. Girls in bikini tops and short skirts were playing handball on the grass, guys with long hair were hanging out, looking stoned. A whole harvest of people in 10-foot peanut costumes had formed a comical guard of honour at the bottom of the long staircase that brought people down into the area from the car park above. Their smiling faces were peeking through the square holes in the front of their costumes, while they hopped about in anticipation of Carter's arrival. We didn't have to wait long.

We saw the entourage first, a mass of hundreds of media people, cameras, popping bulbs and frenzy, spilling down the staircase and across towards the pavilion. It was several minutes before Carter appeared through the melee, a circle of minders pushing and pulling him through the throng of television crews and well-wishers and into the corner of the building we'd cordoned off for the filming. The man coordinating the operation was Mike Hyland, a Capricorn executive at the time. Years later, quite by chance, I met Mike in Nashville and was able to confirm the details of the day and look through his collection of photographs of this amazing experience.

Jimmy Carter told me how much he appreciated the support he got from Capricorn and talked about his love of music, particularly the lyrics of Bob Dylan and Paul Simon. I thought he was charming and sincere. He even wore a *Whistle Test* badge. Some of the news channel crews tried to barge in on the filming, while the security guys did their best to keep stray microphones and equipment away, pushing people back as they encroached into our space. Personally, I didn't care about exclusives, but Carter was strict, and we were the only ones he talked to.

Mike and I spent most of the rest of the afternoon being interviewed about the interview. We even rushed back to the hotel for a few minutes to see ourselves on the CBS 6 o'clock news. Yet the most vivid moment happened immediately after the interview, just as Carter was leaving. One of the security guards suddenly broke ranks and stepped forward towards me, arms outstretched. We're talking American Football player-size here. This man was towering over me, muscles bulging, face red and quivering, his voice trembling as he began to speak. 'I wanna shake the hand of the man who talked to the future president of the United States.' As I took his hand, he began to cry. With tears streaming down his face, he pulled me into a long, suffocating hug, crushing my face into his plaid shirt. 'This man has met the future president,' he hollered. It was hot in there!

Having spent a beautiful day with Dickie Betts at his ranch a few miles from town, recording songs on his porch, we travelled to Miami to talk to Elvin Bishop, another Capricorn stalwart. Formerly with the Paul Butterfield Blues Band, he'd just enjoyed a huge Top-3 American hit with 'Fooled Around And Fell In Love'.

We stayed in Miami overnight, at the Sheraton Four Ambassadors on Miami Beach. Mike, our cameraman John and I were travelling back from the filming late that evening in the back of a cab when we realized that the radio station the driver was listening to was broadcasting live from the hotel. 'There's a club in the basement,' he told us. John and I decided we'd go down, have a drink and listen to the music for a while. 'I wouldn't do that if I were you,' he opined flatly as he dropped us off. As we walked across the marble lobby Mike decided on an early night. A wise move as things turned out.

We could hear the bass beats coming up to greet us as we walked down the stairs and into the club. It was really dark. The only light seemed to be coming from the strobes around the dance floor, each flash of light guiding us as we inched our way across the crowded bar, towards the one available free table. It took us a while, but we got there, sat down, sat back and ordered a drink.

As my eyes became accustomed to the light I began to look around and get my bearings. I could see the outside broadcast desk, close to the dance floor, gyrating with people. I looked around at the people on nearby tables and at the bar. I began to feel uncomfortable. It was dawning on me that we were getting a lot of attention. For the first time I realized that everyone I was looking at was black, that we were the only white people in the entire place. I started thinking about what Phil Walden had been saying, and looked across at John. At exactly that moment I felt a hand on my shoulder. John covered his eyes with his hands.

'You're in my seat,' I heard a voice say. The whole place seemed to freeze.

'There are a couple of other chairs empty ...' I ventured, gesturing around the rest of the table.

'No, you don't seem to understand, man. That's my seat.'

As John sank further down into his gin and tonic I got up and waited as the man seated his girlfriend, then parked myself opposite, on the only vacant chair. John stifled a nervous laugh as I sat for a moment, wondering what was going to happen next. I needed a cigarette.

I realized that my packet of Marlboro and my lighter were across the table, where I'd been sitting. The man and his girlfriend were staring at me intently. As I reached across, the girl curled her lip and disdainfully flicked the packet at me with the back of her hand. The lighter hit me in the chest, the cigarettes went spinning over my shoulder, spilling onto the floor a few feet away. Someone ground them into the carpet with their shoes. This was definitely the time to leave. Fifteen minutes after walking in there we'd made our escape and were knocking on Mike's hotel room door. 'Robert!' he exclaimed after we had recounted our story. 'When are you going to start to grow up?'

The following summer we covered the Bearsville Picnic, a similar event organized by label boss Albert Grossman, held in a forest setting near Woodstock and featuring The Band, Dr John, Mick Ronson and John Sebastian, very much the smiling hippie I expected him to be. All took part in an all-night jam session in the rustic Bearsville studio, their music mixing with the sound of the crickets that filled the scented summer air as I sat listening on the porch outside. The event ended with a spectacular late-night outdoor concert by Todd Rundgren, culminating in a 10-minute guitar solo, during which he climbed up to a narrow platform at the top of a 30-foot apex that dwarfed the stage. The higher he got the more the solo intensified, reaching a peak as he stood astride the apex in his rock-god loveliness. Suddenly, the solo fell away as he launched himself forward off his platform and into the blackness, falling towards the crowd below. Everyone screamed, convinced he was going to kill himself. Instead, at the end of the first bungee jump I'd ever seen, he bounced harmlessly down to the stage and into the encore.

Next, it was on to Los Angeles to meet up with Terry Reid at his house by the sea, to record the now famous interview that began with us stepping through a hole in the side of his house, straight onto the beach. 'I couldn't see the sea,' he explained. 'So I hammered a hole in the wall.'

Despite, or possibly because of its reputation, we often stayed at the Continental Hyatt House on the Strip, the world's most famous rock'n'roll hotel. We were there for five days with Led Zeppelin (the band Terry Reid turned down) on *The Song Remains The Same* tour, their monster Winnebago in the parking lot. The hotel didn't need to advertise the fact that they were staying, it seemed the whole of California knew. The lobby was like Oxford Circus, 24 hours a day. Getting into an elevator was a major problem as the lifts were constantly crammed with people just cruising up and down, hoping that the doors would slide open and in would walk John Bonham,

Jimmy Page, John Paul Jones or Robert Plant.

Mike and I arrived back at the hotel at about 2.30 in the morning, having rushed out to the airport to do a 20-minute interview with Kenny Loggins, who was changing flights and briefly available. The noise in the lobby was unbelievable when we got back. Bonham was holding a party on the sixth floor and hundreds of kids, groupies and Hollywood freaks were trying to gatecrash. I felt like going myself but neither Mike nor I had an invite and security was very tight. It was a happy surprise, therefore, to be joined by one of the band's management team, who walked over with us to the lift.

The three of us just managed to squeeze in, joining the expectant throng as we whooshed up to the sixth floor. As the doors slid open a David Johansen look-alike, made up like The New York Dolls, teetering in silver, thigh-length, stack-heeled boots, began to push his way to the front. A line of black-suited security men met him as he stepped forward, one of them barring his way by extending his arm across the lift doors. 'Where do you think you're going, man?' he asked the New York Doll. 'I'm going to the paaarteee,' was the affronted reply.

'Do you have an invite?' By now, the security man could have just let the lift doors close again, but he was beginning to have fun.

'No, you don't understand, man. I'm going to the paaarteee!!' He pushed hard against that outstretched security arm. It was a big mistake. First an elbow smashed his nose, then a knee jerked up into his groin. As he sank to his knees, the security men stepped forward and pulled him out of the lift, the doors catching the ankle of his trailing silver boot, trapping it for a moment, before the lift doors banged to. As we continued our journey, the occupants of the lift just picked up their conversations again, as if nothing had happened.

Violence and other casual exploitation is an unattractive reality of life around a lot of bands, as overzealous protectors take advantage of the wannabe invaders. Sometimes the band gets to hear about it, sometimes not, but it's always done in their name. It isn't just a band's music that's got the power.

In the mid-70s Led Zeppelin were absolutely awesome, a band at the peak of its powers, with Robert strutting, sliding and pouting around the stage, the audience eating out of his hand. The rhythm section was fantastic, with John Bonham beating out one of the biggest drum sounds ever, while Jimmy's playing was almost miraculous at times, an instinctive combination of feel, aggression and melody.

Through the years I've bumped into Robert many times, including a deeply emotional interview on the British Forces Broadcasting Service in 1993, during which he talked about the death of his son, Karac, 15 years earlier. He'd heard the news while the band was in the middle of the American tour. 'I was really out of it when the phone call came,' he recalled. 'At some party or other, girls everywhere ... I can't really remember. I had to pull myself out of all that madness and come back and face my son's death, in that condition, with journalists and television cameras ... That's when I straightened up. That's when I realized that some things are more important than rock'n'roll.'

My final memory of that week at the Continental Hyatt House was of Jimmy, having had a Harley Davidson motorcycle delivered literally to his hotel room, riding the machine up and down the 13th floor corridor as we were checking out.

A lot of the girls hanging out around the hotel were there more or less full time. As one band moved out, they'd just move in with the next. They cruised the Hollywood music scene, getting backstage and going to the parties, it was an amazing scene.

But there was still more to come, as we left Los Angeles, flew across to New York and onto a Dakota plane for the final short hop to one of the most magical experiences of my life.

James Taylor and Carly Simon had invited us to spend three days with them, filming at their home on the North Atlantic island of Martha's Vineyard. They'd built a fantasy house, like a Disneyland castle, with brightly coloured turrets and set in the middle of a wood. James's sister, Kate, lived in a tepee close by, his brother Alex ran a local store. James took Mike and the film crew on a tour of the island to meet the family. Carly invited me to stay behind and talk. She was elegant, interesting and incredibly sexy. I liked her very much, particularly that touch of vulnerability that led her to stutter a little when she felt nervous. When James returned they performed an impromptu living-room concert for us, rounding off with a version of 'How Sweet It Is', with Carly on piano and James on acoustic guitar. It was idyllic.

By way of stark contrast, the UK music scene was suddenly changing. Punk had arrived and the Americans simply couldn't understand it. To them it seemed like a lot of unattractive, parochial whining. However, to me personally (if not musically) it literally meant the force of change, as I increasingly felt the hostility directed towards me from this new wave of negative thinking. Let's face it, I was the identikit picture of everything the punk generation despised. Long haired, white, middle class, hippie, soft-spoken, son-of-a-policeman, BBC presenter, introducing the dinosaur stadium rock they hated with a vengeance. I was the coconut on their shy, a primary target for excessive bile. No one else was so obviously accessible, no one as symbolically perfect.

Back in Britain, the aggression soon became a menacing reality of my everyday life. People would stop me on the street and hurl insults and expletives. The prevailing atmosphere made it increasingly difficult for me to go to a club to watch a band. Standing in a crowd made me an easy target for abuse, and I was getting totally sick of the gratuitous air of violence, of being yelled at, kicked and spat on. It was degrading, depressing, confusing and unnerving and came as a major shock. I hadn't ever set out to antagonize people in this way, and couldn't understand how I'd managed to do so with such apparent blanket success.

This general feeling of discomfort came to a head in March 1977, first in a confrontation with The Clash at Dingwall's Club in London, then a few days later, in a meeting with the Sex Pistols that had repercussions far wider than I would ever have expected.

It was a Friday evening and I'd been doing some recording at Morgan studios with my good friend and session engineer George Nicholson, with whom I'd worked on the later Wally stuff for Atlantic.

I suggested to George that we stop off at the Speakeasy before going home, and we arrived at the club at about 11.30. As we walked in past the bar we bumped into Jim Diamond, who told us that the Sex Pistols were in the restaurant.

'They seem a bit rowdy,' he confided, with characteristic Scottish understatement. It was the day they'd signed with A&M records and they'd been celebrating. Having gone on a wrecking spree at the record company offices, they'd arrived at the Speakeasy with fuelled-up entourage and were having their own private party in the restaurant. George and I decided to leave and finished up our drinks. A tall, blonde guy in a green boiler suit had been pushing his way through the crowd around the bar and bumped into me as we turned to go. He confronted me immediately.

'When are the Pistols gonna be on the *Whistle Test* then?' he demanded.

'This isn't the right time or place,' was my reply. 'Give me a call in the office on Monday morning.' It didn't matter what I said, he took a haymaker swing at me, cuffing me round the shoulder and knocking drinks off the bar. It seemed to be some kind of signal and suddenly all hell broke loose.

People were punching and kicking their way through the crowd, trying to get to me. People began to scatter as I was pulled round to the other side of the bar for protection. I couldn't see George. Glass was flying everywhere. People were either caught up in the mayhem or screaming in panic, trying to get out of the place.

As I tried to gather my senses I was confronted by about half a dozen Mohican-cut drunks, faces spitting hatred, their fists clutching broken glass. I was in serious trouble here, feeling as scared as at any time in my life.

Three options flashed through my mind as I struggled to maintain my composure. The first was to try to run, but I was in a cul-de-sac on the wrong side of the bar with a wall at my back, and they were barring my way. The second was to fight, but at six-to-one against, the odds weren't favourable. I decided on option three. 'Let's talk...' I began. 'What do you think you're going to achieve by this...' One of them kicked out at me while another tried to slash me with a beer glass as I slumped against the bar. I really thought this was the end of the line. I couldn't even begin to think what injuries I might soon be experiencing. I just tried to protect myself as best I could.

Miraculously, and seemingly out of nowhere, about a dozen guys appeared, forming a kind of human wall between the punts and me, surrounding me in a protective circle as they pushed and fought us through the madness and round the edge of the bar towards safety. I found out later that it was mainly the Procol Harum road crew who, like us, had just popped in for a quiet drink! You saved my life, guys.

I was incredibly lucky to walk out of there with little more than a bruise on my leg and cuts on my back. George was not so fortunate.

As I was being pulled away, Sid Vicious had stabbed a broken bottle into George's face, who'd been quick enough to deflect the glass up and away from his eyes, but the jagged edge had torn into his wrist and opened up a wide, ugly gash right through the top of his head, from forehead to crown. I found him lying semi-conscious in a pool of blood in the reception area of the club. We had to get out of there, but it wasn't easy. The word was out and punk reinforcements were arriving from nearby clubs to join in the rumble and kick a hippie. It took about 20 people to get us through the door, across the road and into George's car. Someone told me that the police later cordoned off that whole block of Margaret Street in an effort to contain the trouble. I drove us straight to the Hammersmith Hospital, where George had 14 stitches in his head wound.

By now, Sue and I had given up the struggle of trying to keep our marriage together in the face of all the madness and Jackie and I had moved into a flat together in Putney, where I arrived at about 8.30 in the morning to find the press already gathering outside. I had absolutely nothing to say. 'Sex Pistol In Storm Over Brawl' ran the page 2 headline in the *Sunday Mirror* on 20th March 1977.

All I wanted to do now was to have a bath and lick my wounds. If those people had wanted to shake me up, they'd succeeded. I felt wretched and deeply depressed. I wondered what the hell was going on and whether it was all worth it. I really hadn't got into music for this.

We were deluged with calls for days, from my family, the press, friends and inquisitive acquaintances. One of the first on the line was Derek Green, the UK boss of A&M Records. 'I'm so sorry to hear about all this,' he told me. 'You'll be glad to know that I'm dropping them from the label. We're making an official announcement on Tuesday.' Next to call was Aidan Day, my old producer on the Radio 1 *Review Show*. 'I've banned all Sex Pistols records from the playlist,' he told me angrily. 'The station will never play them again while I'm here. They shouldn't be allowed to get away with this.'

Some of the calls were more sinister, if not darkly amusing.

"Allo ... Mr 'Arris? You don't know me, but I thought I'd give you a bell to offer you our services. A lotta people were very upset by what happened at the Speakeasy and would like to take a bit of retribution, so to speak. We can do a very good job on their fingers of course, but what I recommend is the eardrums. A bit of perforation would be good. They're musicians, see? They need their ears ...'

'Stop! It's good of you to call ... but no thanks.'

FIVE

'Who's Out for '78?'

THE SEX PISTOLS INCIDENT LEFT ME FEELING SULLIED, INVADED AND very disillusioned. Dark clouds had gathered. The memory of the ugly violence of that night at the Speakeasy was proving hard to shrug off, but I was equally shaken by the wider hostility it provoked. The music press was now wading in with some witheringly personal attacks. Punk was the new thing, said the papers. The *Old Grey Whistle Test* was – old and grey. A piece by Michael Watts in *Melody Maker* accurately sums up the attitude towards me at the time.

> He has undeniably been the most reviled personality both on television and within rock music. 'A wimp' has been the most general criticism. His questioning of interviewees has been deemed less than penetrating, and his eagerness to spread around gentle bonhomie has caused severe irritation. Always the music press has been the most personal and vitriolic. In this paper one writer, now gone, urged that a brown bag be placed over his head on screen; the following week he repeated his demand. Harris has simply had the ill luck to be the cause of outrageous spitefulness in others.

These words straddled a huge, dark pen drawing of myself, looking over my shoulder at three pen quills embedded in my back.

Even *Time Out* endorsed the invective, using a typically cruel Gerald Scarfe cartoon to illustrate a poem in a 'Who's out for '78?' section of the magazine:

> Groovy Bob is glad to serve
> The PR apparat

He snuffles, 'Welcome To The Show'
Then settles back and off they go,
Dull-witted, vain or vicious.
Musicianship with every vice
Bob will opine 'really nice',
Not slack and repetitious.
Long bunny teeth; receding hair;
A tennis shoe; a swivel chair;
Just one more bureaucrat.

No matter how resilient you are, that kind of stuff gets through to you in the end.

Some of the criticism of the programme was justified and I think we handled punk badly. It was a long-established criterion that to appear on the show you had to have an album out. *Top Of The Pops* was the singles show, we were the album show. Our problem was that the New Wave explosion happened on singles and for the first time on newly formed independent labels, not on the albums being released by the majors. The first wave of punk musicians didn't sign to the big multinationals, rejecting the corporate excesses, the big-budget recordings and stadium gigs they said had dulled the music's edge. Consequently, New Wave had been and almost gone by the time the programme began to embrace the second division album bands the bigger record companies were foisting on us. Introducing groups like The Depressions and The Fabulous Poodles felt rather demeaning. We were seen to first ignore this new phenomenon, hesitate, then try to catch up. It didn't work, and in retrospect, we probably should have just stuck to our guns, but the constant criticism was having an impact.

By now, in addition to the introduction of the weekly Newsdesk, presented by the wonderful and eccentric Andrew Bailey, two significant changes had been made to the *Whistle Test* production team. Tom Corcoran had replaced Colin Strong as director of the show and Jill Sinclair had taken the place of Jenny Carson, now expecting her first child. Jill was a dynamic force for change, arguing strongly that the best of the new music should be given more airtime. But I had an increasing feeling that my life was spinning out of control.

Fame seemed shallow, fickle and confusing. Three years before,

Whistle Test had been the hippest show on TV, Britain's No. 1 music show. Our success had been toasted, now I was being roasted. Burnt alive, it felt like. Meanwhile, I hadn't changed and couldn't understand why what had recently been so great had now turned so sour. 'Things have hardened up,' I'd told Michael Watts. 'We are in a very aggressive, very cynical time right now and it's not my time. People don't really want my soft approach.'

He'd described me as being 'very much a child of the 60s. Now 32, Harris has never lost his belief in good vibes and mellow sounds and doing your own thing, and he deeply regrets that there is no longer an open atmosphere, that one's stance is always on trial.'

For 11 years I'd been surfing the crest of a wave. Everything had seemed to fall magically into my lap. I'd never had ambitions to be famous, or even had a major career plan in place. I'd been incredibly lucky, in a 'right time, right person' kind of way. But now things were going against me, I didn't feel like I was coping particularly well. Maybe the critics were right, maybe none of the work really amounted to very much. Maybe I should stop. I didn't know where to go from here, I just knew I wasn't enjoying it any more, and that compromising one's beliefs is never the answer.

Sue remained loyal and supportive throughout, as she and I struggled to retain our friendship following the break-up of our marriage. I was regularly travelling across London to see the girls and we have always been able to talk. But my dark mood pervaded my relationship with Jackie, who was trying to cope with living with a person going through a major identity crisis. She wanted us to settle down now, whereas I didn't know what the hell I wanted to do. I was very difficult company, when I was there. A lot of the time I was concentrating on escape, not from Jackie, but from myself, and the contradictions going on in my head. We were at the point of breaking up when she told me she was pregnant.

Even that didn't hold us together and for a while I moved out and shared a flat with George in West Hampstead, a mile or so down the road from Sue. I was spending a lot of time with Elton John's new lyricist, Gary Osborne, and his then-wife, Jenny, at their house in Regent's Park, a great stop-off place on the way home from the West End. Before writing 'Blue Eyes' and 'Little Jeannie' for Elton, Gary had made his name as co-writer of the massively successful *War Of The Worlds* with Jeff Wayne, a rock concept that featured 'Forever Autumn' by Justin Hayward and narration by the great Richard Burton. He'd also written the English lyrics to a French song called 'Amoureuse', providing a hit for Kiki Dee, a regular visitor to the Osborne household. Another was Tarquin Gotch, who was part of the movie production company that made *Home Alone*, its sequels and a string of films by the late John Candy.

Tarquin lived in West Hampstead, a couple of blocks away from George, in a flat he'd bought from Hazel O'Connor and shared with Kelly Le Brock, who used to come and go around modelling assignments and we all hung out together for a while. He was, at the time, one of London's hottest young record company A&R men, signing the Stray Cats to Arista, getting involved in the career of The Beat and taking Billy MacKenzie to Warner Brothers.

For the next few months Jackie and I rarely saw each other, but we never lost touch and I was there for the birth of our baby, Charlotte, on 30th September 1977. Although my first daughter, Mirelle, had been born only seven years previously, it had still been the convention then for dads to pace anxiously up and down in the hospital corridor outside. Emily had been born two months premature, and was rushed straight off to an incubator but this time I was there and being part of Charlie's birth was very emotional – the joy of seeing her come into the world was overwhelming. The closeness of the whole experience brought Jackie and I back together again and for a while I felt more settled and happy.

The big compensation for the flack we were taking on *Whistle Test* continued to be the regular filming trips to America that fed so much new material into the show. I went to Miami to meet up with The Police at the NASA Headquarters, for the filming of the 'Walking On The Moon' video and to record a conversation with Sting. Frances Tomelty was there too, pushing their toddler around in a buggy.

I'd hitched part of the way to Miami with The Knack, joining them in Tampa Bay and filming an interview with their lead singer, Doug Fieger, on their tour bus, motoring down through the Florida late-summer sunshine. We had to turn the air-conditioning off to do the filming, and with the lights and camera equipment generating so much heat it was like a sauna in the back of that bus. It was the week the band hit the top of the American charts with 'My Sharona' and as we prepared for the interview Doug leaned forward, bathed in sweat, his face a few inches from mine. 'Bob, is it hot in here, or ... is it my career?!'

I really enjoyed the road. I'd recently spent a couple of weeks on an American tour with Queen, working with the band to compile material for a television documentary that, for some reason, was never shown. It was fascinating watching the activity that went on behind the scenes, and seeing the luxuries money can buy. I travelled with them in their private jet, their four individually appointed limousines waiting on the tarmac for them wherever or whenever the plane touched down.

I joined them for the leg of the tour that took in Chicago, Houston and then Las Vegas, the oasis in the desert, where they played at the world-famous Aladdin. I'd driven there once, a 12-hour journey from Los Angeles through the desert, travelling a straight road that looked exactly like the photograph on the *Best Of The Eagles* album cover, in a temperature of around 110 degrees. Halfway across I ran into an unexpected ultra-violent thunderstorm, with attendant flash flooding from wind and rain so heavy I was forced to pull over to the side of the road. It was over an hour before I could get moving again, and I watched in wonder as the moisture miraculously brought the desert to life. The ground seemed to be covered by a green sheen of vegetation splashed with the colours of a thousand flowers, instantly transforming what previously had been nothing but miles and miles of lunar desolation into a beautiful summer landscape.

On the night of the Queen gig, the band had their drivers collect them from the front door of the hotel, four 40-foot white limousines waiting to take them to the venue, arriving one by one at the backstage enclosure. It wasn't a long drive. They were playing in the theatre at the back of the building. Although the Aladdin is a big complex, the car journey from front to back probably lasted no more than a minute and a half. It would have been a lot easier to have just walked through from their hotel suites, but where's the sense of occasion in that?

I always enjoyed watching Queen play live. They were four intelligent guys who applied their minds to their music, be it the theatrical expression of their stage show or the instrumental setting for their strong, operatic songs. They all wrote, the chemistry in the band was exactly right, and they could really rock, driven by Roger Taylor's classic drum style and embellished by the world-class guitar playing of Brian May, so nimble on the frets with those long, thin fingers. And, of course, in lead singer Freddie Mercury they had the showman supreme, someone who simply refused to give less than one hundred per cent. I'll always remember the effort he put into a 9.30 a.m. session at the BBC Langham Studios for my *Sounds Of The 70s* show, veins standing out on his neck as he held the microphone, reaching for the very best vocal performance he could give. I also liked the way the band treated people, particularly the fan club, inviting members to special private concerts and video shoots and generally making them feel a part of what the band was about.

The Aladdin concert, however, turned out to be a very subdued affair. Las Vegas didn't really know what to make of them at all. But I had a fabulous time for the four days we were in town, sightseeing and club-hopping with Roger Taylor and his minder. We gambled (lightly), drank (heavily), saw a couple of Wet T-shirt competitions and spent an evening with the Dick Clark Nostalgia Show, watching The Shirelles and Bo Diddley performing on stage. Dick Clark was famous as the host of the great *American Bandstand* television show, and the evening featured fascinating footage and on-air clips from the programme's rock'n'roll heyday, projected onto a huge screen at the back of the stage.

At the checkout desk the following morning I bumped into one of the guys from the Queen road crew. As we talked, he idly slipped a quarter into one of the hundreds of one-armed bandits scattered around the hotel lobby. To our great astonishment he won the jackpot. Coins spilled out everywhere, suddenly people were rushing around, handing us those little cardboard buckets and helping us to scoop up the money and the tokens. Having settled up his winnings, the cashier gave him a silver dollar, a token given to all jackpot winners by the management. As we waited for my car to arrive we stared at the monster slot machine that sat astride the hotel entrance. It was said to be the biggest one-armed bandit in the world at that time – a glittering, gaudy monument to gambling. It stood about 10 feet tall, used a power station-full of electricity, and only took silver dollars. He didn't know whether to keep his as a souvenir or take a chance of winning the world's biggest jackpot. After some deliberation, he slid that big, shiny coin into the slot. It took the weight of both of us to heave down the heavy, chrome handle and we stood transfixed as all the coloured lights started to flash. One by one, three identical symbols came down into the illuminated windows ... chunk, chunk, chunk. His luck was unbelievable. Sirens went off, the man was a hero. I stayed just long enough to learn that the jackpot he'd won was worth more than 17,000 dollars. And it all started with just a quarter.

I'd been to the Aladdin once before, with Emerson, Lake and Palmer, as part of a *Whistle Test* special, reporting on their American tour. We'd followed them from Montreal, where they'd played the Olympic stadium, the setting for their striking *Fanfare For The Common Man* video, with them knee-deep in snow. They'd filled the place with 80,000 people and 129 onstage musicians, including a full concert orchestra. It was massively expensive lumbering the equipment and personnel around America, a project for which they'd commissioned three chrome-plated juggernauts, issuing instructions that they always had to travel in the order of the letters painted on the roof. First was 'P', then 'L', then E', a very important point, because with 'P' leading, the convoy correctly read E L P when viewed from the sky. The tour couldn't sustain the extravagance and soon the orchestra was disbanded, the band playing the latter part of the tour as a three-piece. Even Carl Palmer had to downsize from the huge suites he used to book at every hotel stop, the rooms stripped, cushioned and especially appointed for his daily workouts with his personal fitness trainer.

We'd featured the band many times through the years although, to start with, I'd never really liked them. I'd been critical of them on air when they came in for their first live studio session some years earlier, calling them 'pretentious', or something like. One of their roadies came over and had a 'quiet word' in my ear about the possibility of me being more complimentary and changing the script before the programme went out.

Despite the early difficulties, I'd become good friends with Emerson, Lake and Palmer, particularly Greg Lake, with whom I enjoyed spending time. Filming with the band additionally took us to New York, Los Angeles and briefly to Memphis. I flew out of London on a Friday morning and with the time change landed in Memphis, via Atlanta, just before the band went onstage that evening. I watched the show, then we took a film crew out to a local restaurant to record the interview, finishing at about 3.30 in the morning. I just had time to get the taxi driver to take me to the Graceland gates before heading straight back to the airport for a 7.30 a.m. flight out, arriving back in London via two changes, at breakfast time on Sunday morning. I'll never do it again. I was jet-lagged for about two weeks.

We also did some filming together at the Compass Point Studio, right by the beach on the island of Nassau in the Bahamas. The band had been asked to organize a playback of their *Love Beach* album for the famous and demanding Ertegun brothers, owners of the Atlantic Records label, who swooped in by helicopter to hear rough mixes of the new recordings. They'd lost a lot of money on the tour and this was a crucial album. I've rarely seen three people as nervous as Emerson, Lake and Palmer were that day, hands shaking on their appointed faders as they mixed together the tracks, the Ertegun entourage an intimidating presence at the back of the control room, puffing on their big cigars.

'When they forced us to make *Love Beach* we were exhausted, frustrated and we had completed most things within our life as a band,' Carl Palmer said. 'We'd taken technology by the ears, as it were, with the Moog synthesizer. We recorded with an orchestra and toured with it. We didn't have a lot more to say musically, and I think we wanted some free time.'

Compass Point was owned by Chris Blackwell, founder of the Island record label. He also owned a house a few miles along the coast, situated on a low cliff top, overlooking the sea, and he invited me to stay for a few days, a wonderful opportunity to completely relax in a magnificent setting. From the pool I could see the housekeeper, Pearl, cleaning fishes on the beach below, throwing the remains into the sea. At the same time every evening a huge manta ray would swoop slowly and elegantly through the clear, turquoise water, circling in to steal the fish heads and remains Pearl was discarding. With the backdrop of the sun setting into the mouth of the cove it was a most beautiful sight, one I was determined to burn into my mind like a photograph. I didn't have a camera with me, but to this day I can still close my eyes and summon up that spectacular scene. Carl Palmer took me deep-sea fishing with Peter Frampton and his manager, Dee Anthony, which was very exciting. We even had a shark bump the boat.

Having completed the filming with Emerson, Lake and Palmer, and with the Average White Band, who were also recording at Compass Point, I flew to Miami to link up with the Bee Gees. We met at Criteria Sound, very much their 'home' studio at the time. The facilities were superb, as we knew from using their mobile unit to record the Macon Picnic, with top-of-the-range engineers, state-of-the-art equipment, and a fully operational film unit.

The band were absolutely huge at that time, having been enjoying a dramatic renaissance of fortune with the success of the *Saturday Night Fever* soundtrack, at that moment the biggest-selling album of all time. On 18th March 1978 they occupied the top three places on the American *Billboard* chart, with 'Night Fever' at No. 1, 'Stayin' Alive' at No. 2 and 'Emotion' by Samantha Song at No. 3 – a track they'd written and produced. With their brother, Andy, at No. 5 with '(Love Is) Thicker Than Water', this was chart dominance of Beatle proportions.

Despite their superstar status they were, as always, friendly, professional and polite, meeting me in reception and ordering us all a pot of tea. We chatted for a while, Maurice unexpectedly telling me about Lulu and what drove them apart. 'She was married to her career,' he told me. I felt married to mine.

They invited me through to a small, dimly lit, black-walled audio booth for a playback of their new LP, the hugely anticipated *Spirits Having Flown*. The backing tracks were almost finished but they were falling behind schedule. Only guide vocals had been added so far and none of the lead voices or harmonies had been recorded. The sheer scale of the project had thrown up a number of problems. They were using 96 separate channels in the recording process, which, with the technology available at that time, had meant hooking together two 48-channel mixing desks. It had worked to start with, but then the desks started slipping out of phase with each other, rendering the backing music useless as it hit the speakers like a cacophony of random sound. An army of technical support engineers had failed to come up with a solution, so they'd been temporally forced to strip back to 48 tracks, at the cost of much valuable time. The Bee Gees were philosophical about it all.

While I got myself comfortable facing the monitor speakers, they took up places just behind me, Maurice leaning over my left shoulder, Barry in the middle and Robin leaning over me on the right. 'Because we haven't recorded any vocals we thought we'd sing it through for you,' he said. 'You can tell us what you think of it and you'll know what you're talking about when we do the interview.' I sat absolutely spellbound for the next 40 minutes or so while they stood behind me and sang right into my ears, giving me a stunning, private, live performance of the album the whole industry wanted to hear.

I heard 'Too Much Heaven', 'Tragedy' and the album's glorious title song, their effortless harmonies filling that tiny room, voices so close that you could hardly prise them apart, instinctively perfect, like the Everly Brothers. I thought about what David Crosby had told me on Radio 1, about when he, Stephen Stills and Graham Nash had sung together for the first time, in Joni Mitchell's kitchen. They had to stop almost immediately, they were so amazed by the way their voices exactly fitted together. 'We started laughing, we couldn't believe it,' he'd recalled. 'I mean, how would you ever know. You can't legislate for a thing like that.'

I get shivers down my spine just thinking about it and skimming back through the memories of those trips to the States, it seems extraordinary that I was the person doing all that. It had been my escape, my enjoyment and, occasionally, my salvation. We'd worked our socks off and had a really fantastic time. I didn't know it then but that final *Whistle Test* trip was to be my last to America for 20 years. Boy, did I miss it!

I found it hard adjusting to reality back home. The UK seemed immediately hostile. I felt jaded and completely worn down by all the ongoing press attacks and found myself increasingly locked within a kind of siege mentality, feeling defensive and suspicious.

Despite the first appearance of Dire Straits in the summer of 1978, a great Tom Petty concert soon after and the foundation-shaking studio performance of 'Paradise By The Dashboard Light' by Meatloaf, the fun was going out of doing the show. The contrast with the American experiences emphasized the increasing panic that was setting in around my inability to see a way forward from here. I felt I'd lost my identity to my television persona, that I'd become 'the Ken Barlow of Rock', as I was quoted as saying. I decided I'd outstayed my welcome and my main thought now was to step back for a while and take stock. I did my last live *Whistle Test* studio presentation, co-hosting with my successor, Annie Nightingale, on 19th September that year.

Whistle Test had completely dominated my life for the previous six years and it felt strange that it had come to an end, but I knew I'd done the right thing. There were no big announcements, no trumpet fanfares. It was just time to get back into radio.

Seeking anonymity and freedom I joined Radio 210 Thames Valley, a small commercial station housed in a converted ambulance depot near Tilehurst on the outskirts of Reading. My first broadcast was on a Saturday afternoon, sitting in on the *Sports Show*, taking reports on all the local matches, reading out the scores and playing a few records. I'd never done a programme like that before but being a keen soccer fan I had a really good time. At 6 o'clock, one of the young station DJs arrived in the studio to do the *210 Club Show* that followed, looking at me apprehensively over the pair of National Health glasses that sat precariously on his crooked nose.

He was armed with boxes, carts, tapes, discs, newspapers and letters, all spilling over the desk as we went through the hot seat changeover. I couldn't believe he needed all that stuff, until I heard his show come alive in the car on the way home. It was a revelation, a cavalcade of news items, sketches, phone calls, correspondence, characters and the occasional burst of music. It was exciting. I hadn't heard anyone as effortlessly madcap since the Everett days of Radio London. As I flashed back up the M4 to London I decided I wanted to be a part of this station, and all the time he was banging home his name. I wasn't about to forget it. This was Steve Wright, six months into a burgeoning radio career.

Radio 210 was owned by Neil ffrench-Blake, an eccentric Berkshire aristocrat. He'd wanted to have his own jukebox of the airwaves so, in the less-regulated days of the mid-70s, he'd bought one and staffed it with an extraordinarily high level of local talent. Steve was part of an original on-air line-up that featured Mike Read and Steve Crozier. Croze became a great mate, supportive and constructive. Many were the nights he put me up – and put up with me.

Radio 210 had a really good atmosphere at that time and we often used to sit around in the evening, talking, playing records, or joining Steve in the studio while he worked after-hours on the characters for his show. Neil used to preside over his apprentices like a benign sergeant major, ever-present cigarette pressed between his lips. 'You're going right to the very top,' he used to tell them all, billowing out smoke over his paper cup full of whisky and water.

He'd married into aristocracy, his wife being a distant relative of the Queen. Somehow, they managed to arrange a royal visit to the station soon after I arrived. The Queen wore a red coat and a black hat with a red feather in it and was accompanied by the Duke of Edinburgh, whom she kept chastizing for being grumpy.

'Oh do buck up, Philip,' she said as I demonstrated the studio equipment to them. 'Try and be nice.' You could tell it was the last place on earth he wanted to be.

I committed myself to a full schedule at 210, and Neil took full advantage. I soon found myself doing 20 hours on-air every weekend. I was on 9 p.m. to 1 a.m. Friday night, 10 till 2 Saturday lunchtime, 9 till 1 Saturday night, 10 till 2 Sunday lunchtime, rounding off with the *Oldies Show* 9 till 1 Sunday night. Steve Crozier would put me up for the weekend at his cottage near the studios. It was a crazy schedule and, after various bits of music logging and administration, I'd arrive back in London around 6 o'clock on Monday morning absolutely worn out. I started the *Oldies Show* one Sunday with The Hollies' 'I'm Alive', just to remind myself I was. But I enjoyed the move across into more mainstream radio and was very much inspired by the work of the guy doing the afternoon show on Capital Radio in London, who remains the best DJ I've ever heard. The late Roger Scott really was something special.

Like his idol, Bruce Springsteen, he was born to do what he was doing. Modest and bright, he had a great voice, a dry sense of humour and a wicked laugh. He made you feel part of his programme, as if he was talking directly to you and, crucially, he never lost sight of the fact that a DJ's primary function is to highlight the music. Roger was a huge influence on me, specifically in two ways.

One was the music mix, which he pitched just left of centre, playing quality rock and pop, some rock'n'roll and 60s singles, album tracks and rarities. He never played rubbish. You could tell how much he was into the music by his casual knowledge of it and by his sense of pulse, which gave his show a rhythm. He played Springsteen, The Beach Boys (his other great love), Queen, Steve Miller, Bob Seger, some soul, the hottest new records and a cavalcade of jukebox gems. It was a rarefied mix that proved to me that it was possible to do a mainstream radio programme packed full of high-quality music and still make it really accessible. Pointers are found in the lyrics of one of Roger's favourite songs, Mark Germino's 'Rex Bob Lowenstein', about a mythical American DJ:

> He lives for his job and accepts his pay,
> You can call and request 'Lay Lady Lay'.
> He'll play Stanley Jordan, The Dead and Little Feat,
> And he'll even play the band from the college down the street.

It's the kind of eclecticism and open-minded musical attitude that I've always thought important. Although written in 1987, the song also predicted radio's increasing reliance on computer-selected playlists and audience research figures, the antithesis of what Roger and 'Rex Bob' were all about:

> Now one day a man in a pinstripe suit
> Took the owner of the station to a restaurant booth.
> His pitch was simple. 'You'll increase your sales
> If you only play the song list we send in the mail.'
> He guaranteed a larger audience
> Less confusion and higher points
> 'But your Drive Time jock won't get to do his thing
> Hey, he's not half bad, tell me what's his name?'

It's a wonderful song, full of irony and still much requested on my shows. Unfortunately, it's proved to be prophetic. Much of commercial radio today has much less to do with programmes than it does with shareholders' bank accounts, a harsh reality of the commercial world. Young broadcasters these days just don't get the same opportunities for self-expression as they did in the past.

The second big influence was on the technical side, particularly the way he used the microphone. Unlike most DJs, Roger didn't use 'ducking' devices, or surge the music up and down while he was speaking. Once a record was going he never touched the faders or chased the fades. He had the great gift of word economy, and set his voice level just above the volume of the non-stop music, blending in with it, letting hooks and riffs breathe as he paced his links around them, lifting his voice or moving closer to the microphone for emphasis. Roger's show was a masterclass in microphone technique. He was sharp, informative and loved his music, the complete professional package. Ask any of my contemporaries and they'll tell you the same. Roger Scott was the DJ's DJ.

I was thriving on the volume of broadcasting I was doing, but getting very tired. The weekend schedule was punishing and I wasn't looking after myself, still seeking escape routes of various kinds and staying up late, particularly when entertaining friends. A typically indulgent Thursday night at our Putney flat finished at about 4 o'clock, when I collapsed into bed. I woke up with a start at about 7.45. It was Miri's Christmas school play that morning and, although I felt absolutely dreadful, I'd promised to be there.

I drove across to West Hampstead through the heavy rush hour traffic hunched over the steering wheel, shifting around uncomfortably in an attempt to ease a dull, aching pain that was beginning to tighten down the sides of my chest. I almost collapsed into the chair beside Sue when I arrived for the performance.

'You look terrible,' she said. 'You should go straight back to bed.' After catching the opening few minutes I took her advice and struggled back to Putney, where I slept for the rest of the day. By the following afternoon I was feeling much better, and was watching the England Rugby Union International on television when the doctor arrived. I even asked him if I'd be OK to get down to Radio 210 the following afternoon. He said probably not, that I'd got a mild case of flu and should take it easy for a couple of days. There seemed no particular cause for alarm. A few hours later, however, things took a dramatic turn for the worse.

The discomfort in my sides returned, only worse this time. It felt like I was in the grip of a tightening vice. I started getting flashes of jagged pain right through the centre of my skull, like a meat cleaver cutting through the bone. It was so horrendous that I started screaming and bashing my head against the wall, trying to cause a diversionary pain. Then I started convulsing.

Jackie rushed me to the Queen Mary's Hospital in Roehampton, where the medical staff spent the next 15 hours working to save my life. As they were wheeling me through to the emergency department, I caught a glimpse of my reflection. My skin had turned yellow and my face had broken out in a hundred red-rimmed spots. How could I have got so ill so quickly?

They could neither sedate me nor give me anything to kill the pain for fear of masking the elusive virus that was doing so much damage. An initial diagnosis suggested a brain infection of some kind and I endured three lumbar punctures that dreadful night, needles inserted deep into my spine to withdraw the spinal fluid needed for testing. It wasn't until later that I discovered I'd contracted a form of legionnaire's disease, linked to pneumonia.

It was almost unbearable, yet equal damage was being done to my pride. I was absolutely frantic about the idea of being seen in this condition, of being recognized. I just couldn't bear the thought of being pushed into a general ward and having to face people. As they transferred me into a small private side ward of the intensive care unit, I felt peaceful relief. For the first time in many hours, the pain lifted and I was suspended in a tranquil silence. I became an observer, having an extraordinary out-of-body experience.

From some indeterminate height I was looking down at myself hooked up to all that life-saving machinery, while white-coated figures bent over me in urgent activity. I felt emotionally detached from myself, yet connected by what seemed to be a silver thread, as thin as a strand of a spider's web. I was hypnotized by an overwhelming feeling of serenity, a certainty that this feeling was not the end of my life, more a stepping stone into whatever came next. It was a tranquil and beautiful feeling. I sensed a tunnel of light, as if into another dimension. Then, click. Everything went black.

I looked up to see my mother come into my music room at my parents' house in Ardington Road in Northampton. I was probably about 13 years old. It was summer and the sash window had been pushed up a little, letting in a breeze that disturbed the net curtains my mum always used to hang. I looked at the pictures on the wall, feeling excited and happy, knowing this was no dream – I was really there. I could feel the breeze on my face. Everything was exactly as it was. Then, click. Everything went black again.

I remember briefly coming to and being hugged tightly by a woman, presumably a nurse, whose voice I didn't recognize. 'Thank God, oh thank God,' she said over and over again, before I fell back into my coma.

I finally opened my eyes and blearily began to take in my surroundings. As I came to, I became aware of someone sitting in one of those big old hospital chairs at the side of my bed. It was George. 'Hiya, man,' he said casually.

'Hiya, George,' I replied. 'What time is it?'

'Ten to five ... Thursday afternoon,' he told me. 'You've lost four and a half days.'

Sue and Jackie arrived, and sat talking together at the bottom of the bed and we all agreed my lifestyle had to change.

My hospital stay lasted 10 days and although initially I felt very weak, the first part of my recovery went well and within a few weeks I started working again. I didn't feel strong enough to go back to radio full time, but I did a couple of interviews and articles and even introduced The Police on stage at a fantastic gig in Slough in early spring. But I continued to feel very low, as if my resistance had been broken. Instead of improving, I started to regress. I didn't seem to have any energy for life and there were so many things about the whole hospital experience that I couldn't explain. The out-of-body sensation and the extraordinary time-travel moment with my mother remained vivid in my mind. Yet I was trying to pretend that the illness had not been serious. Despite my debilitated state and the scars that had now shown up on my lungs, I tried to tell myself that the threat to my mortality had been nothing more serious than a blip. I did not address the possibility that the illness was more likely a reflection of my state of mind and the late-night lifestyle I'd been living. I was in denial.

June Bolan had, by this time, introduced me to Danae Brook and her American husband, John, a student of psychologist R.D. Laing. Everyone knew John by his nickname, Pleasure, a handle he'd acquired at a San Francisco fancy dress party in his youth, where he'd arrived naked, apart from copious leaves, branches and bits of twig and shrub, which he'd entwined around his body. He'd rolled dozens of joints, and had carefully pushed them one by one into all the woody nooks and crevices of this extraordinary creation. He called himself The Pleasure Tree.

Danae was a quality writer. She and Pleasure had two young children and she'd recently published a book about natural childbirth, as well as writing regular features for the national press. They were planning to spend a family summer in Ibiza, at their holiday home near the village of San Miguel in the northern part of the island. The house sounded idyllic, a good 20 minutes' walk from the nearest main road, tucked away in trees, a short distance from Benirras Beach and unknown to tourists. They told me they were leaving the following week and invited me to join them. Pleasure was particularly insistent that it would be good for me and aid my recovery. Jackie couldn't come because of her business commitments, but she also thought a break was needed and promised to join me when she could. I could get fit and have a proper holiday for the first time in years. Filming had usually taken up the middle weeks of summer, but this year, without *Whistle Test*, I was free and we set off in their Citroen Diane for a holiday that was to prove to be a major turning point in my life.

I loved Ibiza. There's something about the atmosphere of the place that seems to loosen people's inhibitions.

The tiny stone house had neither running water nor electricity, and it was my job to prime up all the lights with new wicks and paraffin and every morning pump the water up from the well. I loved bringing up that water and how pure it tasted. It would splash ice cold into the tank on the flat roof above, gradually heating under the hot summer sun to a temperature perfect for a shower and the washing up. At night, I sometimes took a mattress up onto the roof, lying on my back looking up at the sky, drifting off to sleep under a million stars, often to the sound of Mike Oldfield's *Tubular Bells* playing in the house below.

I struck up a close, platonic friendship with a Danish woman called Asta, who was staying with friends nearby, and she was my companion for expeditions to the beach. It was quite a hike to get there, 25 or 30 minutes down a bumpy, rock-strewn dirt track, longer climbing back. Much to our relief, one morning a friend of Danae's offered us a lift in his Land Rover and Danae, Pleasure and the kids also decided to join us for a day on the beach.

By the time we'd all piled in there was very little room left, so I sat on the back frame of the vehicle, supporting myself by hanging onto the roll bar, children either side of me. It was a hot, uncomfortable journey as we sped down that hill, and the impact of the rocks and potholes seemed to jar through my body more and more. I began to hurt. That horrible vice-like pain began to grip my chest again. Arms above my head, I was holding onto the roll bar for dear life and as we bowled onto the beach the pain down my sides was excruciating. Despite my tan I'd turned deathly white and my head was beginning to pound. I began to panic, certain I was getting ill again and wondering what would happen to me in this remote, inaccessible place.

Pleasure took control and laid me on a beach towel under a parasol for protection against the fierce midday sun. He told me not to worry, to breathe deeply and to stay calm. His reassuring voice echoed in my brain as I began to relive the experiences of that first, desperate night in hospital when I nearly died. For the next few hours I was delirious, screaming out in pain as the needle sucked the life fluid out of my spine again while the thunder coursed through my head. Then I was calm once more as I relived the shimmering memory of the out-of-body sensation. I was certain now that I'd experienced a fleeting sensation of an afterlife, that death doesn't end everything.

I began to explore questions about myself that I'd been trying to ignore:

If I'd died, what was my personal legacy?

Had I lived my life in a way that made me proud?

Did I like myself?

For the first time, I realized that mortality is the great leveller. It doesn't matter how much advantage we seek to gain during our lives, our deathbeds will render us identically vulnerable.

I regained consciousness many hours later, just as it was getting dark. I felt absolutely drained. Pleasure put his arm around me as I struggled to sit up.

'You had to go through it,' he whispered. 'You had to exorcize it all.'

I felt completely different, as if I'd been reborn. I'd finally admitted to myself what I'd been through and the pattern of my life that had taken me there. I wasn't frightened any more. I'd been given a second chance to get myself right and I intended to take it. I'd learned a massive lesson about the simplicity of things, that it all comes down to being comfortable with one's self, nothing more or less. When you look at yourself in the mirror, there's a fantastic strength in knowing that you're doing the very best that you can. Treat each day as if it's your last and the revelation dawns that the more you put in, the more you get back. Karma, we used to call it. That's it, the key to a better life. To quote James Taylor: 'Any fool can do it, there ain't nothing to it.'

SIX

Rex Bob Lowenstein

I ARRIVED HOME FROM IBIZA AT THE END OF THE SUMMER OF 1979, feeling fitter and more positive than I had for years. I'd shaken off the shackles and now it was time to start rebuilding my life.

For the past few years I'd been hooked up in the web of 'celebrity', from which I was now keen to unravel. What had been said about me in the newspapers during my last two years on *Whistle Test* had really hit home. I'd defy anyone who's had a real hammering from the press to say it doesn't hurt. It does. In the same way that you're inflated by all the good things you read, so you're hit by the blows. The greater the fame, the harder it can be to deal with. My experience was minor by comparison with that of a Paul McCartney or a Robert Plant. It's very hard to stay level at that kind of stratospheric height. I think it's to their massive credit that they've remained 'grounded' to the extent they have. It isn't easy. I really felt I was starting from scratch.

The idea was to find myself again and go back to my roots. I wanted to establish tighter links with the family. I had neglected my parents and my girls. I wanted to return to what I knew I did best. Radio was where I wanted to be. I also felt there was one piece of unfinished business. I'd left *Whistle Test* with very negative feelings. I really felt I'd run my course. But despite the upheaval it had brought into my life, I still felt very proud to have been associated with the show through what are now seen by many as the halcyon days. When Mike Appleton invited me to call in, it was a wonderful feeling to go back simply for the enjoyment of being part of the programme again.

I visited the new studio set-up at Shepperton, with The Damned playing a live set. After the Sex Pistols incident I'd found it very hard to be objective about punk, but I always liked The Damned, particularly

'New Rose' with its massive energy and its 'Is she really going out with him?' intro, like the Shangri-La's 'Leader Of The Pack'. Mike invited me to introduce Blondie onstage at the Apollo in Glasgow, for the annual New Year's Eve '*Whistle Test* Special'. Blondie had topped the British singles charts twice that year with 'Heart Of Glass' and 'Sunday Girl' and were at the peak of their power and popularity. At the end of a sensational concert we all headed back to the hotel and, as the decade ended and the 80s began, I found myself in the snug bar, enjoying a post-concert jam session – Deborah Harry on vocals, Chris Stein on acoustic guitar and the rest of us banging out percussion and singing along for all we were worth. The evening seemed to round off the decade perfectly. I'd said goodbye to the past. Now it was time to address the future and get behind a microphone again.

I'd already begun a commission from London Radio Productions to work on a multi-part series called *The Moody Blues Story* and I enjoyed meeting up with them all again, particularly Justin Hayward, with whom I always got on well. I rejoined Radio 210, where Chris Yates was as good as his word and had kept my old job open for me, with a more sensible schedule this time. I started broadcasting a Friday evening *Rock Show* and two four-hour programmes through Saturday and Sunday lunchtimes. I absolutely loved it all and soon decided to move to Berkshire, where I rented a small semi-detached house in Southcote on the outskirts of Reading, five minutes from the radio station. Jackie and I had found it impossible to settle together after I got back from Ibiza and, although we've remained good friends, we both agreed that a clean break would finally be a good idea. For the first time for 15 years I was living on my own and happy to see the pace of my life slow down at last. I began to nest build.

An art student friend of Tarquin's moved in for a couple of weeks to help with the decoration, in return for being able to use the interior of the house as a blank canvas. He worked in the colour spectrum from white to black, mixing a light grey wash to cover the walls, then creating rows of squares under the picture rails like paintings – textured blocks of black, grey or white paint. He coated over them several times, maybe black on grey then white or black again, wet paint in all shades of grey dribbling down the walls from the layers on layers. It was unusual to say the least and a real talking point with visitors. 'How on earth do you live with it?' was one of the most regular comments. 'How the mighty have fallen since the heady days of *Whistle Test*,' was another. But I didn't care, maybe apart from the fact that I wished he'd worked in colours. I was really happy there in my odd little semi-detached.

My daughters came down to see me most weekends and we were able to spend quality time together at last. I even got a dog, a slightly neurotic, impossible-to-train labrador-cross called Cassie, bought for me on a whim for £8 by Mike Read from a bloke at a local pub in Theale. She was part of a small litter of puppies playing round our feet in the bar and I'd helped her scramble up onto my knee while Mike, Steve Crozier and myself sat supping our Sunday lunchtime pints. She had a glossy coat, completely black except for a tiny patch of white fur under her chin. I thought she was absolutely gorgeous, curled up asleep on my lap, and when we left the pub I had her blinking in the sunshine under my arm. I'd never owned a dog before and didn't realize the commitment. From then on she went almost everywhere with me.

As well as my own weekend programmes I began to sit in on weekday shows. I even spent a fortnight early in 1980 doing the 210 *Breakfast Show*, not a good idea on the cold, dark mornings of early January. It certainly focused the mind. The station closed down for five hours overnight, so I had to get myself into the studio by 5.45 a.m. and literally switch everything into transmission in time to play the opening theme music and link with the Independent Radio News bulletin at 6. I made it in for the first show with only seconds to spare, making the mistake of explaining my breathlessness on air. A local bookie immediately started taking bets on how many times during the next two weeks I'd oversleep and arrive late. He offered odds for one morning or two mornings, with variations for five minutes late, 10 minutes late and every five minutes up to 30, by which time someone else would have rushed in to man the fort. I'm a late-night person. I hate getting up in the morning. I nearly put a bet on myself but to my own and everyone else's amazement, I wasn't late once.

I started to get to know David Byron, formerly the lead singer of Uriah Heep. He lived nearby in Sonning and Radio 210 was his local station. He was a regular listener and phoned a few times when I was doing the Friday *Rock Show*, often just for a chat or sometimes to ask me for details of tracks I was playing. He invited me over to his place after one of the shows and, having shut the radio station down, I arrived at about 1.45 a.m. The house was magnificent, one of an avenue of millionaires' homes, set in trees in an acre of land, the garden skirting the River Thames. I parked my car beside his white Rolls Royce at the end of the long gravel drive. However, all was not as it seemed. Despite the apparent opulence he was a desperate and embittered man. The Uriah Heep years had taken their toll.

David had founded the band, initially named The Stalkers, in the mid-60s and stayed with them for ten turbulent years, their grandiose progressive rock style yielding seven Top-40 albums before his departure in 1976. Despite their success, they worked and partied themselves to the point of exhaustion, 'a bunch of machines plummeting to a death', according to keyboard player Ken Hensley. Dismissed by the critics as an anachronism, the band became locked in a series of internal arguments following the death of former bass player Gary Thain. In the resulting power struggle Ken Hensley walked out and David Byron was forced to quit. He briefly joined Rough Diamond but they broke up soon after and, following a failed attempt at launching the Byron Band, he was trying to build a solo career out of what remained of his reputation.

The scars of the previous few years were obvious, as was the reality of impending financial disaster. The money had dried up and the rock'n'roll lifestyle could no longer be funded. As he showed me around, I realized that the house was falling into disrepair and the car beginning to rust. I felt desperately sorry for him as he told me how difficult life had become, and could identify with him about the hammering he'd taken from the press. But he was unsettlingly unstable and the atmosphere wasn't good. When he brandished a gun and held it to his temple I felt it was probably time to leave. We spoke a few more times on the phone, but then fell out of touch. He died of a heart attack in February 1985. It can be a brutal business, rock'n'roll. I was pleased to be disentangling myself from the madness for a while.

Radio 210 had a private garden and on sunny days it was possible to feed a few leads across the lawn and broadcast outdoors, so long as there was someone in the studio to play the records in for you. Steve Wright would often trail a mobile broadcast unit down to the A4 at the end of the drive, weighed down by stickers, posters, pens and other station giveaways. He'd flag down passing motorists at random and interview them live on air, stuffing the microphone into their vehicle to see whether or not they were listening to the station, and dishing out loads of 210 paraphernalia. It became a regular *Drive Time* event, a cacophony of music, car horns and traffic jams.

By the middle of 1980 the DJ roster was beginning to change. Mike Read, with whom Steve did the brilliant *Read and Wright Show*, had already moved to Radio Luxembourg, and Steve was about to follow. The innovative Dave Glass was now part of the on-air team, as was Keith Butler, and Neil ffrench-Blake asked me to take another new DJ under my wing. I knew the name Mike Quinn from a hundred black-and-white posters I'd seen when I first moved up to London in 1966. At that time his name was almost as well known to clubgoers as that of Jeff Dexter, except he was much more into dance than psychedelia. Mike was the resident DJ at Tiles Club but I'd heard nothing of him since. Now he was coming to Radio 210 on trial and I was intrigued to meet him. Surprisingly, he'd done very little broadcasting in the intervening years, but arrived at the station with a fantastic record collection and a huge amount of enthusiasm. Not surprisingly, he used Manfred Mann's single 'Mighty Quinn' as his theme song. Later, when he was doing *The Late Show* he'd close down the station every night with 'Goodnight My Love' by Jessie Belvin from 1960, the first time I'd heard that magical record.

He was what's known in the industry as a ducker and a diver. But his heart seemed to be in the right place and I got on well with this likeable rogue, regularly putting him up at my house if he needed to stay over. Over a period of a couple of months he more or less moved in, constantly raiding my record collection for stuff for his shows and getting all my covers muddled up!

Mike was the biggest Rolling Stones fan I've ever met. He travelled to London with me when I interviewed Mick Jagger at his home in Chelsea a few weeks before the release of the *Emotional Rescue* album. Mick was in a great mood, very hospitable and warm, despite the fact that we arrived over half an hour late, having been stuck in the M4 traffic. Mike got him to sign loads of stuff, had his photograph taken with him and I got some wonderful material for a 'Rolling Stones Special' for Radio 210.

As well as all his Stones records, Mike had crates full of northern soul and 60s singles. We constantly played music at the house, listening to new releases for the 210 playlist, choosing tracks for our shows or just listening to our favourite sounds. He loved making tapes of his favourite tracks and one day asked me if I would deliver a cassette for him when I next went to London. My daughter Emily was staying with me for the weekend, and when I drove her back on Sunday afternoon we diverted to the Fulham address Mike had written on the tape box. As we waited in the early summer sunshine for the front door to open, Emily desperate to go to the loo, I had absolutely no idea that my life was about to completely change again.

After the hurt of the past few years I'd vowed to be on my own for a while. I had no desire to start a new relationship and had been taking the opportunity to let my life settle, catching up on lost time with my daughters. Miri was now nearly 10, Emily was seven and Charlie was nearly three. When we weren't together I was comfortable in my own company and I certainly didn't plan to let my life spin into a whirlwind love affair. But that's exactly what happened.

Valentina Scott opened the front door of her house and I handed her the tape. She invited us in and was immediately attentive to Ems, showing her the bathroom then offering her biscuits and a glass of Coca-Cola, a rare treat in my new health-conscious regime.

We stood talking in the kitchen while music, conversation and laughter spilled out of a half-open door along the hallway. Val eventually took us through and introduced us to her friends sitting round a table heaving with plates of pasta, cheeses, bread, fruit, panatone, bottles of wine and pots of coffee and scattered with Sunday review sections and magazines. The atmosphere was convivial and we immediately felt comfortable, sitting down to enjoy the banter.

Val introduced us to her brother Nick, who was sitting slightly aside from the main crowd. Conversation between him and his sister slipped easily into and out of English and Italian, the two languages woven together as they talked, three or four words spoken in English in the middle of an otherwise Italian sentence and vice versa. It was fascinating to listen to and very musical to the ear. Val told us that they'd been brought up bilingual, that the family had spent more or less equal time in England and in Italy and that Nick was one of three older brothers. 'I'm the baby of the family,' she told me, laughing. She was 22, eleven years younger than me.

Above: My first-ever record, Paul Anka's 'Diana', now framed and on my studio wall.

Right: Summer 1947, on holiday with my parents in Mablethorpe. Most often we would spend summer holidays in Pontardawe, surrounded by blue-grey mountains. My parents didn't own a car until I was eight, so each year they would save up to hire the little Austin 7 in which we undertook the eight-hour journey across the Brecon Beacons from Northampton to south Wales.

Above: Marc Bolan and I backstage on the first T.Rextasy tour in 1971.

Left: A letter Marc sent me after publication of the first edition of *Time Out* magazine.

BOB ★

I hope your well, time out is truly a nice thing. I've enclosed the facts below incase their any use to you

Tyrannosaurus REX

2nd LP released late October/november titled Prophets, Seers, & Sages the angels of the ages

on regal-Zonophone

tracks included are Aznageel the mage & the Scenscof Dynasty & 12 others

may your eyes ever shine with happyness love MaR ★

Above: The working hub of the *Old Grey Whistle Test*. Director Colin Strong (left), myself and producer Mike Appleton put final touches to the show in the gallery of Presentation B studio at Television Centre.

Below: A rare photograph of the whole *Whistle Test* team, captured in the studio in 1976.

Above: A memorable and very difficult interview with Van Morrison in my early days on *Whistle Test*.

Below: The Wailers preparing to perform 'Concrete Jungle' and a hypnotic version of 'Stir It Up' in our tiny studio in 1973 – a wonderful image by Alan Messer, our resident *Whistle Test* photographer, now living in Nashville.

Right: A lot of rock 'n' roll stars came into the *Whistle Test* studio, among them Del Shannon, The Everly Brothers, Duane Eddy and Bill Haley (pictured).

Below: A recent shot of Robert Plant and I in my studio 'under the apple tree'.

NOBODY AT WEMBLEY COULD DISPUTE THE U
PASSED SUPREMACY OF BBC-2'S "OLD GREY W
TEST", VOTED BRITAIN'S TOP TV SHOW BY NME RE/
A DEAFENING OVATION GREETED HOST BOB HARRI
PRODUCER MICHAEL APPLETON WHEN THEY CAN
STAGE TO RECEIVE THE AWARD

had done likewise at an mpting to urn the Pool into same feat at the S

Above: *Old Grey Whistle Test* producer Mike Appleton and I lifting the cup at Wembley.

Below: With Gary Lineker, Fred Rumsey, David Gower and Nick Cook at the launch of a pro-celebrity Quick Cricket tournament in 1985.

SEX PISTOL OVER B[...]

ANOTHER storm blew up yesterday over the Sex Pistols punk rock group.

Lead singer Johnny Rotten was said to have been involved in a disco punch-up.

A man was later taken to hospital with cuts to his head, caused by a broken glass.

He was a friend of BBC TV disc jockey Bob Harris, who was also hurt in the brawl.

Solicitors for the two injured men are considering whether to take legal action.

Mr. Harris's manager, [...]

By GEOFF GARVEY

stars in London's Mayfair.

Mr. Harris — host of the B B C-2 pop show The Old Grey Whistle Test — was with recording engineer Mr. George Nicholson, and three other friends.

A tall, blond man is [...] to have approached [...]

Sex Pistols' latest r[...] would be played o[...] TV show.

Mr. Roberge[...] Bob ignored the [...] who then punched [...]

Meanwhile, a s[...] broke out nearby i[...] ing among others Jo[...] Rotten, who was at[...] club with another g[...] member, Sid Vicious.[...] [...]. Nicholson

Disc jockey Harris: He was punched.

PREMIER
From Page One.

Above: 'Kill the hippy!'

Right: The early 1980s and I begin to rebuild my life.

WHISPERING BOB BOUNCES BACK!

For a man close to death three years ago, Bob Harris looked disgustingly healthy when he dropped into Music's offices a couple of weeks back. He's due back on the nation's TV in a few weeks. Bob took time out to tell Grahame Morrison what he'd been up to since leaving 'The Old Grey Whistle Test' in 1979, and why we are due to see him again soon.

During the Seventies, groups climbed over one another to get a spot on 'The Old Grey Whistle Test'. He really wanted [...]

The good thing about Mike was that he'd always be willing to listen to any ideas I might have about bands. It was quite strange how it worked out sometimes [...]

to me, so I let '210' and joined Radio Oxford.

Although Oxford is only about fifty miles or so from London, the contrast between presenting an afternoon's relaxed music programme, and the 'riff-a-minute, dry-iced-laser-beamed' Whistle Test must have made Bob feel he was on a different planet! Helped in no small way by Bob Gorton who Harris describes as, "a great guy to work with." Bob understands radio, he cares about programmes, and he knows how to create the right atmosphere likely to get the best from his presenters", the afternoon programme went very well. One of the highlights of it was the 'big band' spot that soon [...]

express wish that I should take it over, should he die before it was completed.

That means that I am able to do it because Alexis wanted me to do it. I'm not doing it by default because he wants me to be there."

As he talks to the new series, Bob constantly flexis his hands and nervously twists his wedding ring. So much for Mr Cool.

Alexis' express wish

Bob Harris looks to the future. (Pic by Ray Sh[...])

There's thirteen, thirty minute parts, and the hardest bit is decided, but it [...] first programme [...]

Below: My sons Jamie (left) and Ben (the newspaper caption put them the wrong way round) meeting Jason Donovan at Harrod's sale.

PAGE 15

Mail, Thursday, January 4, 1990

THE DAY TWO BOYS MET THEIR IDOL. BUT LOTS OF GIRLS DIDN'T

IT'S not just the girls who think Jason Donovan's great. Yesterday, as the star opened the Harrods sale under siege from screaming female fans, two little boys managed to snatch a quiet moment together with their idol. Brothers Ben, four (left), and seven-year-old Jamie, travelled from their family home in Norfolk.

Fans mob Jason at Harrods

SCREAMING girl fans were pushed to the ground in a stampede yesterday as they struggled to see pop heartthrob Jason Donovan open the Harrods winter sale.

Scores of frantic teenagers [...]

Above: My friend Emmylou Harris who presented me with my AMA Trailblazer Award in Nashville in 2011.

Left: The woman of my dreams. Trudie and I have been together since September 1989 and were married on 24th April 1991.

Below: With Beth Nielsen Chapman at her home in Nashville. A still from our *Back To Beth's* television programme, shown on BBC4 in November 2014.

Mike Quinn was positively beside himself when I got back home. 'What did you think of her?' he asked, bobbing up and down as he followed me into the music room.

'My daughter thinks she's a wild woman,' I announced.

'I thought I might invite her to the show next weekend,' he ventured. 'What do you think?' I thought about it for a second. Greg Kihn and his band were coming in to play live, which I knew would be good fun.

'Perfect,' I replied.

Mike handed me the phone when he called her the following day. 'Shall I bring my pyjamas?' she asked me.

'No, don't bring your pyjamas!' I replied. I put the phone down, realizing that Mike had played Cupid and that I was embarking on an exciting new romance.

Val and I began to spend more time together. She swept through my little house in Southcote, bringing a much-needed feminine touch to the sparsely furnished rooms of grey and black squares, filling them with flowers, rugs and knick-knacks bought from local antique shops. It even looked presentable when my parents came to visit and they took to her immediately, Dad in particular appreciating the trouble she'd taken creating the fabulous meal that was waiting for them when they arrived.

Val was passionate about food and wine. She enjoyed the whole process of cookery, from searching out the particular herb or type of parmesan cheese she needed to complete the ingredients of one of her favourite Italian dishes, to conjuring a glorious meal out of the most forlorn leftovers in the fridge. She loved throwing dinner parties and much of our time was spent surrounded by people, for extended lunches or long evenings of eating, drinking, conversation and music.

Val increasingly involved herself with my daughters, particularly Miri and Emily, often coming to West Hampstead with me, spending time talking with everyone in Sue's kitchen, the most inner of inner sanctums. It was clear to all of us that Val and I were falling in love. Sue and I had never thought to get a divorce but, having achieved the close friendship we'd worked so hard to restore, now seemed a good time, with no recriminations. Her opinion mattered very much to me, particularly regarding the influence of my new relationship on our daughters, so it meant a lot that Sue trusted Val and gave us her blessing.

Val and I began to look for somewhere to live and Steve Crozier told us about a converted chapel of rest he'd heard about in Oxfordshire. Everything was happening very fast, but I had no reservations whatsoever. My track record with relationships up to this point had not been good and maybe because of that I wanted to commit myself unreservedly to this one. I was determined nothing would go wrong, that I would be true to Val for the rest of my life. Within a few months of meeting, she and I decided to get married and began to make plans for our wedding in Italy the following summer.

I had already joined Val on a few trips to Tuscany and could understand why she loved it so much. It was becoming clear that her family was not only wealthy but also had a fascinating history. 'My mum is called Contessa Fiammetta Bianca Maria Sforza,' Val explained. 'Her father, Count Carlo Sforza, was an important Italian politician and anti-Fascist. The Sforza family is one of oldest and most established aristocratic families in Italy and we can trace our lineage right back to the crusades. My parents met at the end of the war when my mother returned from exile in America.'

Val told me how her mother had been smuggled out of Italy during the dark days of Mussolini. 'When my grandfather returned to Italy he resumed his political career but it was made very clear to him by the Establishment that they did not approve of the forthcoming wedding of his daughter to Howard Scott, a divorced, non-Catholic, father-of-two, destitute Englishman!'

Her grandfather, however, was unmoved by any such political pressure. 'What matters now is my daughter's happiness,' he stated and so Howard and Fiammetta married discreetly and lived in Milan, where Howard opened an English-language school. Their wedding present from Carlo Sforza was La Tambura, a villa in the seaside resort of Ronchi.

My first visit to La Tambura confirmed that this was somewhere special. Set back from the inner coast road, it stands square, proud and magnificent behind high hedges and wrought-iron gates, in the middle of its own private world. The grounds are beautiful, scented and serene, shaded by trees and I was absolutely spellbound by the feeling of the place

One of the most memorable nights of my life was spent in the

centre of the nearby town of Forte Di Marmi with Nick, the night
Italy won the World Cup in 1982. The place went absolutely crazy,
people piling into the two main streets on whatever transport they
could muster – cars, coaches, and hundreds of buzzy little sewing-
machine motorbikes, converging with tractors pulling trailers full of
people down into town from the mountain farms. It was a dazzling,
deafening cacophony of horns, klaxons and colour, people dancing,
kissing and yelling with the sheer ecstasy of it all. In the middle of
the main crossroads stood a lone policeman, blowing his whistle
and trying to direct traffic through the gridlock – an impossible task.
Eventually, festooned with scarves and rosettes and with cap askew, he
gave in to the inevitable. He threw up his arms, shrugged his shoulders
in mock apology and joined the throng.

At La Tambura, I felt as if I'd moved into a completely different
world and it was great not to be totally consumed by my work, as I had
been for so long. Italy was bringing a whole new range of experiences
and culture into my life, and when I was at home I had time to spend
with my family instead of rushing off to gigs all the time. The pace of life
was suiting me and I particularly enjoyed talking with the younger DJs
at 210, exchanging radio gossip and discussing the skills of programme
building and broadcasting. My shows felt wonderfully pressure-free, the
atmosphere was good and I increasingly encouraged touring musicians
to come into the studio and play live.

Harry Chapin joined us for lunch on 2nd February 1981 before I
compered for him at the Reading Hexagon that evening. He was a man
of boundless energy, performing nearly 300 concerts every year, half of
them for charities, for which he raised millions of dollars a year. 'I play
one night for me and one night for the other guy,' he explained simply.
Harry had a wonderful narrative writing style and I was particularly
impressed by the captivating 'Cats In The Cradle', which offered a
warning about the consequences of putting careerism above family life,
a lyrical theme that had touched my conscience when I'd first heard the
song in 1974. We'd met a few months after the song had topped the
American charts, to film a *Whistle Test* interview in New York to mark
the Broadway opening of his just-completed musical *The Night That
Made America Famous*. I liked him very much and truly admired the
wholehearted way he threw himself into everything he did.

He loved to talk and was a compelling orator – knowledgeable, challenging and politically driven, a Democratic Party activist. As we sat talking and laughing in the restaurant of our 210 local, he seemed larger than life. At close to six-foot-six and eighteen stone, he commanded the room, ordering a third, then a fourth bottle of red wine while eating at least two dishes from each of the three courses on the menu. After a pot of good strong coffee it was all washed down with a couple of glasses of the best port in the house. I was desperately sad to hear of his death a few months later, killed in a crash on his way to a benefit concert in New York. He loved life so much and had so much to give. Sometimes life just isn't fair.

Alexis Korner was another man of stubborn integrity whose company I greatly enjoyed. I invited him down to Radio 210 to spend an evening with me to record an interview for a special I was planning to mark his forthcoming birthday. As we settled in the studio he gave me a letter. I recognized the writing immediately and asked him how he'd got it.

'Somebody just handed it to me as I was leaving Egton House to come down here,' he stated.

'Did you see who it was?' I asked.

'No, I didn't really take much notice.' Alexis went to get us a coffee as I sat looking at the envelope.

It was from a girl who'd been writing to me for several years. She'd seen me on *Whistle Test* and become fixated, God only knows why. She bombarded me with letters, photographs and all kinds of personal stuff. When I left the programme she became desperate, phoning local radio stations all round the country until she located me at 210. After failing in an attempt to persuade management to send her tapes of all my shows, she went first to the Independent Broadcasting Authority then to the Reading Police, before systematically phoning all the local numbers she thought might provide her with the recordings, including every hi-fi and electrical shop listed in the phone book. The letter, however, was a slightly discomforting new development. No one knew Alexis was visiting me. He hadn't told anyone, nor had I trailed it on air. Neither of us had any idea how she knew he was seeing me that night. It felt extremely weird being in the sights of this person I'd never met who, as well as being obsessive, was also eerily telepathic! I put the unopened envelope in the bin and a few weeks later the letters abruptly stopped. I didn't hear from her again for nearly 10 years.

More disturbing was the fact that Alexis was feeling unwell. He'd been ages getting the coffee and came back into the studio looking awful. It was an hour or so before he felt up to doing the interview but once we got underway he was riveting, talking in that deep gravel voice with all his usual passion and eloquence. We talked about the history of The Rolling Stones and the pivotal role he'd played in the formation of Free.

There is enormous peer affection for Alexis. Many of the great British blues musicians who emerged in the 60s acknowledge their debt to him to this day and many had joined the celebrations at Pinewood Studios a couple of years earlier to mark his 50th birthday, an event he talked about with great pride. His house band that night comprised Charlie Watts, Jack Bruce, Ian Stewart and Dick Heckstall-Smith, joined onstage by such as Eric Clapton, Zoot Money and Chris Farlowe in a two-hour jam session that had lifted the roof off. The whole event had been filmed for possible inclusion in an ambitious 13-part television series called *The History Of Rock*. Alexis told me he was working with director Luke Jeans, whom I'd met with Tarquin Gotch at Gary Osborne's house. They'd recently been to America with Del Taylor, Alexis's manager, recording interviews for the series. He was particularly thrilled to have spent time with Tina Turner, whom he described as being 'the real thing'. He asked me if I'd like to be involved with the project in some way and although it never made the screen I said I would be honoured. It was, as always, wonderful spending time with him but as he drove away at the end of the session I had a nagging feeling about his health. Never the most robust of people, he looked fragile and weary. I really didn't want anything to happen to Alexis.

A few days before the programme went out, Val and I moved to our eighteenth-century chapel of rest in Oxfordshire. The interior conversion was impressive, with an open-plan kitchen at the top end of the ground floor where the altar used to be, font still untouched by the builders. The original stained glass window threw mottled, multicoloured bands of light onto the landing and there was even a small study that became my music room, walls lined with album shelves. The house had a small garden, just big enough for a game of cricket and, as summer arrived, we started inviting friends over for regular Sunday knockabouts on the lawn. We called it the Garden Cricket Club, and much like those long-ago games of football-tennis at Peel Acres, the rules were, of necessity, complex. All overs were bowled from one end at one batter at a time, everyone had a bat and a bowl. Hit the wall of the house and it was a four, over the house was a six, over the fence was out. We split up into teams – our Oxfordshire friends against our friends from London. The games could get quite competitive but were fantastic fun, fielders spread around the garden, sandwiches, cakes and tea on a big trestle table on the patio, beer on tap. The star was usually David Duncan-Smith, an ex-Millfield boy who had to be got out early. Once he got his eye in, a century usually ensued. We even kept averages!

Life felt blissful and the future looked assured, a feeling enhanced by a call from Ted Gorton, station manager of the local BBC station, Radio Oxford. He'd heard that I'd moved in locally and had called to offer me the *Drive Time Show*, Monday to Friday 3 p.m. to 5 p.m. It would be a wrench to leave 210. They'd treated me extremely well and I'd had a really good time there. But I was keen to return to BBC radio and agreed to join the station when I got back from our honeymoon.

Val and I were married in Ronchi a year and a day after we met, on 20th June 1981. Like her mother before her, Val had been refused permission by the Roman Catholic Church to marry an Anglican divorcee, so the ceremony was held at Val's aunt's house, a few minutes' walk from La Tambura, the only other Sforza property in Italy to survive Mussolini's wartime fire raisers. Friends and relatives travelled from all over Italy and the UK to be there, gathering in the shade of the courtyard. I'd ferried a carload of people down myself in the dear old Volvo 245DL Estate I'd bought for the now-regular journeys, including my best man, Steve Crozier, whose minister father performed the ceremony. The organization was unbelievable. My mum even flew for the first and only time in her life! Miri and Emily were bridesmaids.

It was a spectacular day in Tuscany, hot and still, Val arriving in the sunshine with her father in a horse-drawn carriage. The reception was held in a huge marquee on the lawn at La Tambura and Dad was one of the speakers. He and Val's father, Howard, had already begun to forge a friendship.

Val and I then whisked off to spend a night in Forte Di Marmi before flying to Bangkok for a three-day stopover en route to the paradise island of Bali, where we spent the next 10 days. To round off our honeymoon we flew back to Italy to visit relatives in Rome, before returning to Ronchi for the last few days, finally arriving home in Oxfordshire the day before my first show on Radio Oxford at the beginning of August.

I took over on *Drive Time* from Timmy Mallett, who was moving to commercial radio before embarking on a successful career as a wacky children's presenter on TVAM. He was extremely popular locally and the contrast between our two shows must have come as a huge shock for the listeners. One week they were hearing novelty songs and being hit over the head with Mallett's mallet, the next it's all Steely Dan, Jackson Browne and Steve Miller. But the show went really well, the figures were good and soon the programme was extended by an hour to 6 p.m.

Radio Oxford linked with the main networks at certain times of the day. I followed *Woman's Hour* on air at 3 p.m. and usually began my programme in an appropriately mellow mood, developing a feature called 'Sentimental journey' and playing a couple of oldies at the beginning of the show. I did a birthday and anniversary spot at 3.30, researching material that would eventually be published as *The Rockdate Diary* in the early 90s. And once a month I did 'The Singles Cavalcade'. Starting at 3 o'clock on Monday afternoon, I'd spend the entire week playing through every record to have topped the British and American charts that month in years gone by, starting in 1955 and working up to the present day, phenomenally successful with listeners and really good fun to do. Miraculously, it always exactly fitted. Without having to chase fades or drop records I would hand over at 6 o'clock on Friday evening to John Dunn on Radio 2, having just played the current No. 1.

A young trainee used to come in straight from school and occasionally help out on my show, taking phone calls, making the tea and maybe doing a bit of tape editing. His name is Jon Briggs and, to me, he is a model of what can be achieved with the requisite amount of hard work and enthusiasm. He'd been bitten by the radio bug and just loved being around the station, learning all the skills. He qualified for Bristol University but just couldn't bear the thought of breaking away from radio to begin his course. 'At least give it go,' I told him, sounding like my father. 'You can always come back to radio when you've got your degree.' He followed my advice but was back within three months, hanging around in the hope of a job. Sure enough, someone phoned in sick one day and he found himself on air. He was a natural, blessed with a golden larynx and hasn't looked back since. These days he runs his own agency, 'The Excellent Voice Company', is the voice of *The Weakest Link* and does voice-overs galore.

He became a regular member of our garden cricket club and was also in the Radio Oxford team that played the *Oxford Mail* in the annual grudge match on the village green at Marsh Baldon in the summer of 1982. Our opponents had acquired the services of a couple of strapping fast bowlers from the local league who decimated our early batting. After seven overs of mayhem and injury Jon arrived at the crease, me at the non-strikers end, the scoreboard reading 5 runs for 3 wickets. The first ball he faced whistled over the top of his head. The second one hit him a fearful thump under the heart. He collapsed like a pack of cards. No one would have blamed him had he retired then and there but after several minutes of 'magic sponge' treatment he took guard again. Despite our protestations that this was supposed to be a 'friendly' game, the bowler thundered in and delivered a face-high bouncer. To his enormous credit, Jon stood up straight and hooked it to the boundary. That he was out a few balls later didn't matter. The boy had shown that he had guts. Early next over I was hit on the hand. Val said she heard the crack from the boundary. Exit to hospital, leaving my favourite pair of trousers in the pavilion.

I felt truly happy, secure and settled. Mornings were spent building my shows, piling singles into a wooden Schweppes crate. Armed with the crate, I'd arrive at the Radio Oxford studios soon after 2, do the programme, and be back home by 7. Weekends were free. I'd never been so organized before! Mum and Dad were frequent visitors to our chapel of rest and Miri, Emily and Charlotte came to stay with us most weekends. It was idyllic, and soon Val and I were telling everyone that we were expecting a baby. Our first son, Ben, a bright and beautiful boy, was born on 17th September 1982.

A few days later I received a letter from Radio 1, inviting me to take part in their 15th-anniversary celebrations on the *Dave Lee Travis Show* at the Paris Theatre on 30th September and later that day to appear at a concert at the Hammersmith Odeon. It was the first time I'd done anything with the network since I'd lost my *Sounds Of The 70s* programme seven years previously and I was keen to impress. Nothing doing, I'm afraid. Management was frosty, particularly one of the executive producers who, seeing me with a group of DJs gathering for a photograph, shouted to get my attention. 'You! Get out of the shot,' was his devastating command. So, I could knock out any thoughts of returning to Radio 1 then!

That wasn't the only setback. Things were beginning to feel uncomfortable at Radio Oxford. Unexpectedly, Ted Gorton was leaving to join the team producing Selina Scott and Frank Bough on the forthcoming BBC *Breakfast Show* and John Bright, his successor, was not a fan of my programme. 'Why is he playing the American charts on a Thursday afternoon?' he said on his arrival. 'This is supposed to be local radio.' It wasn't encouraging when, six weeks after taking over, he called every member of staff into his office to discuss their futures – with two exceptions. When fellow DJ David Freeman and I discovered we weren't invited, we knew the writing was on the wall. I was a big fan of David's, an intelligent and creative broadcaster and a great bloke. He was popular with the listeners but it was clear that John Bright didn't like us.

My parents arrived at Radio Oxford a few days later with a copy of the *Oxford Mail*. 'What's going on?' my father asked as he handed me the paper. 'Top DJ Faces Axe' read the front-page headline above an article predicting my demise. The tone of the article and the information printed strongly suggested the story had come from management.

'I have no idea,' I assured him. 'This is the first I've heard of it.' I phoned John Bright from the studio and arranged to see him at the end of the show. He was unpleasant and unequivocal.

'Your programme isn't local enough, so as soon as I've found a replacement I'm taking you off air.' There was no logic to this decision and I felt a strong sense of injustice, much as I'd done in my headmaster's office many years before. Only this time I didn't walk out, despite being goaded to by the station manager. I told the local press people waiting in reception the truth, that I was devastated and really didn't want to leave. The reaction was amazing.

The papers began a 'Save Bob Harris' campaign and within days correspondence and petitions started to arrive. Under the headline 'Hands Off Our Bob!' the *Oxford Mail* intensified its campaign: 'Programme organizer Stuart Woodcock said the station had not received any protests from listeners to his knowledge – but we have.' To prove their point, the 'Mailspin' music section published a page full of them.

'His show has the most varied musical content of any show on national or local radio,' said one.

'It seems to be the only programme where you stand a chance of listening to something which is not bland and middle of the road or pure chart fodder,' said another.

Every day the paper carried more protests. I thought it might all just go away, but it didn't. The papers became more insistent as the campaign intensified.

'It really does mean a lot,' I told the *Oxford Mail* in an interview headlined 'Whispering Bob's Show Gets The Chop'. 'It makes it all worthwhile when you get that sort of reaction. It would be very nice to think they will have an effect but we'll just have to wait and see.'

Eventually, John Bright called me into his office and proposed a compromise. My programme would continue, in shorter form, if I increased the local content. We made specific agreements and issued a conciliatory statement. The local press trumpeted their victory and I was able to leave for our summer holiday in Italy with some peace of mind.

I loved the Italian way of life, their passion for food and culture, their expansive temperament, the way they enjoyed a good time and a good row. I admired their respect for their cultural heritage, marvelled at the chaos of their politics. There seemed to be less of a generation divide than exists in Britain; the family unit was still an important part of the social structure. Elderly people got more respect, children were more readily acknowledged and included in whatever was going on.

Miri and Emily were often there with us in the summer or at Christmas and we took them on excursions to see some of the most beautiful cities in the world – Florence, Venice, Milan and Rome. We explored the local fishing ports and mountain villages, tasting the wine and the delicious local cuisine. Val also spent time on her own expeditions, talking to shopkeepers, restaurateurs, local fishermen and farers, as she began the work of compiling information and recipes for the cookery book she was preparing to write.

When we returned, I started my new programme on Radio Oxford, convinced that I was keeping to the arrangements made with John Bright about content. We'd agreed that I'd occasionally feature star guests, and I began turning up at the Apollo Theatre in Oxford or the Wyvern Theatre in Swindon to record backstage interviews with Cliff Richard, Chas and Dave, Jimmy Tarbuck and Tom Paxton. I worked with a local amateur dramatic society, the 4 x 4 Theatre Company in Wallingford, charting the behind-the-scenes progress of their production of 'Godspell', first recording the auditions then following the rehearsals right through to their first-night performance. I cut down the music content of the programme and upped the speech. But ten days into the new regime I received a letter from John Bright, signed by his assistant, telling me I hadn't kept to the format laid down and that he was giving me a month's notice of the show being taken off.

I didn't even bother going to see him; I had no respect for him at all. I thought he was devious, spineless and rude; he didn't even have the balls or the courtesy to sign my letter of dismissal. To me it was entirely predictable that under his divisive stewardship the Radio Oxford audience figures sank like a stone. I felt strongly enough about the way I'd been treated to contact the local radio administration unit at Broadcasting House. They didn't want to know.

If I was ever going to give up on radio it was now. I was really struggling to get any sort of broadcasting work, or even get people to return my calls. In the era of Margaret Thatcher's yuppie-led, synthesizer-laced, chrome-plated 80s, it was clear that I was yesterday. I'd become uncool, past my sell-by-date, a relic of a different era. But radio is what I do. It's my job and my passion. I knew that if I was going to rebuild my broadcasting career I was going to have to grit my teeth and tough it out. I'd begun to answer Mike Appleton's question. I may be a late starter, but perhaps I was beginning to grow up at last.

More bad news arrived on 1st January 1984. Mark Ringwood, a friend from my days at Radio 210, phoned to tell me that Alexis Korner had died. I was desperately sad to hear of the death of such a wonderful man and good friend. I just put down the phone and cried.

By now Val was also working hard on her first book, *Perfect Pasta*, published in October that year, so I was able to provide backup and spend time with our son Ben. We'd acquired a springer spaniel from Val's brother Nick, and Ben and I would take him and Cassie out for walks by the river near our house, or just mess around together. I loved being with Ben and we became very close. He was such a lovely, enthusiastic little boy, so bright. But I was fearful for the future and scared that my career had grounded. At 37, I didn't want to feel that I was all washed up but the reality was hammered home by an encounter at a local pub. 'Didn't you used to be Bob Harris?' enquired the barman as I asked for a pint. It was a cliché but it hurt.

I got in touch with Jonathan Holmes and asked if he could help. Jonathan ran a financial services and management company in Beeston in Nottingham and had a number of top-name clients in a mainly sporting portfolio. I'd contacted him during my last days on Radio Oxford to organize an interview with David Gower, for broadcast in my final week. I'd really wanted to meet David and, with the BBC connection coming to an end, I decided this might be my last chance. He gave me David's number and we arranged to meet at one of the service stations on the M1.

'It's too complicated to give you directions on the phone,' he told me. 'It will be easier if I come and collect you.' As I followed his white Audi through the outskirts of Leicester, I was half-amazed that his mere presence wasn't bringing the traffic to a standstill. David was a huge hero of mine and meeting him was a real thrill. I felt genuinely nervous when we arrived at his house and I began to set up the recording machinery. Interviewing John Lennon, Eric Clapton, Mick Jagger and most of the other major rock stars had never fazed me. But this was England cricket's golden boy, the future captain of England and one of the most elegantly gifted batsmen I'd ever seen. I was in awe of this person.

The house was relaxed but immaculate – pastel colours, lots of cushions and a white shag-pile carpet that submerged my shoes. David handed me a can of beer and I began to settle. I put the can down on the carpet for a moment while we chatted, before it occurred to me that I still hadn't plugged in the equipment. As I stepped forward towards the nearest power point, I managed to kick the open beer can. Becks would have been proud of me. The moment I made contact, I knew it was curling into the top right-hand corner ... of the painting hanging on the opposite wall, beer spurting all over the place, spraying a brown frothy foam down the side of the sofa and all over the white shag-pile carpet. I just wanted to disappear into it.

It's a moment David doesn't remember, thank God, and we've enjoyed a good, if spasmodic, friendship since. It gave me the greatest pride that he invited me to play in a pro-celebrity event on my birthday, of all days, the 11th April 1985. The team included England wicket keeper Paul Downton, fast bowler Fred Rumsey and Gary Lineker in a match to mark the opening of England's first quick-cricket facility, near Heathrow. I even got a 'Well done' from the captain for a sharp piece of fielding at cover. I got to bat and scored 5.

Jonathan Holmes offered to help in my quest for work and arranged an appointment with Jo Sandilands, top person at Capital Radio. We arrived at 2 o'clock and waited 15 minutes. 'You're late!' he said as she walked into the office. It was no surprise that the meeting didn't go particularly well.

As he had done in the past, Steve Crozier stepped in with assistance. He was now working at LBC, the London news station, and invited me in to meet Brian Hayes, the senior presenter. Brian was looking for an expert to join him once a month on his morning phone-in to talk about music and take calls on the subject. He had great authority, was commanding, often brusque on air but had a warm side and a dry, rather cynical sense of humour. We complemented each other well and soon I was invited to present the LBC music review programme for half an hour on a Friday night. To my great surprise and pride, the show won a Sony nomination in 1986, ironic in that it was the only music show on what was otherwise an all-speech station.

I also started working for GWR, a new commercial radio station based in Wootton Bassett near Swindon. I'd arranged a meeting with the managing director, Ralph Bernard, and arrived to find him kicking a football around his office, using his desk as a goal and practising his skills, walls covered in muddy football marks. I thought his attitude was great and immediately liked him. We began an association that lasted for the next four years, starting with a Sunday afternoon show, then adding a Saturday lunchtime show when Ralph took over the ailing Radio West, broadcast from their newly acquired studios in Bristol.

My first GWR show in Bristol followed an outside broadcast from Johnnie Walker, recently back from America. He'd left Radio 1 in the mid-70s to build a broadcasting career in the States. It was a very brave move but just hadn't worked out, and on his return he contacted Ralph, who immediately offered him a job. 'What a turn up for the books this is!' he remarked as he handed over to me. The following week I found myself doing a live outside broadcast with Samantha Fox from a local car showroom. Commercial radio works in strange ways, its woodwork to perform!

None of this work earned much money and, as finances continued to tighten, Val and I began to look for a smaller property, somewhere less expensive to run. George, who was now married and living in Norfolk, recommended we take a look at properties in East Anglia, and we realized we could get much more for our money there than was possible in Oxfordshire. We found a lovely, low-ceilinged cottage with about half an acre of land in the village of Northwold, south Norfolk, and moved in during August 1984.

For a while I commuted, leaving Norfolk on Friday for the LBC shows, staying over with Simeon David at his new flat in Oxford on Friday night, ready to travel to Bristol the following morning, and I loved listening to 'Loose Ends' on the car radio as I drove down the motorway. I'd stay in Oxford again on Saturday night, do my show in Swindon on Sunday afternoon, then drive all the way back to Norfolk. I didn't even have my Volvo – it had been a victim of the economy cuts – so I was doing almost a thousand miles a week in a Fiat Uno! The petrol cost me almost as much as I was earning.

Clearly, I couldn't keep this way of life going and began to search for work on my new local stations. I got a Saturday evening show on Radio Broadland in Norwich and a Sunday lunchtime show on Hereward Radio in Peterborough, staying on in the studio to record my programmes for GWR, which I'd post to the station to be broadcast the following week. It was hard work for low pay, averaging less than £40 a show, but I was doing it to keep myself on the roundabout, just to keep broadcasting.

My career reached a particularly low point on the day 'Live Aid' was broadcast in 1985. I was on air at Radio Broadland, doing my *Bob Harris Music Show*, watching the concert on the monitor in the studio. Mike Appleton collaborated with Bob Geldof to coordinate worldwide television coverage of the event and it was very much a *Whistle Test* day, using all the programme's facilities and expertise. I desperately wished Mike had asked me to be involved. I felt sad and unwanted, like I was a million miles removed from it all. I actually asked for people to phone in to my show, just to reassure me someone was listening. I got one call.

Thankfully, writing was coming to the rescue. Orbis Books commissioned me to write and compile a quiz and information book for them called *Rock and Pop Mastermind*. Despite originally coming into the business through journalism, I'd never tackled a project of this size before and really enjoyed the process of it, spending over a month in Ronchi at the beginning of 1985 to get it finished, working every day from 1 a.m. to 10 p.m. I loved that enclosed world-within-a-world writers retreat into. The book was published later that year.

To promote the book I did a radio tour, which included a visit to the British Forces Broadcasting Service (BFBS). I was interviewed by Tommy Vance and at the end of the programme asked his advice on how to get a job on the station. Funded by the Ministry of Defence, BFBS was able to cherry-pick the very best broadcasting talent and there was a lot of kudos attached to working there. Tommy introduced me to the station manager, Charles Foster, one of the really good guys of the industry, a man of his word. We talked through a number of ideas before he suggested *Black And Blues*, a programme devoted to soul, blues and R&B. This was fantastic, just the sort of thing I wanted to get my teeth into and I started the first series at the beginning of the following calendar quarter. 'You Can't Sit Down' by Phil Upchurch was my theme tune.

It was all very hard work but I didn't mind that. After a period of uncertainty, everything seemed to be stabilizing again. By the time Val and I had our second son, Jamie, on 30th September 1985, I really thought we'd weathered the storm. But the financial structure of British Schools was coming under increasing strain and Val's father was becoming unwell. At the same time, the pace of Val's professional life was speeding up. She was writing another book and working up a few ideas for television, often heading off to London for meetings. She began to close off. Understandably, I thought, she was distracted and preoccupied, considering everything she had on her plate.

A short time later, LBC offered me the weekend *Nightline* show, on air Friday, Saturday and Sunday nights, 10 p.m. to 1 a.m., with an open phone line and guests. It was a challenge I couldn't refuse. I could now let most of the other programmes go and concentrate on this main source of decent income. I'd never done all-speech radio before and relished the chance to talk to the wide range of people who arrived in the studio. I met some of my great sporting heroes – Trevor Bailey, Steve Coppell and Henry Cooper. I discussed fashion with Zandra Rhodes, cookery with Jill Cox and hosted political discussions with Edwina Currie and Frank Field. I even talked pets with a pet expert!

It was fantastic experience and a steep learning curve, with no music to fall back on if a caller swore or the pace got too hot. But I was spending time away from home again, trying to earn a living, unaware that Val now had her own agenda and that the fabric of my marriage was beginning to slowly unravel.

SEVEN

Return to Radio 1

'WHAT ON EARTH AM I DOING ON LBC?' WAS A THOUGHT THAT regularly crossed my mind. I didn't feel qualified to be hosting a late-night phone-in show. I have no real interest in politics or in politicians (except for an overall feeling that they're all more or less as bad as one another), I'm not particularly well educated or knowledgeable, I don't watch a lot of television and I'm not a great one for gossip. I never had any ambition to be a talk show host and probably used to irritate the hell out of listeners who tuned to the station as a refuge from pop radio by insisting on finding reasons to include the odd album track from time to time. But doing those shows gave my broadcasting a huge boost of confidence.

LBC was situated in Gough Square, and I would spend the early part of Friday evenings on my own in a little pub in Fleet Street, having a pie and a pint while reading the newspapers and researching my guests. The guys from the newly launched *Sunday Sport* were often at a nearby table, coming up with their 'Routemaster Found On The Moon' type headlines over a few beers. To them life was just one big laugh.

I do a lot of reading and research for interviews but rarely make many notes other than jotting down a few basic topic headings. I avoid writing out a list of questions because I find I get glued to them. For me the most important thing is to establish eye contact with the interviewee and to listen to what they're saying, and you can't do that if you're constantly looking down at your notes. I work on the theory that the research will be there in my head as my guest and I talk, allowing me to follow the interviewee off subject, if that's an interesting place to go. I have a rough idea in my mind of the ground

I want to cover but other than that I prefer things to be loose, to go for a conversation rather than an interview.

I'd get to the office about 8.30, meet up with producer Cathie Louie to discuss topics for the 'open line' section of the programme and plan the choreography of the show. My programmes went out across London every Friday, Saturday and Sunday night from 10 p.m. to 1 a.m. and I'd often feel slightly nervous as I went down into our scruffy, chocolate-brown basement studio, knowing that the microphone would be open for the whole of the next three hours and that somehow I had to fill that time with reasonably articulate comment and conversation, with only a few notes for support. I had a small screen in front of me with details of the next caller, half a dozen microphones around the table for guests and that was it. I didn't even have a fader to allow me to close my microphone for a moment if I wanted to take a breather. The whole show was driven from the control room through the glass ahead of me and I'd make signals to the engineer when I wanted to end a call or go to an advertising break, often taking instructions back through my headphones.

In this situation it's very important to establish a good rapport with the engineers. How you sound is in their hands and they can be extremely cruel. Tony Fox, a colleague from my Radio 210 days, had also recently joined LBC and made the mistake one evening of criticizing his engineer on air, a cardinal sin. Never blame an engineer, your producer, or anyone else for that matter; always take responsibility yourself. The guy had put the wrong caller through and Tony made a comment that he was incompetent or something like. In a huff, the engineer got up and walked out of the control room, leaving Tony live on air for nearly 15 minutes with no material feeding into the show apart from the listener currently on air. Tony desperately tried to persuade him to stay on the line for a while but the caller eventually got so bored he put the phone down, leaving Tony to keep things going on his own, a dialling tone buzzing faintly in the background. 'Filling' for any length of time is bad enough. Very few people would be able to keep talking for as long as Tony did then with absolutely nothing to work on – a perfect qualification for his current profession of artist management.

Having always been used to a record under my thumb and music to fall back on, speech radio felt very different. Holding a talk show together requires a very high level of concentration and my broadcasting abilities were tested to the limit, but I was learning a lot and it felt good to know that I was holding my own and improving. I also enjoyed meeting the guests who came onto the show.

Willie Rushton told me about his love of Surrey Cricket Club and his background at Shrewsbury School with John Peel and Richard Ingrams. Journalist Ed Harriman described the difficulties of reporting news from hot spots like El Salvador. John Conteh relived the feeling of beating Jorge Ahumada to become Britain's first light heavyweight boxing champion for two decades and explained why he subsequently took the sport to court. My regular experts included Dr Mike Smith, *Oxford Dictionary* editor Tony Augarde, who set fiendishly difficult word quizzes, and legal man James McGovern, who later became my solicitor. We also ran a hi-fi clinic with writer Barry Fox, who would come in with all sorts of magic new electronic gismos, and predictions of a computer-led generation getting their entertainment from game stations and their music from new, indestructible CDs. It was easier doing an advice hour because I could hand the calls over to the expert for a while and just sit back and listen.

A single call could last 10 minutes, especially on subjects of law. Pete Murray, who hosted the Monday to Thursday phone-in, would do the *Evening Standard* crossword while these conversations were going on, sipping coffee from a plastic cup and lining up his lit cigarettes on the edge of the broadcast desk, in the process burning long brown lines into the wood. I was in the control room one evening while he presided over a particularly mundane call to his gardening guru. As the conversation droned on we realized that Pete was falling asleep. Mulling over his crossword clues as usual, his head had begun to nod. The engineer sent a whistle and other low-level noises into his headphones in the hope of stirring him, but to no avail. Finally, he nodded off completely and, as his chin dropped to his chest, his forehead hit the microphone suspended in front of him. The 'clunk' cracked like a gunshot through our speakers and his headphones, straightening him up as if he'd seen a ghost, eyes wide open. The all-year suntan drained from his face for a moment as the shock reverberated through the middle of his head. But he was the ultimate professional as always and just got on with the programme as if nothing had happened, making faces and gestures at the producer, chiding him through the control room glass.

I was particularly pleased to meet Cathy McGowan, who came on my show one evening as a mystery guest to talk about her time on *Ready, Steady, Go!*. I liked her straight away and, although we'd never met before, we had an immediate affinity, based in part on our respective experiences in music television. She was interested in doing some presentation work for LBC so I introduced her to the management, who agreed she could do a few trial programmes. One of these evening shows was with agony uncle Phillip Hodson, whose job it was to advise callers on their personal problems. A teenage girl came on air in some distress. Her boyfriend had left her crying at King's Cross station, after coming down from Manchester to see her and rowing with her all weekend. Phillip began to counsel the girl, suggesting she give the boy another chance. Perhaps he was going through some problems of his own and, despite his behaviour, she should try to understand where he was coming from and make some allowances.

Cathy was unable to contain herself. 'That's rubbish!' she exclaimed before Phillip could go any further. 'I'll tell you what you should do,' she told the caller. 'Dump him. You sound much too good for him.' She'd hit the nail on the head, of course, but the interruption was an affront to Phillip who, turning red with rage, stormed from the studio, complaining bitterly that his professional authority had been undermined, that he'd never been so humiliated and that he would never work with that woman again. Mutually, she and the LBC management decided that the relationship probably wasn't going to work.

Val and I had become involved in the Great Ormond Street Hospital 'Wishing Well' appeal and I asked Cathy if she would help us organize some of the music events we were planning. She was absolutely brilliant, appearing on stage with me to co-host a special fund-raising concert at the Piccadilly Theatre in December 1987 and helping pull people in for a £75-a-head pop quiz at a country club in Buckinghamshire. Guests included Jess Conrad, Dave Lee Travis and an Elvis look-alike, who arrived in a pink Cadillac. We followed that up with a 60s evening at Stringfellows, thanks to the generosity of Peter Stringfellow and the then club manager Peter Stockton. Topping Elvis and the pink Cadillac was a tough one, but we did so in spectacular fashion with the arrival of a Harley Davidson in an explosion of dry ice, smoke, flashing lights and high revs. The bike blasted into the club from the street outside, onto a ramp and down into the basement where it accelerated onto the dance floor, strobe lights flashing, skidding sideways to stop in front of the stage, a stunt that required three days of meticulous planning and rehearsal.

Val's writing career was taking off. She seemed to be able to rattle off her cookery books at will and when she wasn't writing she'd often disappear to London for meetings. I would set off for LBC early every Friday afternoon, spend Friday and Saturday nights in London and drive back to Norfolk in the early hours of Sunday morning, so we spent less and less time together. Leading separate lives is never good for a relationship. I tried commuting but, by the time I'd put the programme to bed and made the two-hour journey home, it was usually well after 5 a.m. and I'd have to leave again at 4 in the afternoon to allow for the M25 traffic. The 180-mile round trip and lack of sleep were just proving untenable. For a while I stayed in London hotels, which was depressing, but I eventually rented a small top room in a house owned by Gill Pyrah, one of my colleagues at LBC.

This large, imposing house was situated in Islington, at the far end of the Essex Road, about a mile from Highbury football ground, but after a while, compared to the tranquillity of our Norfolk village, the area began to seem like an urban hellhole. It was a regular Saturday spectacle to see a group of any number of Arsenal supporters, standing in a long red line, urinating into the front gardens of the houses in the street. The railway track on the other side of the road carried the mile-long nuclear waste trains that boomed their way slowly through London in the middle of the night, rattling the pictures I'd put up on the wall. Within weeks my car had been broken into three times and I found myself constantly getting out of bed in the darkness to peer through the window to check it was still in one piece. I was finding it really hard to sleep and eventually my fears were realized.

The crash that disturbed me sounded horrendous and I rushed to the window to see what had happened. From my third-floor room, high above the street, I looked down in horror as a young joyrider hauled himself out of the battered Renault 16 with which he'd smashed into the back of my parked car. By the time I made it down the stairs he'd legged it with his mates, driver's door hanging by its hinges, steam hissing from the crumpled engine. By then some neighbours had joined me in the street but no one had seen a thing. My car was a total write-off; the Renault, it turned out, was uninsured. I lost my no-claims bonus and what was left of any sense of security. But worse was to follow.

I was due in London on New Year's Eve 1987 for the very final *Whistle Test* broadcast, a 'Best Of' celebration that was to last all night. On the morning of the show I got a phone call from Gill telling me to get to London early as there'd been a break-in at the house. She was away on holiday and hadn't seen the extent of the damage but had been told that the burglars had smashed their way in through the front door, which had had to be boarded up. I arrived to find my room stripped of all belongings – my recording machine, tapes and records, even the clothes I'd planned to wear for the *Whistle Test* special. The air was thick with a stench disgusting enough to make me want to vomit and it took only a few moments to discover the source. Whoever had been in my room had shat in my bed, piles of it soiled the sheets and the duvet. Who on earth would do a thing like that? Animals behave better. I put a handkerchief over my face, donned a pair of Marigolds and deposited all the bedclothes into the dustbin before having a bath and heading for Television Centre. It was the last time I ever set foot in that room. Jim Dowdall put me up for a while at his house in Olympia but alternative sleeping arrangements were not necessary for very long, as it turned out. I'm a great believer in fate – that things happen for a reason. 'Chance' is the only way to describe the way events conspired to influence my departure from LBC.

My producer at LBC, Cathie Louie, had devised a new 'rolling' format for my Friday night show, which I wasn't sure I fully understood. When an on-air test run started to go wrong, Cathie joined me in the studio for a quick briefing. The caller currently on air was launching into a monologue about the state of the country, and for the first and only time in the whole of the three years I spent at LBC, I took my headphones off and left the call running unattended on air while I concentrated on the instructions I was receiving from my producer. When I put the cans back on the line was silent. 'Well, thank you very much for your call. Some good points there. If you want to phone us, don't forget the number ...'

The hotline was already ringing when Cathie reached the control room. The bloke I'd left on air had gone into a foul-mouthed rant about Margaret Thatcher and the evil things he'd like to do to her. Distracted by the production problems none of us had been listening, and his poisonous tirade had even slipped through the ten-second delay system. I thought it was incredible that of all the thousands of calls I'd taken while doing those programmes, the only one I missed was the most explosive of all. Management were apoplectic and, with some relish, told me that my programmes the following weekend would be my last with LBC. Two days later they phoned me again, telling me not to bother going in at all. Out of a job again then.

For a short time I worked on The Super Station, Richard Branson's first venture into radio, helping with its launch as part of an on-air team that included Johnnie Walker, Nicky Horne, Jonathan Ross, Ruby Wax and Janice Long. The idea was a good one, to provide an overnight sustaining service, available via satellite, to commercial stations such as Radio 210 that would otherwise close down between 1 a.m. and 6 a.m. For me personally, however, it just wasn't right. It was the first time I'd worked for a station where Selector chose the music, and I didn't like it.

Selector was a computerized system that was programmed with information regarding the tone and tempo of individual tracks and notes about the style and the time of day of on-air programming. Click an icon and the machine blended the information together, churning out reams and reams of running orders as required. It sounds good in theory but was very rigid in application. Current chart songs and popular oldies would be given 'high' rotation, often coming around as quickly as once every two or three hours and the on-air repetition of such 'core tracks' can be brain-numbing. Although I fought successfully to keep my programmes out of the system, the environment was not sympathetic to my old-fashioned hand-building methods and I soon realized that this was the wrong place for me to be. One of my main strengths as a broadcaster is the enthusiasm I'm able to communicate about the music I play, given the freedom to express it. On The Super Station I felt flat and out of place. Doing it just for the money gave me no satisfaction at all.

My one remaining source of income was BFBS. Charles Foster had extended my hours and I was now doing a weekly three-hour show, broadcast around the world on Sunday afternoons. But it was not enough to support a family and Val was increasingly becoming the breadwinner. We began to change roles, with me looking after the boys while she was working. Val's father, Howard, had become ill and, to accommodate his wish to move to England, Val's family had funded the conversion of our dilapidated coach house. Soon Val's parents moved in, our new neighbours across the garden.

Howard was suffering from Alzheimer's disease and I was shocked by the cruel and degenerative nature of this illness. I knew a part of him was struggling to break out of the nightmare that had grid-locked his brain. Sometimes he would wander out into the garden as if searching for something, a look of panic on his face. Increasingly it seemed as though his body had become merely a shell, and that the soul of the person we knew had died. As the disease took deeper hold, I found it depressing and confusing that the fleeting windows of lucidity had become only painful reminders of the dynamic, deeply intelligent person I'd first met. I felt angry and resentful that he should be suffering in this way, and very sad for Val's mother, who was coping with her usual calm dignity. Val supported her mother in every way she could and my parents often visited from their new home on the north Norfolk coast. Dad would sit with Howard, talking to him and singing him old war tunes and Welsh songs, which he loved. Howard Scott died in 1991.

Without Howard's leadership British Schools had spiralled into debt. Nick did everything he could to hold things together but eventually even La Tambura was sacrificed in an attempt to keep the business afloat.

I spent a final summer in Italy in 1989 while Val was filming material for her first BBC TV series, *Italian Regional Cookery*. Things had got very bad between me and Val, who was no longer showing any interest in our relationship. With Sue and Jackie I'd been the principal force of change, but this time I was the one desperately trying to hold the relationship together. Val was away for much of the holiday, filming in different parts of the country, but I was able to spend a glorious, sunny summer with Ben and Jamie and with Dad, who joined us for a few weeks, probably the closest time we've ever spent together. At the end of the holiday Dad and I drove back to England together, on the way spending a night in Chamonix at the foot of Mont Blanc. Soon after we arrived home I realized my relationship with Val had finally broken down. It was a very difficult time for everyone.

Not for the first time I was becoming increasingly desperate for work. I'd been fired from LBC, left The Super Station and now my marriage was on the rocks. I really needed to start rebuilding again. I sent Jeff Griffin tapes of a couple of my, new three-hour, BFBS shows in the hope that he would pass them on to the Radio 1 management.

I recorded the programmes each week at the main BFBS London studios at Bridge House in Paddington. As always, I'd build the running orders at home and take the CDs and records into the studio with me. I'd be in charge of the recordings myself, loading video cassettes into the two main recording machines and setting the studio clock to 12 o'clock so I could record in 'real time'. The preparation work included timing the music to fit into the three 57-minute segments (punctuated by pauses for the three-minute news bulletins), allowing room for all the music to be played in full, links to be delivered and no early fading. (If you've ever wondered how this works ... take 60 minutes as the hour, minus 30 seconds for a link into the news. From the resulting 59 minutes 30 seconds, take away the time of the final track in that hour [e.g. 4.15] to establish the exact time the track needs to be started to be heard in full [in this case 55.15]. Working backwards, if the previous track is 3 minutes long it needs to be started at 52.15, or 51.45 if you allow time for a link between the two. You can back-time the whole hour this way to fit the maximum amount of music into the mix and always know how long you've got to talk. I usually manage to play 12–14 tracks an hour, blended into a flow.) Equal attention to detail was applied by BFBS to the distribution of the programmes.

Having completed my recordings, I'd deliver the tapes to a control room containing banks and banks of tape-duplicating machinery. There, the programmes would be copied onto labelled tapes and distributed individually to stations all over the world. At that time, BFBS had an estimated total worldwide audience of approximately 24 million. I was really proud of those programmes and the music mix I'd created. I played mainstream rock, vintage blues and R&B, fringe country and roots music, laced with anniversary classics from *The Rockdate Diary*. I'd put B.B. King next to Elvis Presley or Eric Clapton, segue a Simon & Garfunkel track or an Emmylou Harris song into Mary Chapin Carpenter, Bruce Springsteen or Bert Jansch. I've never cared what category of music a record comes from – if I like it, I'll play it. I really wanted Jeff to hear the eclectic nature of those shows. Suddenly it felt like 1970 all over again.

I started calling him to see if there'd been any reaction from Radio 1. 'For God's sake, Bob, stop bothering me,' he scolded. 'Didn't you learn from last time?' As before, I was going to have to be patient. I waited months for them to make up their minds. 'They're worried you're going to come back and say, "Wow, man, listen to the colours",' Jeff eventually explained. The *Whistle Test* image died hard.

Finally, executive producer Stuart Grundy phoned to offer me two weeks sitting in for Richard Skinner on the Radio 1 *Late Show*. As the celebratory firework display exploded in my head I knew this was my big chance, and I intended to grab it for all it was worth. My first programme back on the network was the day after Ben's birthday on 17th September 1989, and serendipity again took a hand in shaping my future.

Johnny Beerling, the controller of Radio 1, was away during my first week and consequently missed the programmes. He was in southern Spain, on a sad mission to record material with Roger Scott, who'd been diagnosed with cancer, for a tribute programme to him called 'Radio Radio'. By chance, Johnny tuned in to BFBS broadcasting from Gibraltar, heard my Sunday show, really enjoyed it and decided there and then that he wanted me on the network. However, I knew none of this when he walked into Jeff's office the following week, hand outstretched, broad smile on his face. 'Welcome back,' he said simply. It was one of the best feelings of my life.

Trudie Myerscough-Walker had, by now, become a part of my life. She was the 24-year-old niece of Val's great friend Robin and we'd first met a couple of years previously. I'd seen her at the occasional party or cricket match and she'd visited our house from time to time with her uncle. We always seemed to gravitate towards one another and talk. I found her bright, positive, enthusiastic and straight as a die. She has a great sense of humour and is stunningly beautiful, with blonde hair and hazel eyes, one of them flawed with a tiny prism. We became so obviously close that people began to think we were having an affair, but we weren't. I loved her company. She was fun to be with and made me feel happy and good about myself, but neither of us thought to take the relationship any further. I was married, it was as simple as that. But when my marriage broke up, Trudie and I began to see one another more seriously.

She worked in Knightsbridge as personal assistant to the then chairman of Harrods, Mohamed Al Fayed, and at the end of her working day I would often meet her in the hushed, air-conditioned luxury of the management offices on the fifth floor of the store. Her desk was situated just outside the door to Mohamed's private suite and he usually came out to greet me and chide me about my beard. Egyptians have an aversion to facial hair and he was always trying to devise ways of tricking me into shaving it off, creeping up behind me with a razor or a shaving brush frothing with foam, a wicked smile on his face.

Mohamed and I got on really well and he became fond of my two boys, giving Ben sweets as a bribe to rub honey into my beard while I was asleep. He's a loveable rogue, Mohamed. He can be crude, mischievous and suspicious but he's an incredibly generous person with a quick wit and a most sensitive eye for beautiful things. Unlike many around him, Trudie wasn't afraid to stand up to him and tell him the truth and he respected her for that. He demanded loyalty but gave it in return and was completely supportive of Trudie when news of our relationship first hit the newspapers.

We'd been to see Eric Clapton play at the Albert Hall, our first public appearance together. Simon Bates was among a crowd of people in a box hired by Warner Brothers Records for the evening. All were very curious as to Trudie's background and fascinated to hear that she worked for Mohamed. Three days later, on the Monday afternoon, I got a call from Val. 'What's going on?' she demanded. 'I've had the press on the phone, asking about our break-up and what I think about you and Trudie. They quoted really nasty stuff you'd said about me, it was horrible.' I told Val that I hadn't spoken to any newspaper and that I knew nothing about it. It was only when Jackie phoned later to tell me there were photographers outside her front door trying to get a photo of our daughter, Charlotte, that I realized the press really were after a story.

The ingredients were really quite juicy ... 43-year-old father of five, rock DJ just about to return to Radio 1, leaves successful writer wife about to begin a major six-part television series on BBC2, for Mohamed Al Fayed's personal assistant, who is 19 years his junior. Mmm, good one. We soon discovered that one of the tabloids was planning to publish a 'Bob Harris exposé' the following weekend. Based on my experiences in the past, my gut instinct was to walk out and face them. The more you try to put the press off the more tenacious they become, so I suggested we just call the paper and arrange an interview, but it wasn't as simple as that. It was very important to get the approval of Radio 1 and mobilize the press office facilities and to do the same at Harrods. Trudie talked to Mohamed while I went to see Johnny Beerling. Both were supportive and promised to give us their full backing.

During the next two days most of the newspapers tried to make contact and on the Thursday morning, from the Harrods media office, Trudie returned the call of Chris Hutchins at the *Today* newspaper. He was amazed to find her so open and co-operative and in return was surprisingly friendly. He even sent a photographer over to take pictures of us together in Hyde Park. He told us that the piece would be in the paper the following day and I phoned Cathie Louie later that evening to ask if we could call in to LBC to see the station's voucher copy, which I knew would arrive at the studio at about 10.30 p.m. Wouldn't you know it, *Today* was the only paper that arrived late that night and we spent an anxious 90 minutes while we waited, but when we finally saw the article we knew we'd done the right thing. Under the headline 'Val Blows The Whistle On Rocker Bob's Bride' there was a wonderful, happy picture of Trudie and me smiling in the sunshine. The story accompanying the photograph was factual rather than sensational. They even described Trudie as 'stunning', and of course they were right. With no further material featured in the weekend tabloids we felt we'd effectively contained any potential journalistic excesses.

I was getting more and more involved with Trudie's world and I was with her at Harrods when Jason Donovan opened the annual winter sale there on 4th January 1990. Both my boys were desperate to meet him. Ben was seven and Jamie was four. Trudie made arrangements for us to wait in Mohamed's office in the hope of spending a few moments with him there. He was at the peak of his popularity at the time and as we waited we could hear the chaos in the store below us. Scores of screaming girls were being pushed to the ground in the stampede as they struggled to get a glimpse of their hero. The situation became so dangerous that anxious security bosses ordered the tour to be cut short and he was whisked up to the fifth floor, security men barring the stairs and the escalators as fans tried to follow him, their shrieks and squeals echoing round the stairwell.

He came through the outer office, exhaling loudly as he entered the calm, quiet atmosphere of the management suite and, as he got his bearings, Trudie introduced him to us. He was friendly and kind – Ben and Jamie were dumbstruck. One photographer penetrated the security cordon and managed to capture them together in a picture that dominated a page of the *Daily Mail* the following day. It's a terrific photograph, Jason Donovan in the middle and the boys with wide grins on their faces, Jamie wearing a Harrods doorman's hat. 'It's not just the girls who think Jason Donovan's great' the caption read. 'Yesterday, as the star opened the Harrods sale under siege from screaming female fans, two little boys managed to snatch a quiet moment together with their idol.' In addition to all her other attributes, Trudie could also work miracles.

A few weeks earlier I'd been in Gibraltar at the invitation of the local BFBS station, sitting in for a fortnight on the *Drive Time* show. Charles Foster thought it would be a good experience and he was right. I loved it. Trudie joined me for the second week and we stayed at the Holiday Inn, right in the centre of town. In the local pubs and restaurants I met many people who regularly tuned in to the show and received direct feedback in the form of comments and requests.

Just before we returned to Britain I got a call from the BBC, put through to me in the office of Dave Raven, the station manager of BFBS Gibraltar. It was from Stuart Grundy, phoning from London to offer me a permanent show on Radio 1, albeit in tragic circumstances. Roger Scott had lost his battle with cancer and died on 31st October 1989. Stuart asked me to take over his Sunday evening programme, 11 p.m. to 2 a.m., starting at the beginning of January 1990. It was the call I'd been dreaming of. Having done my last regular *Whistle Test* broadcast on New Year's Eve 1979, I was returning to the national airwaves exactly a decade after I'd left. It was as if the 80s and I had somehow passed each other by.

A few days before the first show I met up with my new producer, Phil Swern, and we immediately forged a close friendship and working partnership. Phil is one of the most genuine people I've ever met. He's quirky, considerate, creative, generous and constant, he became a cornerstone of my life. He's also one of the world's premier music archivists, with a collection of records and CDs that runs to hundreds of thousands. Together we've raided record shops as far apart as Nashville and Hamburg and his knowledge of music, records, catalogue numbers, dates, statistics, facts and trivia is unrivalled.

Phil and I first met more than 30 years ago when I did some recording at his home studio in Wembley. He was working as a plugger for A&M Records at the time, promoting a wonderful Phil Spector single called 'Black Pearl' by Sonny Charles and The Checkmates, Ltd. and, although the record didn't chart, Phil was convinced that 'Black Pearl' was a hit song. Frustrated by its initial lack of success, he poured his savings into making a cover, an up-tempo version by Horace Faith, which became a Top-20 smash in October 1970. The record launched a production career that included hits by Blue Haze ('Smoke Gets In Your Eyes', 1972), The Pearls (four hits, including the Top-10 'Guilty' in 1974) and R & J Stone (who made the UK Top 5 with 'We Do It' in 1976). He also scored as a writer, penning 'Up In A Puff Of Smoke' for Pickettywitch lead singer, Polly Brown, who took it into the Top 20 of the *Billboard* charts in America.

Phil even has a song on the album *Coming Out* by Manhattan Transfer, submitted to the group by his publisher. He only realized it had been included when he bought a copy of the album from his local record shop. 'I saw the title "SOS" and thought, "I've written a song called that",' he told me. 'When I got home and played the album I discovered it was my song. The publishers had forgotten to tell me the group had recorded it!' It was the British New Wave movement that brought his production career to a close. 'When punk kicked in, I kicked out,' he declared.

Phil got into radio through a quiz show called *You Ain't Heard Nothing Yet* on Capital. Producer Tim Blackmore was desperate for material for the show, and Phil volunteered his knowledge and music collection, beginning an association with the station that was to last several years. Soon he was producing the weekend output of the newly launched Capital Gold, hand-building the programmes in his studio at home.

When Roger Scott moved across from Capital to Radio 1, he took Phil with him, persuading Johnny Beerling to let him produce his Sunday show, which evolved a unique music mix. As well as Bruce Springsteen, John Mellencamp, The Beach Boys, Bob Seger and other Roger favourites, Phil mixed brand-new releases with a pile of jukebox singles, rock'n'roll, doo-wop and traditional country. It was a fabulous programme and essential listening. It was not lost on me that my return to Radio 1 was following a similar pattern to that of my arrival there 20 years before ... choreographed by Jeff Griffin and taking over from a hero and mentor figure, previously John Peel, now Roger Scott.

I immediately felt at home on the Sunday show and was comfortable with the music and the environment. It was fantastic to be back on Radio 1 and it was clear that controller Johnny Beerling had become a big supporter. Within three months I was broadcasting five nights a week, having additionally taken over from Richard Skinner on the Monday to Thursday midnight to 2 a.m. slot, initially with Jeff Griffin producing, then with Phil.

As my Radio 1 career resumed I moved into Trudie's west London flat, or our 'Shepherd's Bush love nest' as one tabloid put it. This was not at all amusing for Trudie's flat mate, Uncle Robin. As one of Val's closest allies he was caught right in the middle of a triangle he didn't want to be a part of. His best friend's ex-husband moving in to share his flat with his niece was something he had neither expected nor encouraged, and it was understandably difficult for him to get his brain around it all. The CDs that gradually cluttered the sitting room became symbolic of the space invasion, and over the next few weeks Trudie and I looked at literally dozens of places, all either unliveable in or way above our price range. We got more desperate to move as Robin's obvious stress increased.

Shortly before my return to Radio 1 I'd joined Tony Fox's roster of artists and he recommended that we take a look at a flat fellow DJ Bruno Brookes was selling. It seemed exactly right for us, with a large sitting room, two bedrooms (one for Ben and Jamie when they stayed), a small study, a kitchen and three tiny bathrooms. The flat took up the whole of the ground floor of a large Hampstead house situated, by coincidence, at the bottom of Platt's Lane, only a few doors away from where I'd lived with Sue in the late 60s. It was a few minutes' walk from Hampstead Heath, less than a mile from Sue's flat in West Hampstead and just 15 minutes from the BBC. Perfect. It even had a small, leafy garden, shaded by the surrounding trees. But this was early 1990, at the height of the property boom, and the value of the flat had inflated to £260,000, way above what we could afford. Bruno came up with a solution.

'I'll lend you half the money, interest-free, for two years,' he suggested. 'After two years you can either pay it back or sell the flat. Your career is expanding at Radio 1, Bob. You should be able to afford to do it by then.' We were apprehensive, but eventually Bruno seemed to make some sense. If we really did have to sell it after two years we felt we'd be able to get our money back and repay the loan. And, who knows, he could be right about Radio 1. After a great deal of thought and some reservations we decided to go for it and moved in at the beginning of May 1990. Bruno had been good to his word and completed a few agreed repairs, using a craftsman called John Monaghan, with whom we quickly became good friends.

My shows on Radio 1 were going really well and the next few months were extremely busy. I was one of the presenters of the network coverage of the Nelson Mandela Tribute Concert at Wembley Stadium, during which I interviewed Lou Reed, Bonnie Raitt and Peter Gabriel in a particularly cold and windy walkway at the top of

Left: Trudie with Robert Plant at Robert's sixtieth birthday party.

Below left: Trudie and Paul McCartney at the recording of an interview for *The Day John Met Paul.*

Below: I have massive respect for Rosanne Cash, with whom I'm pictured in Nashville in 2014.

From the recordings for our *OGWT 40* series for BBC Radio 2, marking the fortieth anniversary of *The Old Grey Whistle Test*. Clockwise from left: Jackson Browne and Brian May, Steve Harley, Alice Cooper and Yusuf Islam.

Top: With Elton John at the Electric Proms at the Roundhouse, London in 2010.

Middle: Presenting the great Duane Eddy with a Lifetime Achievement Award, onstage at the Ryman Auditorium in Nashville in 2013.

Bottom: Trudie and Miles joined me backstage with Taylor Swift on her Red Tour in 2013.

Top: My Mum with her great radio hero, David Jacobs, at my *This Is Your Life* recording in 2003.

Middle: A family picture, clockwise from left, Miles, Dylan, Flo, Catherine, Trudie, Aunt Margaret (now 100 years old) and Mr Monk Monk!

Below: Charlie, Jamie, Ben and Mum at Emily's wedding on Holkham Beach, Norfolk.

Right: Miles looking across the Cumberland River at the Nashville skyline.
Below: Emily's wedding, Holkham Beach, Norfolk, 2004. Below right: Catherine and Flo in our 'Under the Apple Tree' session.
Bottom: Miri, Ben, Dylan and his friend Abi Blain at Miri's 21st birthday party.

Above, left to right: Flo, Dylan, Trudie, Miles, Niamh, Emily, Me, Eliza, Olivia, Miri, Alana, Ysobel, Graeme, Sue and Marnie.

Clockwise from top left: Just some of my beautiful granddaughters: Marnie, Alana, Olivia and Lola Mae.

Above: Onstage at the O2, compering the 2015 Country 2 Country festival.

Left: Broadcasting backstage at C2C for BBC Radio 2 Country with Jo Whiley.

Below: With Charlie, Trudie and Miles at Windsor Castle, following my investiture in 2011.

the main stand. For several weeks in the summer I also presented the British Forces Broadcasting Services' fast moving flagship show, BFBS UK, a two-hour, Monday to Friday early afternoon programme with music and guests which was broadcast live all over the world, a really exciting show to do. I'd get home mid-afternoon, have a nap for a couple of hours, then leave for Broadcasting House at just after 10. I loved the pace of it all but, for me, the biggest event of the year was the Knebworth Festival, on the weekend of 30th June.

Radio 1 broadcast live from Knebworth for the entire day and Simon Bates and I were there to feed live location material into the output. Simon concentrated on the 'news' coverage while I got to hang out backstage. It was brilliant, like a huge *Whistle Test*, and I spent most my time cruising the hospitality area, microphone in hand, bumping into loads of people I hadn't seen for years. It just felt so great to be back!

I interviewed Mick Ralphs from Mott the Hoople and Bad Company, who was smiling as always, and Dave Gilmour, who was his usual studied, circumspect self. I spent some time with Robert Plant and the larger-than-life Traffic drummer Jim Capaldi and bumped into Elton John, who promised me an interview later before disappearing into the artists' enclosure, frustratingly the only area of the site for which we didn't have laminates!

I was working as part of a three-man mobile broadcast unit coordinated by producer Phil Ross, and he was very keen on the idea of doorstepping the security compound and grabbing people as they headed towards the stage. Phil was determined to corner Paul McCartney in particular. We'd been told that he was giving no interviews that day so this represented a major challenge. After a vigil of over an hour, sweating in the hot sunshine, Phil rushed over to find me, literally pulling me back towards the security gate. 'Paul's coming out,' he announced. 'I want you to walk out in front of him and get him to say something.' I wasn't keen to do it. It would be great to get an interview with Paul, but not like that, forcing a microphone in front of his face. As he approached the wire mesh gate, surrounded by people, I stepped away.

Paul walked through and saw me standing a few yards back. I was thrilled to see his face light up and he immediately came over and gave me a hug, onlookers and minders watching bemused.

'What are you doing here?' he asked me.

'Hoping to interview you,' I replied.

'Really? When do you want to do it?'

'Now would be a good time,' I suggested, frantically gesticulating to Phil to bring the recording equipment over. All my experiences with Paul have been warm and friendly and this was no exception.

A few minutes after Paul had left to go onstage I felt a tap on my shoulder. I turned around to discover the smiling figure of Elton John. 'I've come to do the interview,' he said. 'See? I never break a promise.'

It was a wonderful day. Although I didn't get to see many people play, I did catch some of Cliff Richard's set, holding his own in the stratospheric company, Robert Plant and Jimmy Page dynamic together again, and the opening of Pink Floyd's bill-topping performance before Simon Bates told me it was time to go. He'd given me a lift to the site early that morning from the hotel in Luton where we'd stayed the previous night and where I'd left my car. He'd promised to run me back there after the show.

'If you want a lift you have to leave now,' he announced and, with no further explanation, strode purposefully away across the fields and into the darkness. This was all very sudden and I wasn't prepared. I rushed back to the production van, grabbed what stuff of mine I could find in 15 seconds and galloped after him, finally catching up with him a few yards from the car park. 'Do you know which way we're going?' he asked as I arrived puffing by his side.

'Er no,' I replied. 'Have you got a map?'

'Typical!' he snorted, as he slammed the driver's door. I made an attempt to ask the people on the gate for directions to Luton as we left the site, but Simon accelerated on through the checkpoint, grumbling about how late he'd be getting home.

'I think the guy said to go right at the end of this road,' was my only constructive suggestion.

An hour and a half later, as we turned into yet another cul-de-sac on yet another featureless estate, we realized we were completely lost somewhere on the outskirts of Luton. It was all too much for Simon, who suddenly screeched the car to a halt and turned accusingly to address me, face contorted with rage. 'You're ruining my life!' he announced in that deep, beefy voice. I burst out laughing, which seemed to inflame him even more.

'Right. Well, I'll just step out here then,' I suggested. 'I can call myself a taxi from the pub across the road.'

He reached across to stop me getting out of the door. 'I told you I'd run you back and I'm going to do it if it kills me.' We drove the rest of the way in silence. When we finally reached the hotel he continued the farce by driving off as I tried to gather my things from the back of his Volvo, boot lid bouncing up and down as I chased him across the car park. I only managed to rescue the rest of my stuff because he had to wait for traffic. It was as if I'd spent the last two hours in the middle of a sitcom.

The Knebworth broadcast was a fantastic success and a few days later I received a note from Stuart Grundy. 'Dear Bob,' it read. 'At last a moment to say a personal thank you for your work on the Knebworth show. It sounded as if you were enjoying it, despite the hassles. The received wisdom is that it was our most successful epic ever and we won't argue with that. You were bloody marvellous. Thanks again.'

It made me feel great that Stuart sent that note and it was a wonderful characteristic of the Radio 1 management team at the time that they took the time and trouble to do things like that. I have what I call a 'special drawer' in my desk at home where I keep objects of high personal value. In amongst pictures of Trudie, my parents and my children, school drawings (and a sealed champagne cork given to me by American blues guitarist Michael Katon from a bottle he shared with Muddy Waters), is a small bundle of letters from Johnny Beerling. It gave me enormous confidence to know that he appreciated my programmes and was thoughtful enough to praise me for extra effort.

It's amazing to think that at that time Radio 1 was still shutting down for a three-hour overnight break at the end of my show at 2 a.m. The Gulf War changed that. I'd just begun my programme on 7th August 1990 when hostilities were declared. Within a few minutes, senior producer Chris Lycett had joined me in the studio and when Johnny arrived later he took the decision to keep the network on air through the night. It was an exciting, if unsettling night as we constantly crossed to the newsroom for the latest news on the bombing raids, analyzing the lyrics of every song we played in case they jarred or caused offence. ('Eve Of Destruction' by Barry McGuire was probably one to avoid!) The long-term impact of this programme was immense. The circumstance of our all-night broadcast was the lever Johnny had been looking for to force through his desire to make Radio 1 a 24-hour station at last. A few days later I launched the BFBS service to the Gulf, broadcasting live from London at 3 a.m. on 12th August, beginning the first programme with The Bellamy Brothers' 'Let Your Love Flow', a rather forlorn hope in the circumstances. 'Whispering Bob Shouts For Our Boys' ran a headline in the *Daily Star*.

Ordering new CDs from the States for my programmes had become one of life's great pleasures, and to help feed our insatiable appetite for new music Phil and I subscribed to a weekly service called 'Hit Disc'. Originated by Century 21 in Dallas, Texas, it cost a fortune but was worth every penny. Each week we'd receive two CDs, comprising all the new entries from that week's various American *Billboard* charts, maybe 35 tracks in all. I used to love those things plopping through the letterbox every week, always a few days before publication of the corresponding *Billboard* chart. It reminded me of the excitement of getting the Decca label singles a day before their release at John Levers Record Shop when I was a teenager in Northampton.

The Hit Discs began to have a massive impact on the sound of the programme as we discovered and played more and more new names and unveiled UK radio exclusives. We championed Jude Cole's 'Baby It's Tonight', 'Just The Way It Is, Baby' by the Rembrandts and 'For You' by Outfield, an excellent but virtually undiscovered British band, bigger in America than in the UK. We were the first to play 'Losing My Religion' by R.E.M., and tracks from Neil Young's perfectly titled *Ragged Glory* and the Black Crowes' *Shake Your Money Maker* album. But of all the new records we were playing at the time, the one that created the biggest impact with our listeners was 'Walking In Memphis' by Marc Cohn, still one of my all-time favourite records. Soon after its release in the States Marc flew into London for a short visit to plan the release date and promotional schedule with Atlantic Records. After a long day of meetings, stuck in his hotel room and unable to sleep, he turned on the bedside radio and heard 'Walking In Memphis' literally as he tuned in. He stayed listening until the end of the show and the following afternoon I got a call from Joe Reddington, from the promotion department at Atlantic Records, telling me that Marc would like to come into the studio that night and meet me.

'I couldn't believe hearing my record being played on the radio three thousand miles from home,' he told me when he arrived in the studio. 'I had no idea anyone in Britain had heard it.' He went on to talk about his affection for radio and how much it had influenced him. 'Particularly when it came to the running order for *my* album,' he explained. 'I spent a long time getting the songs into the right sequence and getting the flow exactly right, like a mini radio show. Around 1972, when I was about 12 or 13 years old, I used to listen to a late-night DJ on my local radio station playing James Taylor, Joni Mitchell, Van Morrison and Neil Young, all the music I liked. When my mom and dad had gone to bed I used to sneak down to the phone in the hall and call him up. He'd talk to me for ages off-air, about the way he put his shows together and the albums he recommended. The guy had a big influence on me. Listening to you last night reminded me of that show.' I liked Marc's music; he liked my radio programmes – the perfect recipe for a friendship.

Trudie was almost always in the studio with me, answering the phones, organizing the guests and attempting the almost impossible schedule of arriving home at 3 a.m. and then getting up again at 7.30 to get to Harrods. Lack of sleep eventually caught up with her following my appearance with Alan Freeman on the 'nose desk' of the 1991 'Comic Relief' programme. As Trudie and I stepped out of the main lift at Television Centre about 2 o'clock in the morning she collapsed, falling into main reception and dragging me down on top of her. People were stepping over us as they made for the exit. It was spectacular. Everyone thought we were drunk, but we hadn't touched a drop, it was sheer exhaustion. That's when she decided to leave Harrods, have a few lie-ins at last and get more involved in the running of my professional life, applying the energy and natural organizational skills that Mohamed Al Fayed prized so highly.

Trudie and I were now partners emotionally and professionally – a team. I knew how lucky I was to have found her. After the break-up of two marriages and a long-term affair, all involving children, I'd begun to wonder if I was capable of holding a relationship together. But when Trudie and I fell in love I knew, at last, that I'd found the person I'd always been looking for, my floozy, as Jeff Griffin calls her. 'You're not seriously thinking of marrying him, are you?' he asked her. 'With his track record? You must be mad!'

Despite Jeff's best efforts Trudie went ahead with the wedding, becoming Mrs Myerscough-Harris on 24th April 1991. We spent the next few days enjoying our wedding present from Mohamed – a honeymoon at the Ritz Hotel in Paris! It was another world, opulent beyond belief. Our bedroom had a marble fireplace, gilded mirrors, a walk-in cedar cupboard and a massive brass bedstead, the most luxurious environment imaginable.

While we were in Paris Mohamed invited us to visit the Duke and Duchess of Windsor's house on the edge of the Bois de Boulogne. Following the death of the Duchess in 1986, Mohamed had been granted the lease of the villa and had spent millions restoring it to its former glory and painstakingly cataloguing its contents, a process completed by the time of our visit. It was an awesome experience, to see the splendour of the house exactly as the Windsors had left it. We walked through the salon across the Aubusson carpet decorated with ostrich feathers and inhaled the opulent luxury of the library, used by the Windsors as their downstairs sitting room. We saw the Duchess's bedroom, decorated in her favourite 'Wallis' blue, pug dog cushions in all shapes and sizes scattered on the bed and the chaise longue, and we sat on the terrace looking out across the grounds. But, to me, the most memorable items were the rows and rows of tiny women's shoes, cabinets full of them, some in the Duchess's dressing room upstairs, some in the basement museum. She must have had feet as small as a child's. The property was in the charge of the Duke's former chauffeur, Gregorio Martin, who's lived behind the high hedges in that world-within-a-world since 1964, a life similar to that of the character played by Peter Sellers in the film *Being There*.

Johnny Beerling had been very keen for Trudie and I to postpone the wedding for a few days and seriously proposed that we have the ceremony live on air, to launch the new 24-hour service on Radio 1.

Thankfully, we managed to persuade him against. The service began regardless and I suddenly found myself with more output on the network than anyone else – 16 hours a week, Monday to Thursday 12 midnight to 4 a.m. I rarely got to sleep much before 6 a.m. and, as anyone who works the night shift will tell you, the hours mess with your body clock and you feel as if you're permanently jet-lagged.

Phil and I put the shows together between us, meeting up for an all-day building session every Monday at Platt's Lane, Phil arriving weighed down with three or four BBC programme boxes stuffed to the brim with new CDs. I hand-wrote the week's running orders, leaving gaps for new releases or last-minute ideas, sticking strips of paper over alterations we'd made in the absence of cut and paste in those pre-computer days. I'd then deliver the material to our programme assistant, Sue Baines, who would process it all, calling up anything extra we needed from the BBC library.

I kept my BFBS show going and even began to pull in the occasional voice-over job, always lucrative and consequently intensely competitive. It was a fantastic feeling to be earning decent money for the first time for more than a decade, a happy and successful time.

The listening figures for the overnights were genuinely spectacular and the shows were great to do. I broadcast from a small, purpose-built self-op studio on the second floor of Egton House and was amazed at the contact I was able to establish with listeners at that time of night. It was like an intimate, exclusive club, with a membership of approximately one and a half million.

Marillion recorded a great jingle for me, based on The Animals' 'House Of The Rising Sun' and most nights we featured sessions, either pre-recorded in the afternoon, or live on the show. Jimmy Barnes, Janis Ian, Taj Mahal, Alannah Myles, Leonard Cohen, Jackson Browne, David Crosby, Carlos Santana, Garland Jeffreys, Buddy Guy, Restless Heart, Mary Chapin Carpenter, Jimmie Dale Gilmore and Shawn Colvin all came in to talk and play. But one of the most touching moments of all was a meeting with Billy Falcon towards the end of 1991.

At the time, Billy was in the American charts with 'Power Windows', produced by Jon Bon Jovi, and came in to play the song on the show. He told me it was based on his own experience as a single parent when, trying to bring up his kids while juggling the demands of a career as a musician, he'd become desperate, trying to be all things to all people, and feeling guilty that he was neglecting his children. 'I was sitting at a traffic light thinking about what constitutes happiness when this big car pulled up alongside me,' he recalled. 'The driver was a middle-aged guy, sitting there in his air-conditioned luxury and I thought "he must have it all". Then I realized he was on his phone having an argument with somebody, veins standing out on his neck. At that moment a beaten-up old Dodge came up on the inside, two kids sitting back, listening to the radio and laughing, they didn't seem to have a care in the world. The two kids had no material wealth but they were in love and happy, the guy in the Mercedes was rich but stressed out. The contrast was amazing; money doesn't buy you happiness. I just drove straight home and wrote the song. In less than ten minutes it was finished.'

I still get requests for 'Power Windows' and it's a gem of a track, included on the album *Pretty Blue World* on the Jambco Record label. A few days before the interview with Billy Falcon, Trudie and I received some fantastic news. We were overjoyed to discover she was pregnant and our first son, Miles, was born on 2nd June 1992. He was a breach baby, born by caesarean section at the exclusive Portland Hospital in London, funded by Trudie's medical insurance, and I was truly impressed by the VIP treatment we received when we arrived. They took charge of our car, swept us up to our room and generally made us feel special. It was like arriving at the Ritz! It was only when I went back down to rescue the car that I discovered the reason. 'Oh, I'm terribly sorry, Mr Harris,' said the receptionist. 'We thought you were Richard Branson!'

Rachel Hunter was having her baby at the Portland at the same time and it was extraordinary to see the lengths the paparazzi were prepared to go to in their attempts to get some pictures of her, Rod Stewart or the baby. As well as the vigil in the street outside, the first floor of the building opposite was commandeered and overrun with photographers, training their telephoto lenses on the hospital, some even climbing out and balancing precariously on ledges and window sills in desperate attempts to get a better angle.

Trudie is the perfect mother. She read Miles brilliantly and always seemed to know instinctively what was exactly right for him and Miles was a happy, contented child. Within weeks he was sleeping through the night and he used to love to jig up and down in his baby seat while I was playing my music and working on my shows. Our lives seemed idyllic, but nagging worries were beginning to surface.

Shortly before Miles was born I arrived at Egton House one evening to discover Dave Lee Travis waiting for me. He looked uncharacteristically serious as he followed me into Phil Swern's office, closing the door behind him and looking around the room as if to check that we weren't going to be overheard. He had a very powerful presence and I was genuinely apprehensive. 'They're taking us all off Radio 1,' he said in a hushed voice.

I couldn't believe what I was hearing. 'What on earth are you talking about? Things are going really well.'

'You don't understand, Bob. I've been talking to top management and they're going to reposition the network and get rid of us all. You and I will be the first to go.'

I was absolutely stunned. 'But what about Johnny Beerling?' I asked. 'He won't let it happen.'

'You mark my words, it's going to happen. I'm telling you as a friend. I wanted to warn you and tell you to start looking out for other work. Put some eggs in other baskets, your days here are numbered.'

I'd been aware for some time of the increasing pressure on Johnny to make the station more 'hip' but had never dreamed it would go as far as a complete re-vamp, something he was dead set against. In September 1992 I was onstage at the Radio 1 25th Birthday Party Road Show at Astor Park in Birmingham, introducing Del Amitri to the crowd of nearly 130,000 who had turned out despite the dreadful weather – hardly a demonstration of falling popularity! But the political ball was rolling and DLT was ultimately proved to be correct.

Meanwhile, the bottom had fallen out of the property market and we were becoming increasingly worried about our flat. We'd been trying to sell it for months, before our two-year loan period with Bruno Brookes expired, but already the value had fallen by more than £60,000. Despite the cut in price no one came round to view the property and we were beginning to realize we were caught in the negative equity trap everyone was talking about. Paying Bruno interest on his fixed loan of £130,000 at a rate of more than £1,300 a month, as well as a similar sum to keep up the mortgage payments, was crippling us and all the time the value of the property was falling like a stone. By the end of the year things were becoming really scary and our bank manager instructed us that we could no longer sustain these outgoings.

At that moment I knew we were in trouble. Bruno was adamant he was going to get his money and that was that. He wanted his cash and I couldn't pay. Stalemate. The next few months became a battle as Bruno applied increasing pressure to get us to pay the money he thought was his by right. Meanwhile, the press started baying for the blood of the dinosaur Radio 1 DJs, and I was at the top of the list.

EIGHT

'The World Ends on a Whisper'

A CHILL WIND OF CHANGE WAS BLASTING THROUGH RADIO 1. IT WAS becoming clear that Dave Lee Travis was right in his prediction of a major cull. The atmosphere at Egton House was very uncertain as rumours of who would stay and who would go gathered force. The national press was choreographing an increasingly vigorous campaign to see off the dinosaur DJs, with my name prominent in the published lists of potential casualties. Nevertheless, it came as a major shock when, in August 1993, DLT made his stand and resigned on air midway through his programme. Whatever else I thought about it, I had to admire the man's principles. His 'up with this I will not put' speech was a classic.

'As Dave Lee Travis packs his record box and prepares to leave Radio 1, he will leave behind a slight feeling of vulnerability among some of his 20 fellow disc jockeys' wrote the *Guardian* a few days later, with droll understatement. 'While Radio 1 claims its target audience is between the ages of 15 and 35, the average age of the disc jockeys is just over 35. Some have been criticized for being staid and out of touch as the station attempts to inject a fresher, lighter approach and move towards a younger audience.'

Despite assurances to the contrary, I realized that it was all adding up to the end of my Radio 1 career. Let's face it, I'd been deemed unfashionable for the best part of the previous 17 years, ever since being castigated by the punks! In a funny sort of way it didn't really bother me. If I lost the programmes ... well, I'd just have to rebuild again. The fact that I'd successfully recovered from setbacks a number of times in the past had given me some resilience and trained me in the methods of 'moving on'. Of course, losing Radio 1 would be a massive blow, but it didn't represent as big a threat to the very heart of my home life as did the increasingly bitter financial battle with Bruno Brookes.

What made it so difficult from our point of view was the fact that Bruno was pressing for full payment of his loan to us, no matter what. We were desperately trying to sell the flat, which had now lost £85,000 of its value in 12 months. Even at the knockdown price of £172,000 we hadn't received one offer. With the equity on the flat mortgaged to the hilt we had no means of raising the lump sum of £130,000 we owed Bruno and we could no longer support the interest on the loan. I could understand him wanting his money, and never pretended anything other than liability, but the hostility was palpable as he increased the pressure on us. Several times he reduced Trudie to tears on the phone. At the end of March 1993 Bruno served us with a repossession order, giving us notice to quit the property by 5th July.

The hot seat changeovers between our shows at 4 a.m. were a nightmare of tension. I tried not to acknowledge him in any way when he came into the studio, other than to applaud the self-discipline that stopped me from punching him in anger. I'd never before experienced as high a degree of stress as was packed into those two or three minutes at the end of my programmes. What kept me going was my belief in the old-fashioned 60s concept of karma. I knew that whatever he was going to sling at us, I wouldn't lift a finger against him. I knew I didn't have to. My near-death experience had taught me that we make our own hell, and I cursed the obsession with money that made him so difficult to deal with.

As the summer ended I got a call from Matthew Bannister, the new controller designate of Radio 1, asking me to meet him at Broadcasting House. I can remember almost every word of our less-than-two-minute conversation in that bare, strip-lit office. 'Thank you for coming in,' he began, 'but I'm afraid I've got some bad news for you. I'm taking your programme off air.'

'What, from 16 hours to nothing?' Although I was expecting drastic news, this still came as a jolt.

'Yes, we're repositioning the network,' he answered. 'I want you to know that this in no way reflects the standard of your programmes, but we're moving Radio 1 forward. I'm changing the overnights and expanding the music base.'

I looked at him for a moment. My show was arguably the most eclectic on the network. 'You haven't heard my programmes,' I stated simply.

'I'm sorry,' he said. 'I hope you'll continue with some sort of presence on the network ... maybe documentaries ...'

There didn't seem much else to say. I didn't take it personally, and I had no axe to grind with Matthew, whom I'd never even met before. I'd had a fantastic time at Radio 1, had enjoyed a wonderful working relationship with Phil Swern and Jeff Griffin and been staunchly supported by the controller, Johnny Beerling. I couldn't have asked for more and I'd done my very best. I'd loved doing my programmes and knew I was going to miss them like mad. But hey ... life goes on. As I reached the door, I stopped and turned around. 'Just to let you know ... I won't be going to the press to slag you off, or anyone else for that matter. I've loved it here, it's as simple as that.' A lump rose in my throat at that bit, but the difficult part was going on air that night. With all information embargoed until the following Monday, I couldn't even explain why I was sounding so flat.

I'd been supporting a band called Cry Of Love, a four-piece American rock group in the style of Free and Bad Company and sporting an awesome guitarist in Audley Freed. On the strength of the plays I'd given their début album *Brother*, Columbia Records brought them over to the UK for a special showcase gig at the Borderline in London on 21st September, a few days after my meeting with Matthew. Cry Of Love had asked me to compere the show and I turned up to find the place packed to the rafters. During the evening many people made a point of coming up to me, shaking me by the hand and thanking me for playing the band on the radio. The warmth was unbelievable. As I stood onstage looking out at the crowd, the evening seemed to define what I've always thought my job was about – making the introduction between the musicians and the audience, then stepping back while they explored the experience. After a brilliant, high-energy set in that sweaty basement club, the band piled down to Egton House with me for a live session on my overnight show. The evening was a triumphant but confusing experience. If the programme was the success it seemed to be, how come I was losing it?

'The World Ends on a Whisper' ran a headline in the *Independent* on the morning of the final show. Earlier that week journalist Jim White had spent a night sitting in the studio with me, listening to the music, answering phone calls, helping me with the mail and generally picking up the vibe. Jim put together the following article:

Harris's 'repositioning' came as something of a shock for the million or so listeners who regularly tune in to his show. Sitting at the mixing desk in his studio, Harris has a heavy wodge of angry letters, several thousand thick. They come from across the country: from vicars in York, students in Lancashire and the night shift at the Mr Kipling Bakeries in Petersfield, Hampshire. They talk of 'betrayal', 'horror' and 'devastation' at the end of Harris's show. While most disc jockeys simply seem to inhabit another world, Harris found that his job took him into another universe altogether: that inhabited by computer buffs and long-distance lorry drivers, croupiers and hookers, cramming students and bored security guards. He played them an eclectic range of old and new rock, blues, soul, the kind of grown-up stuff that rarely, if ever, makes its way onto daytime Radio 1, delivered in a soft purr that doesn't jar at 3 o'clock in the morning. 'I had no idea there were so many people out there,' said Harris. 'I just assumed I was talking into the ether. I think that because nobody particularly advertised the show, people had to discover it for themselves, and therefore see it much more as their property.'

The article ended with a dedication to Trudie's brother, Brandon, whom I used to phone just after 2 o'clock every morning. The Myerscough family ran a dairy farm in Somerset and Brandon had to be up to load the van for the 4 o'clock milk round.

Musicians and friends called into the show to wish me their best. Nicky Campbell stayed on for a while (I used to really enjoy his show and our conversations at midnight. I saw him years later and he told me that someone had sent him a compilation tape of our 30 best handovers!) and Steve Wright turned up for a while. Marc Cohn phoned from New York, Walter Trout, the world's greatest rock guitarist, rang me from California and blues player Michael Katon called from Hell, in Michigan. Tom Robinson and others dropped by the studio, and

Paul McCartney wrote me a most wonderful letter. Phil and Johnny were there, of course, their futures as uncertain as mine. Even Bruno, to his great credit, was gracious when he started his show. Thanking him for what he said was the last time I ever spoke to him face to face. Having played 'Rex Bob Lowenstein' by Mark Germino, 'I Won't Back Down' by Tom Petty and other appropriate stuff, I chose a Max Bygraves song to play out that final programme. 'When You Come To The End Of A Lollipop' seemed to sum it all up.

After it was over, Trudie and I just stood in the middle of the studio for a few moments, holding each other as tight as we could. As we packed to go, it was a really odd feeling to know that I didn't belong there any more. Finally, we trudged for the last time through the tunnel that ran under Langham Place, connecting Egton House with the main building. It was a very low moment but as we climbed the stairs up to the ground floor of Broadcasting House, I was amazed to discover that the place was bursting with people. I stopped at the top of the stairs and looked at the crowd, them looking back at me in a state of suspended animation. We all stood like that for a moment in a surreal kind of stand off, then someone started to applaud. Gradually the whole crowd joined in as I stood there in disbelief, the ovation echoing around that hallowed reception hall. Unbeknown to me, people had travelled from all over Britain, gathering together in a spontaneous vigil through the night in the streets around Broadcasting House. It had got so cold out there that the security guys had let as many as wanted to into the building to get warm.

As we all went outside, someone was playing Ben E. King's 'Stand By Me' on a sound system they'd set up in the boot of their car. People completely surrounded us, shaking me by the hand, telling me how much they were going to miss me. A gang of bikers revved their Harleys and gave Trudie a white-knuckle ride round the block while two women introduced me to the driver of the taxi they'd hired to bring them down from Coventry. 'We were going away on holiday this week but thought we'd rather spend the money coming down to support you.'

It was very emotional and I really felt I didn't deserve any of this. All I could think of to say was 'Thank you, thank you' to everyone, over and over again.

As chance would have it, Trudie, our son, Miles, and I were on a plane the following day, heading for the Seychelles. We'd booked the holiday months before and it was a wonderful coincidence that it fell exactly at the end of those final few hectic days on Radio 1. It was an opportunity to reflect and relax for a couple of weeks, a break we badly needed. I'd been doing programmes for In Flight, a company providing taped entertainment to airlines, and had opted to be paid in tickets. I'd almost forgotten I'd accumulated them and the company had called to tell me that the option was about to run out. It transpired that I'd saved up enough to get eight people somewhere really sunny and Roy and Karen Webber came with us, with their children Holly and Luke, taking care of the hotel as their part of the deal. Although I'd done the work to earn it, it felt like a free holiday for us, and it was great spending time with Roy and his family, an opportunity we rarely got.

The inhabitants of the Seychelles reminded me of the lyrics of the Blue Mink song 'Melting Pot' – 'multi-racial, coffee-coloured people by the score'. The islands are situated just south of the equator, in the middle of the Indian Ocean, about 1000 miles east of the African coastline. The islanders are gentle people who've absorbed any number of cultural and genetic influences and there was no community tension of any sort on those crime-free paradise islands.

We stayed on the island of Mahe, roughly the same size as the Isle of Wight and by far the largest in the group, with a population of 40,000. It is a stunningly beautiful place, with an all-year-round temperature in the 80s and regular rainfall. The climate produces lush and colourful jungle vegetation that reaches the fringes of the bleached white beaches edging the clear turquoise sea. Outside of the capitol, Victoria, there were few people, very little traffic and, astonishingly, no predatory insects despite the tropical climate. The only inconvenience of any description was the persistent mouse in our hotel room that defied all attempts at capture, forever scrabbling up and down the curtains and waking our toddler in the middle of the night! Miles was 18 months old and the great wonders for him were the hundreds of tiny fish that used to gather in shoals round our feet whenever we went paddling and the peacocks that strutted about making the 'cwaark' sound that always made him jump.

Despite our hasty exit from the flat in Platt's Lane we'd been lucky enough to rent a small farmhouse in Oxfordshire, overlooking one of the largest village greens in England. I'd loved Oxfordshire when I lived there in the 80s and Trudie felt she'd had enough of London. It was a lovely place to come home to after our holiday in the Seychelles and we both felt confident and rested for the first time in months. It didn't last long.

We were woken at 7.30 the following morning by a hammering on our front door. Two bailiffs had arrived to impound my record and CD collection in lieu of our debt to Bruno, who knew the collection was valuable and intended to sell it off to recover at least some of his money. Apparently the law was on his side. We discovered that technically I no longer owned my records, that it was at the discretion of the bailiffs as to whether I kept them or not and that we had seven days to appeal. 'We suggest you call a lawyer,' they said, as we all sat drinking tea in our kitchen. 'We'll wait while you make the call, otherwise we're instructed to remove the collection.'

It was a desperate situation. Our future depended entirely on my records and my ability to build and broadcast my shows. Without the raw materials – well, God knows what I was going to do. Theresa Mulgrew at Cole and Cole in Oxford had agreed to represent us and issued a stay of execution. After a couple of hastily arranged meetings, we arrived for the High Court hearing in the Strand the following Wednesday morning, a very bleak experience. We tried to explain that I needed my CDs and records to allow me to hand-build my programmes in the way that had become my trademark, that they were my 'tools of trade'. Bruno's contention was that I didn't need them and that as a fellow disc jockey he should know. He never built his programmes and therefore didn't need music at home. It was the job of a producer to choose the tracks and anyway, the BBC library was full of anything I'd ever want. It was only a last-minute plea that persuaded the Master of the Court to allow us a little more time to put some kind of case together. We were due back in court on 15th December. I had 14 days to save my future.

I arrived at BFBS to record my show in a state of shock. I'd come very close to losing my livelihood and I was shaking visibly as acting station manager Marc Tyley took me through to his office for a while to calm down. I sat there, staring out of the window at the Westway traffic, feeling scared and hopeless. It seemed that, despite having managed to keep my career going all these years, sometimes against the odds, this time I really was beaten.

I've always spent hours putting my programmes together, getting the blend and the tempo of the music exactly right. I specifically concentrate on segues, playing two, three or four tracks back to back in a seamless run, integrating a diverse range of musical styles in a 'no boundaries' musical mix. For me, programme building is a labour of love, a wonderfully enjoyable, creative and spontaneous process. I never conform to any set format and follow my instincts completely when it comes to selecting the tracks. I've always had the freedom to express myself in this way and knew that Bruno's solicitor's suggestion that all this could be achieved in somebody's office at the radio station an hour or so before a show was completely unworkable for me.

As I moved through to the BFBS studio to begin my recording session, I had absolutely no idea what I was going to do next. It was almost impossible to concentrate on the broadcast and I was struggling with it all when Andy Lowe, the BFBS librarian, edged his way into the studio. 'I don't want to disturb you,' he said, 'but I wondered if this might be helpful.' He put a letter down on the desk in front of me and waited while I read it through.

He'd written that his job was to oversee the BFBS library, one of the most comprehensive CD and record collections in the world; that in all his time with the station he'd only ever seen me use the facility for the occasional track and that I always delivered the music myself from my own resources. He went on to explain that the concept of 'programme building' was integral to the station's definition of my working relationship with them, that my shows were unique and that the idiosyncratic nature of the musical choice was at the core of their appeal. What's more, he said, he would be prepared to stand up in a court of law and offer this professional observation and opinion under oath. This was the answer. I looked up to see a smile on his face. 'I don't know how to thank you, Andy,' I said with relief. 'I think you might just have saved my life.'

As word of the dispute between two erstwhile colleagues at Radio 1 spread through the industry, people started phoning to offer their support. As well as Andy Lowe, Marc Tyley and producer Phil Ward Large from BFBS, Johnny Beerling, Phil Swern, fellow disc jockey Johnnie Walker and Tim Blackmore headed a number of Britain's top independent radio producers who all wrote affidavits in support of my 'tools of trade' contention. Colin Larkin, editor of the Guinness music reference books, sent a long letter describing the value of album sleeves as a research tool and in all we collected a dozen affidavits to be presented in court. Sky News and the national press were waiting for us as we arrived for the hearing.

Torturously, the matter was not resolved. Bruno's solicitor tried to dismiss the credibility of the affidavits by saying that they were all from friends of mine who 'would say that wouldn't they' and insisted that they should all come into court and testify in person. The next hearing was set for 24th February and everyone turned up for me. It was a bit like *This Is Your Life*, with everyone offering touching and heartfelt testimony of support, sticking to their guns under vigorous and, at times, unpleasant cross examination. I was on the stand for over two hours myself, a surreal and intimidating experience for me. It was even more difficult for a heavily pregnant Trudie, watching from the spectators' gallery, who was now expecting our second child and thinking she may give birth at any moment! Only agent Tony Fox and fellow disc jockey Liz Kershaw had written letters on Bruno's behalf but neither appeared in court. Not surprisingly, Tony no longer represented me.

The whole process took up so much time that we were instructed to return to court for a fourth hearing in May to enable both sides to deliver their final summing-up, but even then we didn't get a decision. After what seemed an unbearable wait, Cole and Cole finally called us on 12th August to tell us that we'd won, that the court had accepted our 'tools of trade' contention and that my collection was mine once again. It was a moment of enormous relief. Bruno immediately appealed, lost the appeal and had all costs awarded against him, the worst possible outcome as far as he was concerned.

Meanwhile, BFBS had been keeping me going. Since losing my shows on Radio 1, I'd once again had no other source of regular income and, with the court case running, our finances were devastated. When Charles Foster offered me a three-month series of daily BFBS UK shows in the spring of 1994 I jumped at the chance. I was also keeping busy as one of the judges for that year's Sony radio awards, listening to hours and hours of taped programmes from radio stations large and small. But the pressures of the court case and our financial situation were affecting me. I'd developed a frozen shoulder, an inconvenient and horribly painful condition: stress related, my doctor told me. I was aware that, although we'd won the court battles, we hadn't won the war. Bankruptcy was now hanging over us like the sword of Damocles.

Jude Howells, deputy manager of Greater London Radio, had been following the story in the press, and out of the blue, she called me. 'It suddenly occurred to me that maybe you'd like to come in and do some shows for us,' she said. 'We'd love to have you.' It was all very casual and warm. I started broadcasting for the station in the summer of 1994 and it only took me a few programmes to realize that GLR and I were made for one another.

I started by doing a three-hour programme on Saturday nights, but quickly expanded into the weekdays, broadcasting on Monday, Tuesday and Wednesday nights from 8 to midnight in what became the most enjoyable broadcasting experience of my career to that point. The money was absolutely hopeless and did little to ease our financial plight, but I knew instinctively that this was the right place for me to be.

Oddly, a few weeks after starting I got a call from GWR, offering me a berth on their networked late-night 'love songs' show, broadcasting from Swindon, not far from us in Oxfordshire, with a financial package that could have begun to solve our problems. The terms and conditions were that I'd only have one 'free choice' track an hour in among the back-to-back Phil Collins, Simply Red and Mariah Carey records that constituted the bulk of their playlist. It took me a nanosecond to turn it down. I knew I'd hate it and that the programmes would sound completely unconvincing. Twelve months on, when the current generation of Australian middle management people moved on, I'd be out of a job and I wasn't ready to go out to graze just yet. In contrast, GLR offered the opportunity of exposure to a whole blast of fresh new music.

The station's playlist was strongly indie-based, with bands like Oasis, Blur, Dodgy, Red Hot Chilli Peppers and The Lemonheads defining the station's sound, with disc jockey Gary Crowley, in particular, unearthing any number of fantastic new gems. Blues, soul, punk and reggae punctuated many of the daytime shows and it was clear that everyone had a reasonably free choice on air. Peter Curran was doing a dryly intelligent teatime show and Johnnie Walker was sounding as good as ever in the mornings. The lovely Mark Simpson was spreading his gentle bonhomie and the late Charlie Gillett was broadcasting his alchemic mix of world and roots music every Saturday evening. It was a stimulating environment and Jude Howells and station manager Steve Panton were very encouraging, giving me the confidence to push the musical boundaries of my own programmes to the limit.

More and more new names began to pour into the shows as I increasingly sharpened my taste for independent and roots-based music. Leah Andreone, Beth Orton, Audio Sound System, Black Star Liner, Galliano, Lucy Kaplansky and the Afro Celt Sound System rubbed shoulders with the Primitive Radio Gods, Robben Ford, King L, Chris Smither, Eliza Carthy and John Hiatt in a liberating fusion of styles. I was championing teenage guitar sensations Kenny Wayne Shepherd and Jonny Lang, giving first plays to David Gray, Collective Soul and Canadian band Tea Party and playing tracks from Skip McDonald's brilliant *Little Axe* album.

It was a massive commitment, doing all the listening and building 15 hours-worth of programming every week. I worked four days from around 10 a.m., putting the shows together then driving to London for the broadcasts, getting back home about 1.30 the following morning, then doing the same the following day. With my BFBS shows and the occasional voice-over or writing commission it was a hectic, time-consuming schedule, but worth every minute.

GLR was desperately underfunded and that, in fact, was the *quid pro quo*. Come in and enjoy yourself but we can't afford to pay you very much. The equipment was from a bygone age and the two main studios had both seen better days. Facilities were in such short supply that bartering over an empty tape spool or the use of an editing razor was not uncommon and the station relied heavily on volunteers for programme support, particularly in the evenings, mostly to help out on the phones. I'd inherited a helper called Doug from my predecessor, Simon Barnett, but he was leaving soon, so I needed to build a backup team.

I set up a competition, offering a 13-CD box set of Columbia label classic re-issues and a visit to the studio as prizes. The winner was Alan Watts (Motorcycle Alan), who drove all the way from his home in Southampton to collect it. From then on he made the journey every Tuesday evening to help on the show.

The atmosphere of those programmes was wonderful – very easy and loose, people calling in, live sessions and loads of back-to-back music in carefully crafted segues. People would call us up for dedications and information about the tracks and Doug invited a few of the regular callers into the studio just before he left. So began the formation of my amazing programme team. Hugh (The Man with the Tie) began to sacrifice his spare time between his bank job and drama group rehearsals to come in and help on a Monday night. University student Kirsti Reeve (Clued-in Kirsti) applied her awesome mind and computer skills to setting up a Bob Harris website, further developed by Roy Webber's design company The Works and now a major music resource maintained through all these years by the amazing Les Kneeling. It was Kirsti who taught me basic computer skills and developed the templates I still use for programme building to this day. And there was Backstage Patrick.

Patrick had been caught up in the atmosphere of the show and joined me at GLR almost every night. He was amazingly in tune with what I was trying to do and began to organize sessions for the programme, all done in his spare time. He liaised with the record and promotion companies to get some of my favourite musicians into the studio to talk and play live and organized sessions from the bright and brilliant Dave Matthews and the venerable Dr John. Tom Paxton, Christy Moore, Mary Chapin Carpenter, The Hamsters, Lynn Miles, Bruce Cockburn, The Hellecasters, Dar Williams and Judie Tzuke all did sets on the show, often bringing friends into the studio, joining the team and helping to create a kind of club atmosphere on air. The 'feel' really did communicate to the listeners, who seemed to sense how much we were enjoying it all. It was fabulous to be in the middle of one of those sessions, mixing a two-track sound on the antiquated BBC desk for Fairport Convention, Peter Frampton, Paul Rodgers or Iris DeMent, amazed at how lucky I was to be doing this job. Richard Thompson and June Tabor provided the night that best defined the whole vibe.

Patrick is the biggest Richard Thompson fan I've ever met. He knew every lyric of every song and was visibly nervous on the night Richard came in to play live. Patrick took up a seat just to the right of the microphone and there must have been at least a dozen people in the studio while Richard was performing, warm applause greeting every number. He was midway through 'Beeswing' when he stopped singing, having apparently forgotten the lyrics to the song, repeating the chord a couple of times while he sorted out the next line in his mind. Exactly on cue, Patrick sang it for him, Richard picking up from him again a few words on. The look of pride on Patrick's face was a picture as everyone burst into applause. At the end of the set, everyone moved through to the production room to join June Tabor, who was appearing later that evening. As I watched through the glass, she and Richard began to rehearse together and when she came through to join me, Richard came back in to accompany her for a magical, impromptu performance.

I loved the freedom to be able to spend an hour or so with artists in this way and we subsequently featured Steve Earle, Jackson Browne, Lou Reed, John Hiatt and blues legend Jimmy Rogers in interview and 'unplugged' specials. And it was on air at GLR that I celebrated my twenty-fifth anniversary, the first major milestone in my broadcasting career. *Time Out* advertised the event as follows:

They reckon his musical tastes make Phil Collins sound like Iron Maiden. They say he lurks somewhere between low cred and no cred. They misread his urbanity as showbiz phoniness. And such stories probably led to his axing from the new, youth-orientated Radio Wonderful. But they're all wrong. Bob Harris arouses irrational affection in these quarters and fortunately for us fans, the Whisperer has found a natural home at GLR. Monday's show marks his 25th year of jockery, his ginger whiskers gently wagging to the usual mix of live session and more new music than he played on 1FM, so don't mention AOR. Happy birthday, Bobby.

My three-year-old son, Miles, sat with me for most of the evening at the broadcast desk, fascinated by everything, behaving impeccably and occasionally munching on the microphone-shaped cake baked specially for the occasion. My daughters Miri and Emily were there, Miri with her new baby daughter, Marnie, my first grandchild, who was four months old. The Team was in, Fish, ex-lead singer of Marillion, turned up and Robyn Hitchcock and James Reyne played live sets. I was particularly pleased that James was there because his song 'Take A Giant Step' was very important to us. Not only had it been one of the great anthems of the Radio 1 overnight shows, but the title had also, in a funny way, been symbolic, an inspiration to Trudie and me as we addressed the ongoing problems in our financial life. Take A Giant Step, then another. Be positive and just keep going.

Two weeks later on 2nd September 1994, our second son, Dylan, was born – our sunny baby – a happy, smiling, loving boy, blessed with the deepest of voices. Before he could speak he would express his general contentment with life with a resonant, growling gurgle.

When we moved into our Oxfordshire farmhouse we did so on the understanding that it was a long-lease arrangement, but shortly after I started on GLR, the landlords changed their minds. Their daughter was getting married and they were giving her the house as a wedding present. We were given two months' notice to leave and had to be out by 4th January 1995, so we began the process of looking at properties day after day, a joyless experience. With virtually no money we couldn't afford anywhere big enough to house the music room that was essential for my work, yet so many of the smaller houses we saw seemed so dark, damp and depressing – and the closer we got to Christmas, the more desperate we became.

Finally, we found the house we live in now, situated in south Oxfordshire, set in the privacy of a large garden and perfect for the children, a world-within-a-world environment. I knew it was exactly right for us and it provided an immediate spur to my determination to work our way out of our financial troubles.

Having failed in his attempt to strip me of my record collection, Bruno was now pursuing a 'divide and conquer' strategy. Trudie and I had both signed the original agreement with him regarding the loan and he now singled out Trudie and hit her for the money. I'm still perplexed as to why he thought we'd ever be able to write him a cheque for £130,000, just like that. The only possible explanation was that maybe he thought the Harrods chairman would fund us. Mohamed had called me in a few times to discuss plans to start a Harrods record label and build a £20-million studio on the roof. I advised him against the idea. He later bought a radio station instead and sank his millions into Fulham Football Club, but he was never going to bail us out. Trudie and I truly didn't have the resources to pay the loan in full and in the spring of 1995, Bruno issued Trudie with a bankruptcy order. Twelve months later I went under too.

In some ways bankruptcy came as a relief. At least we could draw a line and begin again, but it was a bleak and difficult experience, one that profoundly affected the day-to-day running of our life. You have to declare yourself the whole time and it's impossible to get any credit of any description. It took us a while to get even a personal bank account again and the restrictions on us were draconian. We weren't allowed a cheque card or charge card and the account would be closed if we went one penny into the red. Almost everything had to be done in cash and several times we went through periods of up to two or three weeks when we didn't have enough money to go food shopping. It was a strange feeling, heading up to London sometimes, maybe to an important meeting or lunch, knowing that in my pocket I had only the fiver Trudie had somehow managed to squeeze out of the housekeeping money. Avoiding my round became a reluctant art form, new clothes were exclusively for the children, holidays were completely out of the question. But I never doubted that we'd come through it all.

My illness had taught me to take things on, to address the difficult issues and try to overcome them. The tougher our problems became, the more I was determined to fight back. 'Don't you worry, Trudie,' I kept saying to her. 'I've got this really strong feeling everything's going to be alright.'

'Ah ... listen to you, you bloody old hippie,' was her usual reply. 'You don't have to deal with the practicalities of life. You creative people, you're all the same. What's it like on Cloud 9 then?'

Despite my optimism, things did get really bad. The worry of our financial plight caused Trudie to have a miscarriage in the summer of 1996. I was at home looking after the children while she recovered in hospital when a reporter from the *Daily Mail* turned up on our doorstep, wanting some quotes about my bankruptcy! (I didn't particularly resent him being there. But let's face it, who would ever want to DO that job?) I invited him in and he sat at our kitchen table, bombarding me with questions about our money problems while I tried to pacify toddler Dylan, missing his mummy and crying on my lap. At that very moment Jude Howells phoned from GLR, and was very sympathetic when I described the scene. 'Just tell him to fuck off,' she advised. I think the guy actually took pity on us because the paper didn't carry the story, we were relieved that there was very little coverage in the newspapers of our stigmatized state.

We'd slipped several thousand pounds behind with the rent and were getting really scared about what was going to happen. If we lost the house we knew we'd go under and the landlords were beginning to threaten the possibility. We had only a few days left to raise the money when, out of the blue, a £6000 cheque arrived from the BBC for sales of *Whistle Test* to distant territories around the world. We couldn't believe it when we opened the envelope. It was the turning point for us.

The first hint of Trudie's impending miscarriage had happened in Somerset, on an otherwise wonderful summer weekend. I'd turned 50 a few weeks earlier and, with her brother Brandon approaching his thirtieth birthday, we decided to pool resources and have a combined 80 years bash, lavish not an option. Family and friends joined us for a most wonderful picnic in lovely evening sunshine, by the lake in Stourhead Gardens, followed by a game of cricket on the local ground on the Sunday afternoon, organized by Trudie's older brother, Justin. My Mum and Dad drove down from Norfolk for the weekend and Miri, her then-partner, Rob, and their daughter, Marnie, arrived from London.

The centrepiece of the picnic spread was a huge cake, made by Trudie's sister Grace, in the shape of a record player, with a big chocolate arm resting on a replica of a 7-inch single. Grace was there with her husband, Lewis, and their children, Max and Agnes. Trudie's little sister Jo was giggling with her gaggle of girlfriends while Robin, Trudie's patient uncle, enjoyed another glass of red wine with grandmother Jane on that peaceful, balmy evening. Trudie's great friend, Fiona Ronaldson, was there and, at the centre of it all, were Trudie's parents, Simon and Angela Myerscough-Walker.

The first thing you notice about Simon is that the thumb and two fingers of his right hand are missing, the legacy of an encounter with a

19-millimetre cannon shell in the post-war Sussex countryside when he was twelve. He'd been exploring near the rusting wreck of a German fighter plane and picked the thing up to have a look. The explosion killed his little brother and detonated bits of shrapnel into his body. He spent the next two years of his life in and out of hospital for surgery and repair, an experience that probably explains his amazing resilience.

His father, Raymond, was the definitive bohemian, living the life of an artist at odds with the real world. A qualified architect and teacher, skilled in the art of 'perspectives' (a rare and valuable ability to create a drawing of a finished building from the plans), he'd turned his back on the prospect of wealth and conformity and decamped to the countryside, where the family lived variously in a marquee in the middle of the Sussex Downs, in a small farmhouse in the middle of a 50,000-acre forest and in a caravan miles from anywhere. Together with his sister and brothers, Simon never attended school, their father preferring the virtues of home education and freedom of spirit. As soon as he was old enough, Simon began working on the local farms.

Simon and Angela met in their teens and have hardly been separated for more than a day since. Angela is one of the most capable women I've ever met and, side by side, she and Simon have invested their life in farming, gradually building up to the dairy business they and Brandon were running when I first met the family. Since then, as for all farmers, times for the Myerscoughs have been very tough.

In our case, there were signs that things were beginning to improve as offers of work slowly started to trickle in. Satellite television music channel VH1 transmitted a *Whistle Test Weekend*, 48 hours of nonstop studio and film material, to mark the programme's twenty-fifth anniversary, an event promoted by a poster campaign that featured a particularly alluring photograph of my good self, all long hair and faraway smile, emblazoned with the slogan 'The best of the *Whistle Test*, the worst of Whispering Bob's tank tops'.

Many of the old team gathered to reminisce in front of the cameras with Mike Appleton, Mark Ellen, Andy Kershaw, David Hepworth, Trevor Dann and myself holed up in a studio for a few hours, exchanging stories and anecdotes about our time with the show. Billy Bragg, Robyn Hitchcock and Rick Wright from Pink Floyd added their thoughts during an evening touched by a genuine sense of camaraderie between us all. I put together a 'My Top 10' for the channel and was invited by programme manager Mike Kaufman to present the late-night *Nightfly* video music show for a few weeks while regular host Tommy Vance was away. Building those programmes was fantastic fun and I really enjoyed being on television again.

VH1 were broadcasting from the old TVAM building near Camden Lock in northwest London, acquired by parent company MTV and transformed from an already radical space into a kind of futuristic pop music amusement arcade, the studios and work areas linked by stainless steel stairs and bridges. I was halfway through a programme one morning when the lights went up and we were all asked to stop filming. Mariah Carey had turned up for an appearance on MTV.

The forecourt had been cleared so she could park her trailer, in which she sat ensconced for almost three hours. She'd insisted that all staff be brought outside to applaud her into the building and there was a lot of 'she's leaving the trailer, everybody get outside' followed by 'er ... no she's not, everyone back in again' going on during that time. Work virtually ground to a stop with the constant interruptions as she kept the staff on tenterhooks. The delay was caused, it transpired, by her desire for canine company.

'I want to be interviewed cuddling a cute little puppy,' she is reported to have said. 'Puppies,' she directed the people from her record company. 'Get me puppies!'

All available pedigree mutts having been corralled from local pet shops and God knows where else, she finally flounced triumphantly from her trailer, through the building and onto the dimly lit studio set. There she arranged herself on the bed where she was to do her 'intimate' interview, pouting provocatively as she stroked the orange puppy nestling on her lap. The demonstration of single-minded star behaviour was awesome, a relentless, self-obsession-fired promotional momentum that later propelled her into the richest recording contract in music business history, reportedly worth £20 million an album.

A few days later I compered the Guildford Festival, somewhat more down to earth. I introduced Big Country, Eddi Reader and the return to the stage of the legendary Peter Green, making only his second appearance in front of an audience after an absence of more than 25 years. At the height of his powers with Fleetwood Mac he'd been one of the most confident, powerful and expressive guitarists in the world, able instinctively to fuse his traditional blues playing with the band's British rock style. He'd written some of the most distinctive and moving songs of the era, a string of hits including the awesome 'The Green Manalishi', which was climbing into the charts when he left the band in 1970. The pressure of fame and expectation was too much for him, however, and the psychological and mental problems that ensued led to him shutting down on music altogether. At one point he grew his fingernails so long that he was unable to play and a pathological reluctance to appear in public had only recently been overcome. Watching him on stage that night he looked bewildered and frightened, like a big, shaggy rabbit in the glare of the spotlights. His voice sounded shot and he was leaning so heavily on the other members of the group that I thought his talent was all but lost. But, as the set dragged towards what seemed likely to be a wearisome close, he located unexpected resources of energy and launched into a version of Don Nix's 'Going Down', good enough to evoke the images of glory days gone by, laced with intuitive licks and a driving groove. He even got a thumbs-up from Eric Clapton, dressed in black and standing almost unnoticed in the shadows at the side of the stage.

I briefly returned to Radio Oxford, in its new guise as Thames Valley FM, to do a three-hour show on Sunday afternoons, Motorcycle Alan and good friend and team member Graham Brown would come in with me most weeks to help out on the phones. Fairport Convention, Sam Brown and local band The Unbelievable Truth did sessions for us and Trudie would often bring Miles and Dylan in for the last half hour so they could get the feel of the studio and see where their dad was doing his work. The children never blinked an eyelid at hearing me on the radio, although Miles would occasionally get frustrated that I was programme building or writing yet again, just at the time he wanted a game of football – all part of the joys of working from home.

I was delighted to discover that my GLR programmes were beginning to find an audience at Radio 2. Some of the programme producers started phoning, telling me they were listening in the car driving home after work and enquiring as to the source of some of the tracks I was playing. It was becoming clear that the station was about to undergo some changes and I was eventually invited to record a pilot programme at Broadcasting House and a *Rock Show* pilot with producer Robin Valk at Pebble Mill and both tapes were submitted to the Radio 2 controller, Frances Line, at the same time. Both were rejected. 'Bob Harris. Isn't he a Rock Jock?' she queried, but the announcement that Jim Moir was to be Frances's successor gave me renewed hope that there might be a place for me on the network after all.

I'd met Jim a number of times at Television Centre when he was Head of Light Entertainment on BBC1. We'd always got on well and he'd once told me that he was a fan. Soon he was on the phone, inviting me to lunch to talk about doing some programmes for Radio 2 and I asked if I could bring Phil Swern with me. Following our enjoyable partnership at Radio 1, Phil and I had vowed to continue working together whenever we could and this seemed the ideal opportunity to reunite. I also thought that Phil was probably more in tune with the 'sound' of Radio 2 than I was at that time and that he'd be able to smooth off some of the rough edges my musical tastes had acquired.

'What are the boundaries?' I asked Jim as we sat chatting together at the restaurant.

'Just bring in all your lovely music,' he answered, offering us a two-week run through Christmas, starting on 21st December 1996.

My son, Ben, was staying with us for a few days during the lead-up to that first show and couldn't believe the pressure I was putting myself under. 'I've never seen you so stressed,' he observed. 'Why can't you chill about it?'

'If I was going out on Saturday to play at Wembley,' I explained, 'you wouldn't expect me to just jog out onto the pitch. You'd surely expect me to prepare, get myself into the right state of mind. Saturday is my Cup Final. I honestly believe it's the most important radio show I've ever done.'

Two factors informed this opinion. First, Radio 2 seemed the obvious place for me to be, now moving to embrace the very audience that had been with me from the start. Second, I knew that if the station didn't employ me, in the long term I probably wouldn't be working. Dark rumours of a GLR 'repositioning' were in the air and anyway, however much I loved it, they weren't paying me a living wage. Commercial radio was now uniformly computer programmed and there didn't seem any other obvious place for me to go. While most stations were all about 'streaming' and digital jukeboxes, Radio 2 has adamantly remained true to the concept of individual 'programmes' and I knew the station represented my only long-term opportunity to go on air in Britain with the freedom to express myself. So, it had to be Radio 2, or we'd probably be off to America.

Phil and I spent ages putting that first show together and eventually decided to start with The Beach Boys. 'Add Some Music To Your Day' seemed an appropriate choice, followed by 'Dance With Me' by Orleans, Shawn Colvin's 'Sunny Came Home' and tracks from Jann Arden, Jackson Browne, Jackie Wilson, Little Milton, Leann Rimes, Joni Mitchell, Lynn Miles, Van Morrison and The Beatles (George's spine-tingling acoustic version of 'While My Guitar Gently Weeps' from the *Anthology 3* collection). We ended the show with Steve Winwood's 'Back In The High Life Again', because we really hoped we would be. Jim Moir was on the phone less than a minute after we came off air.

'We need to speak about your future,' he told me. I looked across at Phil.

'YES!!'

The Bob Harris Show began its regular Saturday night slot on Radio 2 in April 1997.

Just over a month later our little Flo was born, Florence Jayne Myerscough-Harris, on 21st May, the eighth and last of the children in my extended family – and I am so proud of her. She is a bright, beautiful, sensitive girl, loved and protected by the big brothers she adores. We are a tight family unit.

I settled in quickly at Radio 2, broadcasting from a new self-op studio on the first floor of Broadcasting House. I was mostly building the programme myself this time, with Phil acting as my support system, and for a while we kept a lid on the volume level of the music and made sure we laced the new stuff with plenty of tracks people knew. But gradually, as people like Johnnie Walker, Jonathan Ross and Mark Lamarr joined and the music policy of the station sharpened up, we gradually took the constraints off.

I think Radio 2 is a 'world-class station', where the range of programming is unique and I'm very proud to work for the most popular radio station in Britain and to be working in an environment of high-level professionalism.

Almost immediately, the listening figures for Saturday nights started picking up and within two years we'd almost trebled the numbers, to me a confirmation that there really is an audience for the kind of music I play. Trace my programmes right back to 1970 and you'll discover they're very consistent, that I've always been true to the music. I've got a lot of faith in my ability to pick good tracks and the management at Radio 2 give me the freedom to play the people I really believe in and I hope my programmes demonstrate what a good time we're in right now. I know you wouldn't know it by following the mainstream charts, but there's a fabulous wealth of music out there, just under the surface. In my case, I've been lucky enough to discover whole new seams of it through my *Bob Harris Country* show and the music of Nashville and Austin, Texas.

It was a big surprise when Radio 2 first offered me *Bob Harris Country* late in 1998. I've always enjoyed country music and featured it on my shows, right from the early days of *Whistle Test* when we were playing Poco, The Eagles, Pure Prairie League, The Flying Burrito Brothers, New Riders of the Purple Sage, Neil Young and Little Feat. I'd featured sessions from Shawn Colvin, Mary Chapin Carpenter, Suzy Bogguss, Jimmie Dale Gilmore and others on my Radio 1 and GLR programmes and have always respected the fact that country music is all about a good song. I've played Steve Earle, Hank Williams, Johnny Cash, Rodney Crowell, Lyle Lovett, The Jayhawks, Buddy Miller and Patsy Cline.

Dave Shannon, the programme's producer at the time, first called me in December 1998. We'd already met, in April 1994, when I was compering an Alexis Korner tribute concert at the Opera House in Buxton, Derbyshire, a wonderfully ornate and intimate old-fashioned theatre and one of my favourite venues. Jimmy Page and Robert Plant topped the bill that night, playing together for the first time in years. I was introduced to Dave backstage and immediately liked him – he was one of the good guys. A Belfast boy, he had terrific knowledge of music, great dedication to it and a fabulous, sometimes wicked, sense of humour. Dave was one of the few people who could make me really laugh. For many years he produced the *Paul Jones Rhythm & Blues Show* on Radio 2 and later worked with Mark Lamarr on his *Rockabilly* series, the Sony 'Music Programme of the Year' 2000, and produced the country slot from the days of Wally Whyton in the early 90s.

Dave told me that Jim Moir's decision to ask me to do the show was based on his desire to let the programme explore the fringes of mainstream and unearth the new artists who were going to take the music forward. He was very keen for me to stamp myself on the show, hence the title *Bob Harris Country*, to demonstrate the personal nature of the musical choice. It felt like a big responsibility. I understand how passionate and protective people can be about the music they love and I wasn't sure the regular listeners would approve of the choice of what must have appeared to them to be an interloper from Planet Rock.

When it became clear that the programme had abandoned the big-hat middle ground that had previously been its territory, in favour of Lucinda Williams, Buddy Miller, Steve Earle and other left-of-centre performers, the die-hards reacted with venom. We got so many letters from people who thought they'd been abandoned that I eventually took a load of them onto air with me to discuss grievances. I was at pains to point out that I hadn't slammed the door shut on them, but that if they wanted back-to-back Jim Reeves, why didn't they just pull his *Greatest Hits* collection off their shelf at home and put it on? I read out a letter from a listener who'd sent me a list of ten names he wanted me to feature as 'core' artists on the programme's playlist. Six of them were dead. It seemed to me that we needed to move on.

The whole idea was to inspire the sort of excitement in the new acts that the older listeners had felt when they had discovered the artists 'of their day'. I didn't abandon the traditionalists, and made a point of playing music, in a range of different styles, by the artists that I believe are loyal, in their own way, to the various traditions, rules and values of country music, even if they might bend them around a bit.

Most people 'got it', thank goodness, and we began to attract a whole new audience. To my astonishment, the programme added over 300,000 to the listening figures, despite my left-of-centre musical tastes. 'God knows what'll happen if you actually play some country on the programme,' joked Lesley Douglas, Jim Moir's No. 2. *Radio Times* published a couple of complimentary articles about the show. Even Jeremy Clarkson declared himself to be a fan. Writing in his column in the *Sun*, he rejected the test car he was driving on the basis that the road noise was so loud he couldn't hear me whispering!

Before we started the series, Dave thought I needed to immerse myself in Nashville culture so, in March 1999, we set off to spend time in Music City, meeting and greeting, setting up contacts, going to gigs, listening to the radio and recording sessions. It was the first time I'd been to the States for nearly 20 years, and that month proved to be the most enjoyable of all the times I've ever spent there.

Despite having done so much filming for *Whistle Test* in America in the 70s, I'd never visited Nashville before and our first stop, on the Monday night, was the Station Inn, the world-famous Mecca of Bluegrass, to see the opening night of a forthcoming tour by Steve Earle and the Del McCoury Band, in support of their album *The Mountain*. The gig was a very big deal and the old, rustic venue was absolutely packed, tables swilling with beer amid the hubbub of conversation, everyone aware of the one suspended silver microphone, highlighted in a shaft of spotlight on an otherwise dark stage.

Bluegrass music is played on traditional instruments and the Del McCoury Band line-up highlighted acoustic guitars, mandolin, banjo and fiddle, with Steve adding lead vocals and guitar. All the members of the band stood around one microphone for the performance with no other amplification, the soloist stepping forward to the microphone to play as others moved aside to give him space, all of them constantly shifting position to produce the best ambient balance in a brilliant exhibition of dextrous choreography.

The microphone was a work of art, a signature microphone, developed over many years by Steve Earle's Twang Trust production partner, Ray Kennedy – in my opinion one of the best studio engineers in the world. Their Room and Board studio is located close to Music Row, and has produced some of the most radical music to come out of Nashville, mostly recorded on the analogue equipment Ray has collected over the years. He has tape machines from Abbey Road, and Beatles memorabilia galore in the beautiful control room environment he's created. The place is regarded as something of a museum, with old 45s, music scripts and Elvis records housed with other sundry bits of fascinating memorabilia in soothingly lit glass cabinets.

Ray mixes on a relatively antiquated 16-track desk and rarely uses e.q. (equalization) or echo. He believes the best sound is located within the relationship between the instrument and the microphone and that's where the time is spent, in pre-production, getting the dynamics of the sound exactly right for every member of the band. He mostly records as live, with no production tricks and the minimum of overdubs, sparingly used for emphasis. Buddy Miller's approach is much the same and if I were producing today, they would be my models.

After having recorded sessions at Gretchen Peters' beautiful woodland home and later with Gillian Welch and David Rawlings, we met Sara Evans on the day she hit No. 1 in the American charts with 'No Place That Far'. RCA Records had hung a huge banner all the way down the side of their building, congratulating her on the achievement.

I interviewed Steve Earle, puffing on his pipe in the middle of the chaos that was his E-Squared label office and Dave and I made our début on Nashville radio on 98 WSIX with Gerry House, host of the most successful breakfast show in town. The power of that programme was awesome – everyone in the business listened. Whenever we were introduced to someone new from then on, the reaction was the same: 'Oh, you're the guys from the BBC. Heard you on the *Gerry House Show*.' We couldn't have had a better calling card.

We visited the Reba McEntire headquarters, a fully self-contained operational building, complete with miniature indoor fountain in the air-conditioned marble reception hall, three-storey office suite, galleries and recording, television and radio studios.

But the highlight of the trip was a visit to Emmylou Harris's house, to record an interview about the forthcoming release of *Return Of The Grievous Angel – A Tribute To Gram Parsons*, which she had overseen. In all the years I've known her, I've never heard anyone have anything but a good word for her. She is a respected and much-loved figure in Nashville and a genuinely caring person. Emmylou reminisced about her first meeting with Gram Parsons and the recording of the tribute album, and it became clear the extent to which 'chance' has played a significant part in her life. 'If there was a church of serendipity,' she reflected, 'I would be the high priestess.'

The week ended with a session by the admirable Texan songwriter Robert Earl Keen, followed by a raucous gig later the same evening by Robert and his band, supported by an Austin group called Reckless Kelly at the Exit Inn, another well-known venue.

I've discovered that country music people are admirably friendly and accommodating. Highlights included meeting Beth Nielsen Chapman, after she won the Song of the Year award for Faith Hill's *This Kiss* in 1999, and a conversation at the 2000 event with Tia Sillers, a few moments after she received Song of the Year award as lyricist of 'I Hope You Dance' recorded by Lee Ann Womack. I discovered that the Tia Sillers CV also includes the lyrics for Kenny Wayne Shepherd's 'Blue On Black', a blues-influenced song I played regularly on Saturday nights. I was impressed she'd written it, she was amazed I knew the song, a 'Bob Harris moment' as Richard Wootton put it. But the major coup for us was Shania Twain.

Having swept the board the previous year, Shania attended the 2000 event, punctuating a year-long break from the industry, to pass on her Female Vocalist of the Year crown to Faith Hill and afterwards wandered through to meet us. Artists often come into the studio surrounded by publicists, who rush around telling you you've only got two questions maximum and creating agitation. But Shania arrived on her own, knocking tentatively at the door of our small dressing room studio and asking if it was OK to come in. She stood for a moment, looking like a princess in her purple silk gown, before joining me to record what I was later told was the only interview she'd given all year. She was charming, natural and unpretentious, telling us how much she'd needed to take a break after seven years of solid work and how good it felt to do normal things again for a while. She is a genuinely nice person.

Little could I have known after that first trip the impact that Music City would have on my life. Nashville and I established an excellent relationship. I really enjoy the atmosphere of the place and the fact that I can get at the music easily, through any number of venues and record shops. All the music business infrastructure is packed into Music Row and the surrounding area, with major labels, indies, management companies, venues and equipment hire all on tap, creating an atmosphere that's very conducive to music-making. Steve Earle told me that Nashville has a population of just over a million, 900,000 of whom are songwriters, and that young hopefuls travel from all over America and Canada to plug into the resources.

Because of the competition you have to be good to succeed in

Nashville and the smaller labels and emerging fringe artists I support recognize that my show represents one of the few but welcome opportunities to get their music heard in Britain. A number of the people I've introduced on the programme, like Slaid Cleaves and Kevin Montgomery, have subsequently been able to tour the UK on the strength of the plays I've given them, a fact which gives me enormous pleasure. That is precisely my appointed role, to bring good music to people.

NINE

Music City USA

THE FIRST EDITION OF THIS BOOK WAS PUBLISHED TWO DAYS AFTER the most brutally devastating day in modern history. On that fateful morning of 9th September 2001 – 9/11 – I was in a small basement studio at BBC Broadcasting House, recording a major career interview with an artist who was to be more affected than most by the events of that day.

The interview was with Yusuf Islam who, in December 1977, had formerly embraced Islam at the Regent's Park Mosque in his home city of London, changed his name and rejected the life he had formerly known as Cat Stevens, one of the most successful artists of the 1970s, a man whose work virtually defined the concept of the sensitive singer songwriter.

Following a brief career as a 60s pop star, Cat Stevens had released his breakthrough album *Mona Bone Jakon* in April 1970, with the follow-up *Tea For The Tillerman* coming out just as I started my broadcasting career on Radio 1 in November that year. It was a stunning and beautiful album, featuring 'Father and Son' and 'Wild World', tracks I played regularly on my *Sounds Of The 70s* show, alongside 'Morning Has Broken', 'Moonshadow' and 'Peace Train' from his next release *Teaser And The Firecat*. I truly loved those records. He was also a frequent *Whistle Test* session guest and through the next few years our friendship grew. Like many of his friends from those early days, I'd always known him as Steve.

We chatted and reminisced in that little studio about his life and his music. I recalled to him a time in the mid-1980s, when he came in to my *Nightline* show on LBC radio, to talk about the Islamia Primary School that he had founded in the borough of Brent in 1983, the first-ever

Muslim school in London. The fact that it was the first radio interview he'd done since he adopted the Muslim faith was a story in itself, and my producer, Cathie Louie, and I were excited as we headed down to LBC reception to meet him.

We revisited that moment as we discussed his conversion to faith and his rejection of the rock-star lifestyle in the late 1970s. It was wonderful to spend time with this warm, affable, creative artist and he told me that the turning point had come when he was swimming on the Pacific coast, near the home of Jerry Moss who, with Herb Alpert, owned A&M, Yusuf's American record label. Caught in a strong current, he found himself being pulled further and further out to sea, desperately fighting to save himself from drowning.

'There was no one on this earth to help,' he told me. 'I just called out and said "God, if you save me I will work for you", and at that moment a wave came from behind me and pushed me forward.'

The following year his brother David gave him a copy of the Koran on his birthday and so began a deep devotion to his faith, at first radical and intense, in recent times more mellow, that has seen him become a respected and articulate spokesperson for Britain's Muslim community and a passionate advocate of tolerance and peace in an increasingly divided world.

Our conversation had lasted more than two hours before I finally had to break away to join American country star Gary Allan, who was waiting for me in a nearby studio to record a session for *Bob Harris Country*. As Yusuf and I walked into the control room, the first images of the burning twin towers were appearing on the monitors above the mixing desk. The sound was down and we gave the screens very little attention. I assumed the engineers were watching some kind of disaster movie and I briefly stepped out into the corridor to have some photographs taken with Yusuf, before he left and I returned to join Gary and his band in the studio.

Gary was a big star at the time and I'd been looking forward to meeting him. He'd just received a platinum disc for sales of his third album *Smoke Rings In The Dark* and was promoting his new record *Alright Guy*, which contained songs by two of my favourite writers – Todd Snider from East Nashville, who wrote the title song, and Bruce Robison, who had contributed a hilarious track called 'What Would

Willie Do', an ode to fellow Texan Willie Nelson '... he loves all the people no matter what their races, hell, he even made a country song with Julio Iglesias!'

It was only when we returned to the control room at the end of the recording that the full horror of the 9/11 attacks began to sink in. Gary had brought his band and representatives from his Nashville record label into the BBC with him and by now they were absolutely traumatized as we stood transfixed, staring at those screens, watching the smoke pouring from the crumbling Twin Towers. Some of them were crying, hugging each other for comfort. None of us knew what to say. Time stood still in a terrible combination of grief and silent panic.

The emotional impact and knock-on effect for all the visiting Americans was horrendous. At the moment they most wanted to get home to be with their loved ones they couldn't leave. All airports were on lock-down for days. It still seems strange to me that exactly at the time the attacks were taking place, I was discussing the Koran and the Muslim faith with Yusuf Islam.

The echoes of that awful day stayed with Yusuf too. On 21st September 2004 it was reported that he and his daughter had been arrested on a flight to America. He was due to meet with some musician friends in Nashville. Instead, the flight was diverted to Maine, where he was taken to a military base and interrogated by the FBI. 'Yusuf Islam barred from the US for suspected potential terrorism-related activities' the story read. A few days after returning to Britain, he appeared on prime-time TV in the States in a transatlantic interview with legendary American talk show host Larry King, who asked him 'Where were you on 9/11?'

'I remember exactly where I was, Larry. I was in a BBC studio again, just down the road from here, having an interview with Bob Harris.'

Yusuf's American ban was rescinded two years later but the fact that he had been heading to Nashville when he was arrested only deepened my sense of coincidence because, by now, my own relationship with Music City had become one of the most important in my life. In total, I have now visited Nashville more than thirty times and I owe a huge debt of gratitude to my former producer Dave Shannon for opening my mind to this incredible place.

Dave died of cancer in February 2013 and I miss him very much. He was a fine musician and a kind, gentle and generous man. I never heard him say a bad word about anyone. He was a true professional, and a humorous, creative and supportive producer. His former production assistant, Sue Welch, wrote a lovely tribute that appeared in the BBC *Ariel* magazine soon after Dave passed away, saying '... he made the working day fun and everyone had huge respect for this quiet, humble man', sentiments that perfectly express my own feelings about him. He fostered a fantastic team spirit around *Bob Harris Country*, which exists to this day, and I am now blessed to work with Al Booth and Mark Hagen who have become close friends and partners in the creative process that produces the show. We all love country music and we all love Nashville!

Nashville has become the music capital of the world. In a rapidly changing industry, the traditional music business infrastructure I discovered when I first went there is still flourishing and despite its very high density of well-known stars, the city is relatively paparazzi free. It's a mix of facilities and freedom that is attracting artists from all styles of music. My old mate Joe Brown and his wife, Manon, have just bought a house there; Dave Stewart recorded his two most recent albums at John McBride's famed Blackbird Studio and has made a wonderful and eccentric film expressing his love affair with the city. The Rival Sons travelled from Long Beach, California, to work at the West Nashville studio of producer Dave Cobb, to make the brilliant and edgy *Great Western Valkyrie*, voted the 2014 *Classic Rock* magazine album of the year. Ed Sheeran moved to Nashville for several months, the Black Keys relocated from Akro, Ohio, in 2010 and opened the Easy Eye Sound Studio, and Jack White started Third Man Records in the middle of what is an incredibly vibrant and creative scene.

Founded in 1779 and originally called Fort Nashborough, Nashville is also the capital of the state of Tennessee. Located on the Cumberland River in mid-Southern America, it rapidly grew to become a thriving port and eventually a major railroad and transportation hub. It is an important university town, known as the Athens of the South, and is a major medical centre, home to more than three hundred health care companies. Called the 'Buckle of the Bible Belt', it is also deeply religious. My guess is that there are probably more churches per square mile in Nashville than just about anywhere else in the world and it was religion that originally brought music to the city. Printing presses proliferated for Bible production, drawing in the sheet music publishers who put the first structures of the music business in place, bringing in the forefathers of the songwriting community that is a massive part of what makes the city such a friendly and creative place today.

Central to the growth of the music scene was the Ryman Auditorium, a stunning and imposing building situated right in the heart of downtown Nashville, which first opened its doors as a Tabernacle church in 1892. As time went by, the sound of gospel gradually gave way to the twang of country as the Ryman became home to a live-performance radio show called the *Grand Ole Opry*, the longest-running radio programme in the world, now broadcast from the stage of the iconic, custom-built Grand Ole Opry House near the banks of the Cumberland River.

Founded in 1925, those early Opry shows were blasted across America by the awesome transmitter power of radio station WSM, known as 'The Air Castle Of The South'. It was possible to hear the transmissions right across the States and up into parts of Canada, and the Opry drew fans into town in huge numbers. Honky-tonks and record shops sprang up in the streets around the Ryman as downtown Nashville began to generate the wild vitality that makes it one of my favourite places in the world.

I have a special personal relationship with the Ryman. Known as the 'Mother Church of Country Music', it feels like a sacred place to me, with its hard, polished wooden pews (take a cushion if you're going to a concert!) and stained glass windows, the colours from which bathe the upper-tier balcony in a gentle, coloured light. The auditorium and Confederate Gallery seat more than two thousand people and there is a museum area at the back of the building housing some truly iconic country memorabilia.

In 2009 I was thrilled to narrate a documentary on the Ryman made by Al Booth for Radio 2, and joining one of the many public tours of the place was like walking in the footsteps of giants. Hank Williams, Johnny Cash, Patsy Cline, Elvis Presley and countless other stars have played there. And it was one of the proudest moments of my life when I stepped out onto that stage myself to receive the Trailblazer Award presented on behalf of the Americana Music Association by Emmylou

Harris in September 2011. Robert Plant was honoured that year too with *Band Of Joy* winning in the Album of the Year category. Who would have predicted in the 1970s that the Rock God lead singer of Led Zeppelin and the long-haired hippy host of the *Old Grey Whistle Test* would be embraced by the Americana community at the Mother Church of Country Music! As he and I reflected on the journey that had brought us both to this wonderful moment, Trudie and Robert's manager, Nicola Powell, joined us side stage, Robert joyfully donning the Wolverhampton Wanderers cap and scarf they had bought for him, before falling to his knees and lifting a hefty glass of red wine in celebration.

The Americana Music Association was founded by Jed Hilly and a small, enthusiastic group of like-minded visionaries in 1999 with the aim of 'helping American roots music secure an elevated and secure place in the artistic and commercial life of the nation' – a lofty ambition they have achieved magnificently. From support for young artists to presentations to the president, the AMA has grown organically year by year to become the hugely influential organization it is today, a movement respected and acknowledged by iconic stars and major media alike. Americana is now one of the best-selling music genres in the States, with younger artists such as Mumford & Sons, Old Crow Medicine Show, The Avett Brothers, The Civil Wars and The Lumineers joining blue-chip stars such as Emmylou, Rosanne Cash, Steve Earle and Lucinda Williams in the *Billboard* Top-30 album charts.

The first AMA Honours and Awards show took place in 2002, moving to the Ryman three years later, where Al Booth and I have set up a mini studio each year in a tiny office next to the stage, monitoring the performances and speeches and recording the interviews and reactions that form the basis of our coverage of the ceremony on Radio 2. It's a fabulously enjoyable but highly pressured evening, at the end of which Al and I usually head out of the stage door, across the alley and into Tootsie's Orchid Lounge to unwind, soak up the atmosphere and down a couple of well-earned margaritas!

The bar is situated on Lower Broadway, the epicentre of Nashville's raucous nightlife, a loud, exciting cacophony of sound. Call into Tootsie's, Robert's or any of the many downtown honky-tonks and beer joints and I guarantee you'll hear some of the best playing you've ever heard ... by musicians you've probably never heard of performing on the window stage for tips. Those spit-and-sawdust venues are where many of the major stars first learned their trade, playing from early morning to late at night, and that tip jar was what kept their show on the road and paid their rent.

It isn't easy making it in Nashville. The level of musicianship is incredibly high. Chris King, a young, hopeful British musician, recently told me of his own experience on arriving there with his guitar on his back. 'So you think you're a guitarist?' said the cab driver who picked him up from the airport. 'Well, the guy who delivers the pizza to your hotel tonight will be a better player than you are!' It only took a short while before Chris realized that he was right, but he also soon discovered that Nashville has a very supportive music community; that big stars will step forward to help young hopefuls if they believe they have the talent and the work ethic. Most of the musicians who are now household names have played those window stages themselves, devoting their lives to music and hoping to be discovered, and they know how much it means to get a helping hand. I find this spirit of generosity and support hugely attractive and I've been blessed to forge what I know will be life-long friendships with some truly great people in this wonderful music city.

One of the most exciting of the many big personalities in Nashville is Scott Borchetta, known as the 'King Of Music Row'. Having followed his father into the music industry in the mid-1980s, Scott worked his way up from the post room at MTM Records, through stints at MCA and Universal, to become the founder and CEO of Big Machine Records ('we called the label Big Machine, because who the hell's gonna tell us we ain't!'), starting a sales explosion that has seen the company become the biggest independent label in America today.

I like Scott very much. He's a massive rock music fan, particularly the big-hair bands of the late 1980s, and I simply cannot think of anyone else in the world who could've persuaded some of the biggest names in country to turn out for the recording of *Nashville's Tribute to Motley Crue*, one of the more unexpected compilation albums of recent times. He has an amazing knack of making me feel good and he encourages me to tell stories of my *Whistle Test* days. He loves to hear about Marc Bolan in particular and told me that he played T. Rex covers in his first band.

There's no disputing that he's brought these influences to Music Row.

The predominant sound of Big Machine is a powerful and commercial blend of country music and rock, and like all great label bosses Scott has an unerring instinct for the great opportunity. 'Think about it ... how many massive rock bands have come out in the last ten years?' he asked me. 'Less than a handful. That lane was virtually empty, so we decided to fill it.'

The country traditionalists may shake their heads in disapproval but it's a blend that has taken artists like Florida Georgia Line, Brantley Gilbert, Thomas Rhett and The Cadillac Three to the top of the charts, bringing a new, young, predominantly male audience into the music and selling millions and millions of records in the process. No wonder Scott has been able to build a collection of supercars and vintage automobiles to die for, a garage full of classic American heavy metal.

Central to the growth of Big Machine has been the phenomenal crossover success of Taylor Swift, who Scott signed as a fourteen-year-old in 2005. She is bright, mega-talented, frighteningly focused and is currently the biggest star in the world. When she played the Bridgestone Arena in Nashville on her 'Red' tour in 2013, no less than eighteen equipment trucks pulled up outside, containing the rigs and technology that powered a stunning Cirque du Soleil-inspired extravaganza, one of the best and most spectacular live shows I've ever seen.

Taylor puts concentrated thought and energy into every aspect of her career and connects with her audience in an amazing way. She is a PR specialist and before the show she invited Trudie, Miles and me to join her in a hospitality area she'd set up backstage, where she'd created what looked like a big kids' party room, with a soft-drinks bar, bowls filled with brightly coloured sweets and a Diet Coke dispenser. Taylor is tall, intense and looked absolutely stunning in black shorts and black top, a black hat perched on top of her long blonde hair. I was very impressed that Miles managed to keep a lid on the obvious excitement he was feeling as she walked into the room. With her wide eyes, pale complexion and bright red lipstick, she looked like a porcelain doll.

She introduced us to her mother, the equally driven and almost as famous 'Mama Swift', who, before the doors opened, took us on a tour of the stage and the phenomenal technology and hydraulic wonders it contained, with lifts, pulleys, computer screens and no less than eleven different mini dressing-room areas for Taylor's various costume changes. I've been around rock'n'roll tours for most of my life but I had never seen anything quite like it.

Like many of the artists on the Big Machine roster, Taylor has opened the door to a new audience for country music, including my daughter Flo, who is a massive fan. I am thrilled that Flo loves music as much as she does, taking it with her everywhere and consuming it in bite-sized chunks on her iPhone, from iTunes, YouTube and Vevo. Despite my best intentions, however, she is still somewhat resistant to the wonders of Americana but I am consoled by the fact that Kacey Musgraves is one of her main artists on shuffle, in a mix that also includes 365-days-a-year Christmas songs, Michael Bublé, the Vamps and One Direction. Flo's big dream is to meet One Direction but this is (as I write) an ambition unfulfilled, even though her Daddy is supposed to be able to fix theses things! All attempts have so far failed, despite the best efforts of my friends and fellow Radio 2 DJs Dermot O'Leary, Steve Wright and Sara Cox, but at least Flo did get to meet the Vamps, who were guests at the O2 when Taylor brought her show to London in 2014. And I am happy to report that Flo also loves the music of Beth Nielsen Chapman, a central figure in our lives.

Beth is a truly lovely person and a dynamic and creative force. In addition to winning the Country Music Awards Song of the Year for 'This Kiss', she is a multi-Grammy nominated artist and the writer of songs covered by an amazing array of stars including Bonnie Raitt, Martina McBride, Willie Nelson and Michael McDonald. She is an environmental activist and the creator of a beautiful recent project called *The Mighty Sky*, a beautifully crafted album of songs about the wonders of astronomy, co-written by Beth, songwriter Annie Roboff and Rocky Alvey, director of the Vanderbilt Dyer Observatory in Nashville. The concept has now been translated into a syllabus for schools and Trudie has been at the heart of the project from the start, helping Beth organize concerts, lectures, lessons and events to take the wonders of the universe into the classroom.

Beth has experienced extreme pain in her life. She lost her first husband, Ernest, to cancer in 1994, an emotional trauma that informed the writing of the songs for her album *Sand And Water*, released three years later. The title song is so moving yet inspiring that Elton John chose it to replace 'Candle In The Wind' in the set he performed on his world tour in 1997. Three years later, Beth herself was diagnosed with breast cancer, which through sheer will and determination she successfully fought. She has been a source of inspiration to me in my own battle against the disease in recent years.

When I took Miles with me to America for the first time in 2010, Beth organized a welcoming concert for us at her beautiful Brentwood home. House concerts and 'guitar pulls' are a regular feature of life in Nashville but for Miles and me this was a new and very special experience, with an 'A'-list gathering of Rodney Crowell, Siobhan and Ray Kennedy, Keb Mo, Gary Nicholson, Darden Smith and Mary Gauthier swapping guitars, stories and songs in a joyous and spontaneous evening of amazing music.

Three years later, Beth recreated the evening for us with a line-up that this time included Jason Isbell, Amanda Shires, Kim Carnes, Kim Richey, Angel Snow, John Fullbright and two wonderful English singer-songwriters Chris While and Callaghan. This time we took a camera crew with us, capturing the unique atmosphere for a TV special entitled *Back To Beth's*, made by our production company WBBC. The film was shot by director John Williams, produced by Trudie, edited by Miles, and shown on BBC television in November 2014.

The show also featured Kimmie Rhodes who, to quote Emmylou Harris, 'Has the voice of a beautiful child coming from an old soul. She touches us where the better angels of our nature dwell, and I believe we need that now more than ever.' My family has also been deeply enriched by our friendship with Kimmie.

Miles met Kimmie for the first time when we spent a few days with her and her late husband, Joe Gracey, at their house in the countryside just outside of Austin, Texas, during our time in America together in 2010. Kimmie has a studio there, housed behind the stained glass windows of a beautiful outbuilding at the top of her garden, and had just put the finishing touches to her *Dreams Of Flying* album, produced by her son Gabe. The album includes a sensitive and touching version of Donovan's *Catch The Wind*, which she taught Miles to play on the new guitar Ray Kennedy had helped him choose in Nashville a few days earlier.

Kimmie is from Lubbock in Texas, birthplace of Buddy Holly and the great Joe Ely, such a lovely person, who, with Butch Hancock and their wives, joined us that night for Mexican food and a guitar pull. After dinner, Kimmie's daughter Jolie invited Joe to join her on a version of 'True Love Ways', which, amazingly, he said he had never played before. It took him only a few moments to learn the chord sequence before they performed a beautiful version of that classic Buddy Holly song, with Kimmie singing harmonies and Butch playing Miles's new guitar. He said how much he loved the sound and tone of the guitar and sat picking and strumming it for most of the evening, before passing it around for everyone to sign. It was a truly lovely evening, a very happy memory.

The following day, Miles and I borrowed Kimmie's little white two-seater Mazda sports car for a trip into Austin along Interstate 35. The top was down, the sky was blue, the temperature was close to 100°F and old-time country star Ray Price was blasting from the radio. 'Miles,' I said as we sped through the sunshine, 'it really doesn't get much better than this!' Three years later, my son Dylan was sharing a similar experience with Kimmie, driving her to New Orleans on his own American adventure.

A few days after that first magical house concert at Beth's, Miles and I were invited to attend another fabulous evening at the home of our great friend, publicist Kissy Black. Hosted by her husband, Jeff, it was a 'Stage It' internet event, with performances from another top-of-the-range gathering, which this time included Gretchen Peters and Suzy Bogguss (both of whom took part in our *Back To Beth's* TV show), Matraca Berg and her husband, Jeff Hanna, from the Nitty Gritty Dirt Band, Jessi Alexander and Jon Randall, Grammy-nominated multi-instrumentalist Sam Bush and my Nashville Brother Eric Brace. All played brilliant, heartfelt sets but the revelation of the evening was Mike Farris, who absolutely blew me away. You may not know him, but he is the real thing.

His music is an amazing amalgam of gospel, blues, honky-tonk and Stax-driven soul and his voice is a gift from God. Life for Mike Farris has not been an easy ride. He has battled personal issues and drug addiction that threatened to wreck his world but he has come through them all to emerge as one of the great artists of our time. 'Out of the arms of defeat, he has done a victory lap. He takes people who are hurting, who are broken, who think they are alone and through just the sound of his voice he lets them know they're not ... that's magic,' says

Mary Gauthier. Buddy Miller goes further. 'Mike Farris has enough heart, soul and power to light up a city. He mixes up the elements and turns them into something new, beautiful and uniquely his own'.

Shortly before Miles and I saw him play at Kissy Black's house, Mike had enlisted the help of some of Nashville's top musicians to record a charity EP at the historic Downtown Presbyterian church for the victims of the devastating floods that swept through Tennessee in May 2010. When the Cumberland River burst its banks, the music community was hit particularly hard. Parts of the Grand Ole Opry House were completely submerged and water flooded into the basement of the newly built, state-of-the-art Schermerhorn Symphony Center in downtown Nashville, causing the destruction of two Steinway grand pianos, valued at more than two million dollars.

But for many musicians, the damage at the massive Soundcheck storage facility was the most profound. Many of the major country stars stored their tour equipment and personal instruments there. Between them, Vince Gill, Brad Paisley and Keith Urban lost literally millions of dollars worth of gear, including guitar collections they had taken a lifetime to build. Eric Brace took Miles and me on a tour of some of the flood-damaged areas of town. It was a heartbreaking experience to see the extent of the devastation and realize how many lives had been affected.

Eric is one of my closest friends. He and his wife, Mary Ann, have embraced my family into their home, and when we were filming our *Bob Harris: My Nashville* documentary in 2013, their house became our operational base.

Eric is the boss of Red Beet, an indie record label located across the Cumberland River on the east side of town. East Nashville is very cool indeed. With its rebel musicians, arty vibe, funky venues, trendy coffee shops and vinyl record stores, Eastside is Nashville's very own version of Greenwich Village and the Red Beet catalogue is full of gems by Todd Snider, Elizabeth Cook, Jon Byrd and other free spirits from that colourful, bohemian neighbourhood. While we were there, Eric unveiled his latest project, a folk-opera called *Hangtown Dancehall*, a three-year labour of love co-produced with Washington writer Karl Straub, which they premiered at a sold-out showcase at 3rd and Lindsley, a 400-seater venue in the centre of Nashville.

Inspired by the traditional song 'Sweet Betsy From Pike', it is a musical tale set in the mid-1850s in the wild days of the California gold rush. The sixteen-piece band that brought it to life onstage that night included Austin vocalist Kelly Willis, one-man orchestra Fats Kaplin and Bluegrass star Tim O'Brien. I was so impressed by the whole idea of it that when we returned home I contacted Sir Tim Rice for advice as to how to realize it into a full-blown musical production. Having listened, he described the project as 'muscular and tuneful' and generously offered to spend some time with Eric, who flew to Britain especially to meet him at his favourite restaurant in Hammersmith by the River Thames, where we had a spirited and laughter-filled lunch that lasted well into late afternoon.

Recently, Eric has been working on a passion project – a soulful new album by Jerry Lawson, the long-time lead vocalist with the legendary *a cappella* group The Persuasions. Scan through other Red Beet records and you'll come across a tribute to Tom T. Hall, which Eric produced with his main creative partner, writer, historian and musician Peter Cooper, and Lloyd Green, arguably the finest pedal steel guitar player in the world. It's a project I feel connected to in many ways, not least because Tom T.'s unlikely No.1 single 'I Love' was all over the radio when I first arrived in America with *Whistle Test* in 1974. Entitled *Songs Of Fox Hollow*, the album contains interpretations of Tom T.'s children's songs, including a new version of 'I Love' by Patty Griffin, 'The Mysterious Fox Of Fox Hollow' by Eric and his band Last Train Home, and a totally wonderful version of the impish 'Sneaky Snake', featuring Buddy Miller on lead vocal and the brilliant and distinctive guitar playing of Duane Eddy, the Titan of Twang.

Over the past few years, Duane and his wife, Deed, have joined our closest circle of friends and it has become a tradition for Mark Hagen, Trudie and I to meet them on our first night in Nashville and go out for a curry! I absolutely love these moments, because they give me a chance to hear Duane's stories. It's like talking to my record collection.

As a young rock'n'roll enthusiast in the late 1950s, I was buying some of the best American records ever made. Elvis Presley, Buddy Holly, the Everly Brothers, Chuck Berry, Bo Diddley, Little Richard, Ricky Nelson – these were absolutely magical and mythical names to me growing up in a small town in England – and Duane knew them all.

As my collection grew, Duane's singles became the backbone of it. From 1958–63, he had no less than twenty-one Top-50 singles in the UK and I bought every one of them, first on the London American label, then on RCA. It actually brought a lump to my throat to visit the legendary RCA Studio B with Duane during the filming of the *Bob Harris: My Nashville* documentary to see Miles sitting at the piano Floyd Cramer had played in his 'slip note' style on countless hits recorded there by Roy Orbison, Patsy Cline, Jim Reeves and Elvis.

In the era of the instrumental, Duane's singles were the template, sounding completely different from anything else I'd heard before. He was the first guitarist to have a signature model guitar and he played his Gretch in the deep lower registers accompanied by a chunky sax and the wild yelling of his group the Rebels. The atmosphere he and producer Lee Hazelwood created on those records was electric, pioneering, totally funky and massively influential, and Bruce Springsteen, Hank Marvin, Neil Young and Mark Knopfler are among many musicians who have acknowledged the role Duane's music has played in their lives. The biggest UK hit 'Because They're Young' was even adopted by my friend and fellow Radio 2 DJ Johnnie Walker as his theme tune.

I first met Duane more than forty years ago when he visited Britain to work with Dave Edmunds, another massive fan. He came in for a live conversation on *Whistle Test* and it was great to meet this genuinely modest man and talk about those fabulous early days, and it has been wonderful to see how his popularity has remained throughout the decades since. In 1986, Art of Noise recorded a Grammy-winning version of one of his biggest hits 'Peter Gunn', and the following year he made a record with Jeff Lynne, George Harrison and Paul McCartney. On his last trip to the UK in 2011, Duane released the brilliant *Road Trip* album, produced in Sheffield by Richard Hawley. He also sold out the Royal Festival Hall and played at the Glastonbury Festival. We love Duane in Britain.

In America, he was inducted into the Rock and Roll Hall of Fame in 1994 and the Musicians Hall of Fame in 2008. Recently, he has recorded with Beth Nielsen Chapman and Mary Gauthier, in addition to playing on projects for the Red Beet label. John Fogerty calls Duane 'the first guitar god' and I was deeply honoured to present him with a Lifetime Achievement Award on behalf of the Americana Music Association on the stage of the Ryman Auditorium in 2013.

The Red Beet label office is run by Lindsay Hayes, one of our favourite people in the world. She is truly super-dench! Dylan, in particular, has established a close friendship with Lindsay and her partner, Jesse Lafser, a recording artist and songwriter whose work has been compared to that of Gillian Welch and Mary Gauthier. After Trudie, Miles and Flo had returned to the UK following our 2013 filming trip, they became our East Nashville guides. I'd stayed on to spend a few days with Dylan before he set off on his own amazing three-month adventure across America, which took him to New York, Atlanta and New Orleans with Kimmie Rhodes, and a week in the sunshine at the 30A Music Festival on the northwest coast of Texas with singer-songwriter Callaghan and her husband, Steve Massey.

Steve and I first met when he was working as Head of Events at Cancer Research UK, in charge of a fund-raising project called Sound and Vision (about which more later) and I was massively impressed by his dedication and dynamism. We quickly became good friends and soon he invited Trudie and me to see Callaghan play an acoustic set at a private showcase. It was a difficult gig in front of an unresponsive audience but I thought she handled it brilliantly and I loved the warmth and intelligence of her music. Steve was hugely encouraging and although they had only just become a couple, I could tell how proud he was of her.

As Steve devoted more and more of his time and organizational brilliance to Callaghan's career he would call me on a regular basis for advice and I really enjoyed feeling so connected to them both. She was a huge fan of singer-songwriter Shawn Mullins and sent him some of her demos, asking for advice. To her joy and amazement, he invited her join him in Atlanta to do some recording sessions that led to him producing her album *Life In Full Colour*, which was released in 2011. And when Shawn asked Callaghan to support him on his forthcoming tour, she and Steve moved to America full-time to build her career there. It was a very brave decision and it has been very hard work but it has paid off. She has done gigs in almost every state of the Union, travelling thousands of miles a month to get her music in front of people, playing tiny venues and house concerts, gradually building an amazing database of fans and reinvesting every dollar earned. Crucially, Callaghan and Steve have retained financial and artistic control of her career. I would suggest to any aspiring artist that this is a template to follow, one that so impressed the editors of *Billboard* magazine that they ran a four-page article about Callaghan, unprecedented exposure for a relatively unknown artist. As I write, she has just played a series of headline concerts and released a beautiful new record called 'A History Of Now', fan-funded through a successful Pledge Music campaign. She and Steve have now moved from Atlanta to Nashville, where their apartment acts as a house, a studio, an office and a rehearsal space, their centre of operations. It was also where Dylan spent much of his time during his three months in the States.

It is such great fun being with Dylan. He does, as Steve puts it, have 'great energy'. He is gregarious, knowledgeable and charismatic and the few days we spent exploring Nashville together were very special to both of us. As I'd done with Miles three years earlier, I took him to the home of Alan Messer, with his old, black El Dorado parked outside. The house dates back to the turn of the nineteenth century and sits on an avenue a few blocks from the famed Music Row – and is an extraordinary and eccentric building. When he moved in, Alan took a sledge hammer to the place, knocking the whole of the interior back to its original shell before aiming a super-high velocity water jet at the inside walls, plaster and rubble gushing out of the front door and into skips in the street outside. The result of all this aqua-energy is a space stripped back to the bone – wood framing, beams and original brick visible through the bare, unpainted, rough-hewn walls onto which he has hung examples of his magnificent photographic work. The effect is minimalist, somewhat unsettling and unique.

Alan was with me in the studio for the best part of four years during my time presenting *Whistle Test* in the mid-1970s, taking pictures of all the artists who appeared on the show, in performance, in rehearsal and behind the scenes. He took all of the most stunning stills you see from that time, including Freddie King, Curtis Mayfield, Bob Marley and the Wailers and perhaps the most iconic and well known of them all, a striking black-and-white image of a bandana-wearing Ry Cooder.

Alan began his career as a music photographer working for Dezo Hoffmann in the late 1960s, capturing off-guard moments with The Beatles, the Small Faces, The Rolling Stones and notably Bobbie Gentry, for whom he took the cover photograph for her first album *I'll Never*

Fall In Love Again in 1968. Following his time with *Whistle Test*, he took his entire archive with him and moved to Nashville in 1978, where he became a close friend and confidant of the late Johnny Cash and his wife June, sharing happy and informal times with them in America and Jamaica, capturing many of the best memories on film. Following their deaths, he staged an exhibition of portraits in tribute to them in Memphis in 2005, to rave reviews.

Leafing through his collection of contact sheets is an amazing experience, a gallery of the recent history of rock and country music. He sees the world in a unique way through the lens of the camera that never leaves his side. He has worked on many album shoots through the years with such as Lucinda Williams, Tia McGraff and Kimmie Rhodes, and in 1988 won a Grammy for his silkscreen for the O'Kanes' album *Tired Of Running*. Despite the fact that he has been in Nashville for more than thirty-five years, Alan has hardly picked up even a trace of an American accent. He is a proud English genius abroad.

The following evening, Dylan and I went to the Bluebird Cafe, where Callaghan was taking part in an 'in the round' songwriters' workshop. Situated in an unassuming strip mall a few miles from Downtown, the Bluebird has become a Nashville institution, an intimate venue holding less than a hundred people where songwriters form a circle in the centre of the floor, playing together and exchanging the stories behind their songs, audience participation encouraged. The selection process is totally democratic, mixing established hit makers with young hopefuls, a place where budding songwriters can cut their teeth. Kathy Mattea was the first major star to be identified with the Bluebird and she still makes regular guest appearances to this day. Country mega-star Garth Brooks was actually discovered there, filling in for a writer who missed the gig, and Taylor Swift played at the Bluebird way before she signed to Big Machine and hit the charts.

With its unique atmosphere and historical significance, the Bluebird has also become one of the main locations for the ABC TV drama series *Nashville*, the popularity of which has seen sightseers and music fans from all over the world flocking to the venue, creating queues round the block and a demand for tickets they are struggling to cope with. Initially, many of the scenes for *Nashville* were actually filmed there, but when the disruption became too much, ABC simply built a virtual

Bluebird Cafe in one of the two vast hangars that house the film sets. They have perfectly recreated the interior of the cafe and the minute attention to detail is absolutely awesome. Every bulb, bottle and bar stool has been exactly reproduced, as I discovered when Dylan and I were given a tour of the film lot by one of the major stars of the series, Sam Palliado.

Sam is a young Cornish actor and musician who is living the dream. Having appeared on British television in the Sky comedy drama series *Little Crackers* and with Matt LeBlanc and Stephen Mangan in *Episodes*, he applied online for a part in *Nashville*, sending some songs and a short section of dialogue he'd recorded in a couple of hours on the computer in his bedroom. It worked, and within days he found himself on a flight, heading to Los Angeles for an audition. He was nervous and excited but one look was enough. 'Are you Sam Palladio?' asked the casting director when he walked into his office. 'You are *so* hired!'

Sam is a genuinely modest and lovely person, as we discovered when Mark Hagen invited him to perform a session for *Bob Harris Country* in 2012 at Audio Productions, our Music Row studio of choice, which is where our friendship began.

In *Nashville*, Sam plays the part of Texan musician Gunnar Scott, a role that has completely changed his life. The series has become a phenomenon in America, propelling its cast to superstardom and fast-tracking them onto the stages of the Ryman and the Grand Ole Opry. In a town usually blasé about its superstars, Sam is constantly stopped for autographs and selfies everywhere he goes by fans, with whom he is kind, smiling and generous. He says that being asked for pictures and autographs by his country music heroes and superstars such as Brad Paisley and Carrie Underwood completely blows his mind!

During our visit to the *Nashville* set, Sam took us to meet actor and musician Charles Esten, who plays the character Deacon Claybourne. He was in his trailer, strumming his acoustic guitar and practising a song for a scene he was filming in a few hours' time. The quality of the soundtrack is a key factor in the success of the series: producer T Bone Burnett and musical director Buddy Miller encourage the top writers in town to submit original material and the fact that the actors actually sing and play these new songs themselves, rather than miming to recordings, is crucial to the authenticity and credibility of their performances. As we sat talking on that late-November afternoon, Charles put down his guitar for a few moments to muse on the impact the series was having on his life. 'You'll never guess what I'll be doing on Friday,' he said. 'I'm going to be turning on the Christmas lights at Graceland, fake snow and everything. It's all totally surreal!'

The more I became inspired by the city of Nashville and the people I was meeting, the more I began to talk about them, on my radio programmes and to my friends in Britain. Robert Plant, in particular, was fascinated by my description of the Nashville music community and asked me to make up a few CD compilations of some of my favourite artists.

He told me he'd been driving home through the Worcestershire countryside one July evening, listening to my show on Radio 2, when I played a track by Alison Krauss. He'd never heard her before but was so stunned by Alison's voice that he'd pulled over to the side of the road, turned up the volume, stepped out of his car and stood under the stars listening to her beautiful music drifting into the warm summer air. 'It was', he said, 'like hearing a sound from another planet.'

As well as being blessed with the voice of an angel, Alison is a world-class violin player and a wonderful producer. She is quirky and funny and the warm, gentle sound she creates has won her no less than twenty-seven Grammy awards, as a solo artist and with her band Union Station. She is America's most successful contemporary Bluegrass star.

During the past fourteen years, Alison and I have recorded many sessions and interviews together, and the next time Al Booth and I were at Audio Productions, she joined us to play a new acoustic set, arriving with the surprising and intriguing news that she and Robert had been discussing the possibility of working together. Initially, it seemed an unlikely combination but she explained that her older brother, Viktor, was a massive Led Zeppelin fan and that she had grown up with the sound of Robert's voice echoing round the family home. I felt excited, imagining the blend their vocal styles would create. The album they were planning to make turned out to be one of the most successful of their respective careers, the award-winning *Raising Sand*.

The catalyst for the project was producer T Bone Burnett, with whom Alison had worked on the old-time music soundtrack for the film *O Brother, Where Art Thou?* Released in 2000, *O Brother* proved to be an absolute blockbuster, selling more than seven million copies, inspiring and profoundly influencing a whole new generation of young, roots-based musicians like Mumford & Sons and Old Crow Medicine Show to make natural, organic music. 'It was like a depth charge,' T Bone explained to me a few years later. '... and all the bubbles are now coming to the surface.'

Shortly before *Raising Sand* was released, Robert told me that he and Alison were planning a short promotional tour in America and that he would love me to go to one of the gigs. Looking at the dates, I realized that their proposed appearance at the New Orleans Jazz and Heritage Festival was four days after my wedding anniversary, on 25th April 2008. 'That's it!' said Robert. 'You and Trudie have to be there!' We invited Roy and Karen Webber to join us on what turned out to be an incredible few days.

Robert, his manager, Nicola Powell, and his tour entourage were staying at a hotel in the centre of New Orleans and we arranged to meet them there on the morning of the gig. When we arrived, the receptionist told us that they'd gone to a local cafe a few blocks away for breakfast. As it happened, we didn't need the directions they'd left for us because, as we walked down the street, we could already see the crowd of people gathering outside the cafe, none of them more than twenty-five years old, faces pressed up against the windows.

There is a whole new, young audience for Robert's music in the States, through his work with Alison, with Buddy Miller and the Band of Joy and his latest group, The Sensational Space Shifters. There was even a dedicated Led Zeppelin station on the New Orleans radio dial and when we left the cafe to head for the tour bus he was immediately swamped by excited fans who simply could not believe they were in this moment.

The New Orleans Jazz and Heritage Festival has come a long way since its modest beginnings in the early 70s when Mahalia Jackson and Duke Ellington played in front of no more than a few hundred people. Each year since then it has grown to become more and more important, expanding into the massive and truly eclectic international gathering it is today. Robert and Alison's set was part of a week-long schedule of music and events that pumped more than $300 million into the local Louisiana economy, revenue that was seen as a hallmark of the area's recovery after the devastation of Hurricane Katrina, the scars from which could still be seen in parts of the city – bleak rows of empty, flood-wrecked houses, their contaminated contents piled up in mountains at the end of each deserted block.

The main concert stage was located at the Fair Grounds Race Course and as we pulled into the site it was clear that this was no ordinary festival. The dry, dusty backstage compound was huge, housing the production offices, trailers, dressing rooms, bathrooms, chill-out areas, catering facilities, generators and general infrastructure needed to support an amazing line-up of stars, a bill that featured (among many others) Stevie Wonder, Santana, Randy Newman, Al Green, Diana Krall, Elvis Costello and Billy Joel alongside local Louisiana legends Dr John, Allen Toussaint and the Neville Brothers.

Shortly before Robert and Alison began their set we made our way to the side of the stage where we met Sheryl Crow, who was on later that afternoon. I like Sheryl very much. She is a real trouper, a performer who gives it everything she's got. Over the past few years, she's embraced and been embraced by country music and recently came in to play an acoustic set for *Bob Harris Country* while on a whirlwind promotional tour of the UK, a moment that also provided a wonderful and unexpected reunion with her accompanying guitarist Audley Freed, whom I'd previously met in the 1990s when he was in the band Cry Of Love. 'I don't want anyone to think I've jumped on the country bandwagon,' Sheryl told me. 'I've always loved the music. The Nashville music community is the best there is.'

We stood talking for a few minutes next to the side-stage sound monitor desk, looking out at the vast festival arena in front of us, and what a sight it was. The crowd seemed to go on forever, a throng of thousands of smiley, happy people in a swirling sea of colour; flags and banners waving, blown by the gentle breeze on that warm, sunny afternoon. It was beautiful to see and as Robert and Alison began their set, Trudie and I made our way out into the crowd and onto the grass bank in front of the stage to soak in the atmosphere.

The previous year, I had recorded an interview with Robert for a documentary I was making with my brilliant editor Neil Myners called *Who Knows Where The Time Goes*, which won our production company WBBC a prestigious Sony Silver Award. The programme told the story of the life of Sandy Denny and was broadcast on Radio 2 to mark the thirtieth anniversary of her death. Sandy had begun her career in the late 1960s as the lead singer with Fairport Convention, the group that basically invented a whole new genre of music – folk rock. She went on to make a series of sublime solo albums and was voted top female singer in the *Melody Maker* poll in 1970, the year Robert first won the award for Male Vocalist of the Year, and he was a massive fan.

'I remember how proud I was when we were both voted top vocalists in our field. We ended up on page five of the *Daily Mirror*, hugging each other and having a great photograph. She and I gravitated towards each other. We were such young souls to be in the middle of it all.'

English folk music was always an important ingredient of the Led Zeppelin sound and Sandy was unique in being the only guest outside of the group ever to have appeared on any of their albums. The track she recorded was 'The Battle Of Evermore' on *Led Zeppelin 4* and Robert described the thrill he'd felt hearing their voices blending together for the first time.

'When Jimmy and I began writing "The Battle Of Evermore", it was obvious it was a two-voice part. To hear her first vocal response was one of those great moments when you've written something and somebody takes it to a whole new place. We had to get it so that the one voice cascaded over the other one without actually ever dominating. It was beautiful; a spectacular moment for both of us.'

Robert and Alison also touched the heights in New Orleans on that glorious afternoon, playing through the songs on *Raising Sand* and backed by a band as good as anything I've ever heard – T Bone Burnett and Buddy Miller on guitars, Dennis Crouch on stand-up bass, Stuart Duncan on fiddle, mandolin and banjo and Jay Bellerose on drums, Alison's violin playing weaving patterns across the tapestry of sound. It was both dreamy and funky, and as Trudie and I lost ourselves in the music, thoughts of Robert's work with Sandy Denny flooded into my head and the amazing combination of their voices, a sound he'd found so inspiring. At that exact moment, he announced to the crowd that he and Alison were going to sing a Led Zeppelin classic. When 'The Battle Of Evermore' began, I thought I was going to cry. Trudie and I hugged each other. 'We are blessed to be here,' she said. And she was right.

TEN

A Rocky Road

THE TIME WITH ROBERT PLANT AND OUR FRIENDS ROY AND KAREN IN New Orleans had come as a much-needed boost; a happy moment in the middle of a period in my life that sometimes took me to the edge of despair.

Trudie and I were making our way through the dark, busy streets of Soho, heading towards the Borderline, a music venue just off Charing Cross Road in London, where we were staging a showcase to mark the release of a new Americana CD I'd compiled as part of an on-going *Bob Harris Presents* series, all packed full of my favourite music. It was 2nd February 2007 (my daughter Emily's birthday), and a very important event for us, one we'd been planning for weeks. Three of the acts on the compilation – Eve Selis, Grayson Capps and Alana Levandoski – were playing live and we'd invited Bob Paterson, Lisa Redford and other friends and key music industry people to join us. The gig was a sell-out, so we knew there would be a great atmosphere, and I couldn't wait to get up onstage and get the evening started.

We were running slightly late and, as we hurried through the rush-hour throng in Soho Square, my mobile phone lit up. It was a call from Miles, who was back at home. He sounded flustered and alarmed. 'The Health Centre just phoned,' he told me. 'They wanted to speak to you. They've given me the number of a hospital and said you have to call straight away to make an appointment.' I could hear how worried he was. 'Are you ill?' he asked me. 'What's going on?' I think I succeeded in sounding reasonably calm and reassuring but my mind was starting to race. I tried to call the hospital from the middle of the street but I couldn't get through, so Trudie and I decided to head straight to the Borderline and use a landline to phone the hospital from there.

We arrived to find a large crowd of people outside the venue, many of them gathered round a big old Volvo that Eve Selis and her band were using as a tour bus. The front window had been smashed and Eve was standing amid the broken glass, stressed and animated, explaining that the car had been broken into during the band's soundcheck and some of their equipment had been stolen. As we stopped to sympathize, I felt totally distracted. I really felt for Eve, it was a horrible thing to happen, but I was absolutely desperate to get inside and make that call to the hospital.

A couple of weeks earlier, I'd noticed a trace of blood in my urine. At the time I didn't think anything of it. I had been feeling tired, but we work very hard, so that's not surprising; other than that I felt well. Sensibly, Trudie had insisted that I get it checked out, so I booked myself in for a routine blood test at my local health centre in Abingdon. It was a decision that probably saved my life.

The manager of the Borderline let me use his office phone but there was no privacy at all, and in the middle of the pre-gig chaos the news from the hospital was not good. My blood test had revealed an abnormally high level of Prostate-Specific Antigen, a protein that is produced by the prostate gland. The level of PSA in the blood is often elevated in men with prostate cancer. A healthy reading is anything below 4.0 ng/mL: mine was 22. The hospital told me that there was no time to lose and that they wanted me there at 9 o'clock on Monday morning to undergo a biopsy to determine the extent of the problem. I was adamant that I would not be attending, that I just had to take a few days to work everything out. It was a deeply uncomfortable conversation and I absolutely was not ready for this.

The Borderline was now packed with people and by the time I put the phone down we were late with the start of the show. People were coming in and out of the office urging me to hurry up. Alana was already at the side of the stage waiting to go on but I was by no means sure that I was even close to being able to do this. How the hell was I going to walk out in front of the crowd and put aside all the worries going through my head?

'You've got to do it,' said Trudie. 'We can't pull out now and let everyone down, just do it! You'll get into it, the gig will take your mind off everything and we can talk about it all later on.'

As always, she was right. I took a deep breath, gathered my thoughts and made my way through the corridors, out onto the stage and into the spotlight, summoning up the smile with which I greeted the audience. The show must go on.

The evening was a blur, to be honest, as were the next few days. I immediately booked myself in to see Michael Robertson, my doctor for the past twenty years. He referred me to a specialist and while I was waiting for the appointment, I had a top-to-toe medical. The readings were frightening. My PSA level had already risen to 34 and I was beginning to feel more and more tired. I was desperately trying to tell myself that basically things were OK, that the biopsy results would be fine, but I was wrong.

A prostate biopsy is not a glamorous experience. It's messy, bloody and extremely painful. The procedure uses Transrectal Ultrasound Imaging to guide ten needles through the lining of the rectal wall and into the prostate. Each needle takes a sample of tissue, each sample is analysed, producing a rating out of 10, known as the Gleason scale: the higher the number, the more threatening the cancer. It was with horror that I discovered mine was a 9 and it was clear that I was in serious trouble. What's more, my consultant told me that I had a particularly aggressive type of cancer and there was a strong chance some cells may have escaped the prostate capsule and got out into my system. If they hadn't, we were talking about cancer management. If they had, we were talking about a few months ...

Trudie was waiting in the hospital reception area and as I emerged, ashen-faced, from the consultant's surgery, she ran towards me. We just held each other there for a few minutes in a state of shock, trying to let it all sink in. Miles, Dylan and Flo were waiting for us when we got back home and we sat down with them in the kitchen to explain, as best we could, what was happening. They listened attentively to everything we said, after which Dylan had a serious question to ask. 'What's for supper?' Children have a great way of putting things into perspective!

It all felt surreal as I paced around our house. I couldn't think what to do with myself, so I decided to head over to my studio and listen to some music. The studio sits under an apple tree at the bottom of our garden and is the centre of my creative world. It houses my CD collection, most of my vinyl albums and is where I do all my writing, my listening and where I build my programmes. I make my radio documentaries there and it's also where Miles and I film our WBBC *Under The Apple Tree* sessions. It's a very personal space and I must've made that walk across the garden hundreds and hundreds of times. This time, though, it felt completely different. As the studio came into view the enormity of what was ahead of us finally hit me; the uncertainty, the lack of any sense of control of the future. What if we hadn't caught it in time? What if I'd only got a few months left? I broke down, collapsing onto the grass under the weight of it all. I sobbed my heart out, I just couldn't help myself. It felt like my whole world had crashed into bits. I only knew that I was going to have to put every ounce of energy I had into fighting for my life. As my mind began to swirl into panic I suddenly remembered the famous John Lennon quote: 'Life is what happens when you're busy making other plans'. How bloody right he was.

The mood in the house was sombre, to say the least. Trudie told me that she felt completely helpless. 'I can fix most things,' she said, 'but I can't fix this.' But then she had a brilliant idea. She remembered how fastidious Mohamed Al Fayed had been when she worked for him in the early 90s, how he was a stickler for hygiene and always had a medical team on hand. She thought that maybe he'd have a contact who might be able to help us, so she called him and explained my diagnosis. He was instantly sympathetic and massively helpful.

'Give me five minutes,' he said. Exactly five minutes later he called back. 'I've arranged an appointment for Bob with Professor Roger Kirby, one of the top prostate cancer specialists in the world. He's a very busy man, so make sure that Bob is on time for the appointment tomorrow ... And Trudie, be sure to tell him to shave his fucking beard off!!'

The next few days were fraught and hectic as I went in and out of hospitals and clinics for various CTI and MRI scans and blood tests. Finally, with all the images, X-rays and notes in front of us on his desk, Professor Kirby was ready to give me the results. 'You are a very lucky man,' he said. 'We've literally caught it just in time.' I was overjoyed. I knew the next few months would be testing but suddenly we were talking management, not termination.

There were now some difficult choices to be made and we began to discuss the options. I could have what is known as a radical prostatectomy to completely remove the prostate and the cancer with it. This sounded like a comprehensive answer but there can be serious consequences such as incontinence and a loss of sexual feeling. There is a horrible finality about the phrase 'permanent erectile dysfunction', not a great prospect, I decided. Another possibility was brachytherapy, where small radioactive seeds are inserted directly into the tumour, but I didn't want that either. In the end, I opted for eight weeks of radiotherapy, preceded by a course of hormone therapy, which replaces the male hormones in the body with female hormones. It's a process that effectively switches off the production of the testosterone that feeds the cancer, thereby reducing the tumour to a size that can then be zapped by the radiotherapy lasers. The hormone therapy is administered by regular injections into the stomach, first with a small injection to anesthetize the area, then with a needle that, to me, looked large enough to pierce my stomach wall.

The side effects were much more profound than I expected. As my breasts began to grow, my waistline began to thicken and my moods began to change, I realized the extent to which the treatment was mounting a major attack on my sense of my own masculinity. My emotions were all over the place and always much closer to the surface than I wanted them to be. I was suffering random hot flushes, waking up in the middle of the night drenched in sweat ('menopausal' Trudie called it). I was up and down to the loo and constantly worried about being caught short, not a good look! I was starting to feel seriously down, and more and more tired. Even a family holiday at Disneyland Paris didn't lift my mood. All I wanted to do while we were there was sleep.

I was determined to keep working right up to the start of my radiotherapy and everyone at Radio 2 was massively supportive. Lesley Douglas, the network controller, told me to take as much time off as I needed, that I wouldn't lose a penny in wages. Phil Swern, Al Booth and my production team were wonderfully flexible, moving recording and session dates around, sometimes at the last minute, to accommodate my various hospital visits. Johnnie Walker had been through his own extreme cancer experience and regularly called me with words of encouragement, which I really appreciated. I did my last show on 4th August 2007, with Joe Bonamassa playing live in the studio, before I took four months off to get myself well again.

Life became a routine and I surrendered to the process. Monday to Friday I caught the same morning train to London, arriving at the Cancer Clinic at 11.30. External beam radiotherapy has to be carefully planned for it to be as effective as possible and I'd spent a lot of time with my oncologist and guardian angel Heather Payne to make sure everything was right. I had a final CT scan, which took X-rays of the exact area to be treated, and got three tiny tattoos on my torso to enable the radiographers to position me accurately in the machine for the radiotherapy beams to have maximum impact. After all this initial preparation, the sessions themselves only lasted a few minutes, so I was able to leave the clinic just after noon, with the whole of the rest of the day ahead of me. I hadn't had free time like this for years and I began to enjoy the feeling. Heather had told me how much more effective radiotherapy can be if backed up by exercise, so I started walking the two miles or so back to Paddington station each day, making sure to plan the route for emergency toilet stops!

With time on my hands I could see friends for lunch at my favourite tea house, Patisserie Valerie on Marylebone High Street, and I regularly met my first wife, Sue, for a coffee at a sweet cafe overlooking the canal at Little Venice, before catching the train back home. Sue and I have known each other for more than fifty years now and throughout this whole time she has been one of the central and most important people in my life. It was lovely to have these moments to relax and catch up on news about our girls, their partners and their children. Miri's daughters, Marnie and Alana, were now twelve and ten and, following her break-up with their father, Miri had met a new partner, her future husband, Graeme. Emily and her husband, John, had married on 30th June 2004 in a beautiful wedding ceremony held on a windswept Holkham Beach on the North Norfolk coast – one of my favourite parts of the world – and Ems also had two girls: Niamh, who was six, and toddler Ysobel. They all live close to one another in North London and are a tight family unit, with Sue and her partner, Dixie, an integral part of the grandchildren's daily lives.

As I write, Sue is now seventy, but she hasn't retired. She is still doing what she was doing then and has always done: caring for people. She is a social worker at St Mary's Hospital in Paddington, helping elderly patients during their rehabilitation after serious illness, offering advice and support and, if needs be, visiting them at home to check on their welfare and safety. She is a force for good in the world and I always love seeing her.

Despite the rigours of my treatment, I have happy memories of those few weeks. The weather was mostly warm and sunny, I was getting lots of exercise and I was enjoying the freedom from the pressures of work. I couldn't believe I was feeling so well, better than I had for months. I was beginning to feel like a fraud! Gradually, though, the impact of the radiotherapy started to kick in.

The effects were cumulative. The further into the treatment I got, the more bleak and sluggish I felt. As the exhaustion grew, I stopped wanting to see anyone and stopped exercising. All I wanted to do was get home and go to bed. The skin on my stomach was dry and sore, I lost my appetite and energy for life and began to plunge into a horrible depression. I hated myself for being so sluggish, weak and pathetic but all I wanted to do was pull the covers up over my head and shut out the world.

I was feeling particularly gloomy one evening, propped up on my pillows as usual and staring blankly at the TV screen, half-asleep, as Dylan wandered into the bedroom to see me. 'What are you watching?' he asked as he sat down. I wasn't even sure. It turned out to be a Nigella Lawson cookery programme. As we focused on the screen we saw her melt some butter, dark chocolate and golden syrup in a saucepan, stirring in broken biscuits and marshmallows before pouring the thick, bubbling mixture into a foil tray, spooning on a final covering of melted chocolate for good measure.

'Pop it into the fridge for a couple of hours to let it set,' she explained, 'and you have rocky road, the perfect simple snack.'

'Oh wow! That looks amazing!' said Dylan, and he was right. Even with my diminishing appetite, my mouth was watering.

'I'll make you some!' I told him. 'When you get home from school tomorrow, we'll all have rocky road for tea.'

Dylan looked incredulous 'What, seriously?' he smiled. 'You, cooking?!'

I am not known as a chef. I occasionally do a fry-up or make the children sandwiches, but generally I only use the kitchen when Trudie's not around because she gets so irritated with my ineptitude and the general mess I usually make. Nevertheless, the thought of creating a delicious dish for everyone was making me feel genuinely excited and on my way back from the clinic the following day, I called into our local village shop and picked up all the ingredients. When I got in I downloaded the recipe from the internet and set to work and by the time Trudie appeared in the doorway after the school run, there was a tray of rocky road in the middle of the kitchen table, next to a pot of tea, places laid for everyone. It was the best evening we'd all spent together for a long time and I felt so happy that I was able to do something for the family again instead of them having to do everything for me. In retrospect, it seems such a mundane event, but it was a turning point. I realized I could not allow myself to be defeated by my illness, that I had to start to fight.

The first thing I addressed was my fitness. I was determined to work off my lethargy and 'man boobs' and begin to like myself again. I pulled the exercise bike out of the garage, bought a mat and some weights and devised a workout, building up slowly. I climbed up and down our stairs over and over again, using the rails on the landing for push-ups. I made notes in my diary and later bought a fitness app for my iPhone to keep a detailed daily record of my progress. Trudie bought me a free-weights bench for Christmas and by the time I returned to work at Radio 2 at the end of 2007, I was looking and feeling much better, the effects on my radiotherapy receding.

I was still a long way from getting the all-clear, however, so to further help my recovery the late, great Jon Lord recommended that I have a consultation with the naturopath Bob Jacobs, founder of the Society for Complimentary Medicine. The Society was a beneficiary of the annual Sunflower Jam fundraisers – rousing rock concerts featuring Jon, members of Deep Purple and their friends and organized by Jon's wife, Vicky, and her sister Jackie, who's married to Ian Paice, the drummer in the band. Sunflower Jam was set up 'to work towards providing access for all to complimentary and integrated treatments in the fight against cancer and other diseases by funding and supporting research, treatment and education', a noble vision that I have supported as compere of some the events.

The results of the blood tests Bob carried out on me were not great, but I completely bought into the idea that what the radiotherapy had taken out of my system, he could put back in, through minerals and vitamins. He told me to think of every day as a battle in my fight with cancer. 'Win the daily battles and you'll win the war,' he said. I found him sincere and inspiring and a few minutes later I left his office with a bag bursting with jars and containers full of all sorts of supplements and boosters and a bill for almost £500. It was just about the best money I've ever spent. I began to feel the benefits almost immediately and for more than two years Bob Jacobs became a vital part of my recovery regime.

My daughter Mirelle was also a wonderful source of support. She had studied homeopathy for several years, graduating with a degree in 2002 before founding a community practice in Primrose Hill in London, offering alternative therapies and advice on health issues and diet. Unlike conventional medicine, homeopathy takes a holistic view, looking at the physical, spiritual, mental and emotional factors affecting a person, so Miri was very tuned in to what was going on in my head.

A few months after my diagnosis she had told me she was expecting a baby and I was absolutely thrilled to hear the news. She'd had a tough time following the break-up of her relationship with the father of her two daughters, sometimes struggling with the balance between the demands of bringing up Marnie and Alana as a single mother and her restless ambition to establish her career. Now her life had stabilized, anchored by her new partner Graeme, later to be her husband, a man who truly loves her.

Shortly before she'd discovered she was pregnant, Miri had committed her medical skills to the NHS, enrolling on a four-year course of nurse training, initially working in the accident and emergency department of her local hospital, sometimes seven days straight without a break. She was now well into her pregnancy and at the end of one particularly stressful twelve-hour shift, she began to feel seriously ill. She was rushed into an emergency ward at the Elizabeth Garrett Anderson Hospital in central London, where she gave birth to a baby girl on 11th March 2008. Olivia was four months premature and weighed less than 740 grams.

Within moments the tiny baby was put on a ventilator to keep her alive. Seventy-two hours later, she had a massive brain haemorrhage – a Grade 4 intraventricular bleed. The damage was potentially so profound that the doctors warned Miri and Graeme that, even if she survived, Olivia was likely to be severely disabled. The news was terrible but there was worse to come. Shortly after Trudie and I returned from a trip to New Orleans, Olivia was rushed to Great Ormond Street Hospital suffering from Necrotizing Enterocolitis, a life-threatening disease that necessitated a massive operation to remove a part of her bowel. Her condition was so serious that no one expected her even to last the night. Prayers were said at her bedside. Yet, against all the odds, Olivia survived, almost motionless in her incubator, wired up and helpless, hanging on to life by a thread. Miri moved into the hospital to be with her and, over time, she very slowly began to improve and gain strength. For me, in my own battle with illness, her fighting spirit was an inspiration. After three months she came off her ventilator, after six months she was allowed home. The doctors told Graeme that it was unprecedented for a baby to survive what she'd been through, but survive she did.

At exactly this time, I got a call from Steve Massey, in his role of head of special events at Cancer Research UK. He'd heard that I was receiving treatment and wondered if I would be willing to appear at a charity fundraiser he was organizing, an annual event called Sound and Vision, held at the world-famous Abbey Road studios in London, where The Beatles did the bulk of their recordings. He said he'd like me to join the founding patron of the event, Sir George Martin, onstage for a few minutes to talk about the impact of cancer on my life.

Sound and Vision takes the form of a live auction of rock and pop memorabilia donated by some of the world's biggest music stars, photographers and artists and Studio 1 was transformed into a colourful and magnificent art gallery for the event. Striking, iconic images, paintings and photographs of icons such as David Bowie, Jimi Hendrix, John Lennon and Deborah Harry lined the studio walls, alongside gold discs, signed guitars and other unique rock'n'roll souvenirs. The Brand New Heavies and 10cc played storming live sets, there was a champagne bar in the middle of the studio and, as the auction got started and the evening went on, the atmosphere became more and more rowdy. I took to the stage, expecting to struggle for attention, but as I began to speak the room fell silent and I knew my words were having an impact. There is no cause closer to my heart than the work to find a cure for cancer and my emotions were still very raw as I stood up there in the spotlight, urging people to donate. In the end, once the online auction revenue and other donations were added to the total, the event raised more than £165,000 for Cancer Research UK and I was very proud to have been a part of such a worthwhile and wonderful evening.

A few days later Steve was back in touch. He asked if I would consider permanently joining Sir George as co-patron of Sound and Vision and I was honoured to accept his invitation. He also invited Trudie and our production company to be at the centre of the organization of the next event, with specific responsibility for artist recruitment, and we were thrilled to get involved. Being an integral part of such an important initiative was a hugely exciting prospect. Our production company WBBC was about to move into new offices in our village (previously the HQ of our local Truck Festival) and the wonderful Genevieve Wills (now an Ambassador Relations Manager at UNICEF) had joined us to work on some of our bigger projects and we soon set up a meeting with the special events unit at CRUK. Steve Massey was joined by Jacqueline Fitzgerald, Kirsty Jones and Ali Cleveland and we immediately knew that we would love working with this sincere and caring team.

As we began to put together the plans for Sound and Vision 2009 we had lunch with Giles Martin to talk about his dad's involvement; we liaised with Drive, the production company responsible for staging the event; we invited Roy Webber and his design team at The Works to get involved with the look and the branding; and we called our friend Colin Hall in Liverpool to ask him if he could locate some rare Beatles memorabilia for our auction. Colin and his wife, Sylvia, work for the National Trust as custodians of John Lennon's childhood home, Mendips, and 20 Forthlin Road, the small terraced house where Paul McCartney lived as a child and where more than 180 of the Beatles' hits were written.

Both houses have been meticulously restored to the homes that Lennon and McCartney would recognize from their younger years, using photographs and eyewitness accounts to replicate the original fixtures, fittings and furniture – and walking in was like stepping back into another era. There was a picture of John that particularly resonated with my own childhood memories of the 1950s, wearing his school cap, blazer and short trousers, long socks pulled up to his knees, satchel on his shoulder. I've got a picture of me looking exactly the same. All kids looked the same in those days. I loved seeing copies of some of his favourite vinyl 45s, scattered on the bed in his little box room at the top of the stairs. There was 'Baby Face' by Little Richard, 'Tom Dooley' by Lonnie Donegan, and 'Only The Lonely' by Roy Orbison, and positioned on the shelf behind John's bed head, next to a somewhat battered Gallotone Champion Guitar, was a magazine of the time, opened at a colour picture of Elvis. It's giving me shivers just thinking about it. Colin recently told me that when Bob Dylan had visited Mendips he also stood there in silence for several minutes before declaring 'It was cold in my bedroom too'.

Visiting the houses with Colin and Sylvia was a fascinating experience that gave me the inspiration for our award-winning WBBC documentary *The Day John Met Paul*, broadcast on Radio 2, for which I recorded a major interview with Paul McCartney. The programme told the story of Paul's first encounter with the Quarrymen at a summer fête held in a field next to St Peter's Church in Woolton, a leafy suburb of Liverpool, where they were playing among the fairground stalls and tea tents on a makeshift stage on the back of a flat-bed truck. Paul was only fifteen and he'd ridden down to the fête on his bike especially to see them play and to try and meet their rebellious and charismatic lead singer, John Lennon. After their set, the band invited Paul to hang out and jam with them backstage before their gig at the church hall later that evening. There was a lot of banter but they were knocked out that Paul could play piano and knew all the words to Eddie Cochran's 'Twenty Flight Rock', which he played on John's acoustic guitar. Paul told me that when he handed the guitar back to John he got a whiff of his 'beery breath' and was not impressed – 'They had a gig to do!' – but they hit it off immediately and two weeks later, John invited Paul to join him in the group. Shortly afterwards George Harrison also became a member and the rest, as they say, is history. No one knew it at the time but the events of that day, 6th July 1957, were to change music forever.

It was fascinating hearing Paul tell the stories of his time with John at Mendips. As you approach the house, there is a small, glass-encased vestibule outside the front door where the two of them used to rehearse, with just enough room for them to stand shoulder to shoulder, their guitars pointing in opposite directions as they played and sang. It was a space that gave them a unique and very 'live' sound, their harmonized voices bouncing off the glass surfaces all around them. Paul became more and more animated as he told us how much John loved the sound in there and as I listened a huge penny dropped in my mind. I'd always thought that the slap-echo that John favoured so often (listen to 'Come Together' or almost everything on the *Rock'N'Roll* album for reference) was his attempt to recreate the vocal sound of 'Be-Bop-A-Lula' by Gene Vincent, one of his favourite records. Not so. It was an attempt to recreate the voice sound he'd experienced with Paul, all those pre-Beatles years ago, in the vestibule at Mendips.

The Day John Met Paul was turning out to be a fantastic project and as well as spending quality time with Paul, Neil Myners and I also recorded a wonderful interview with the surviving members of the Quarrymen in my studio, our conversation underlining to me the significance of Lonnie Donegan's cover of the Leadbelly song 'Rock Island Line', which had hit the UK Top 10 in January 1956. To my mind, it is without doubt one of the most important British records ever made.

'Before then we were listening to things like "How Much Is That Doggie In The Window?" and "The Ballad Of Davy Crockett",' they told me. 'But this record had an energy that was totally different from anything we'd heard before.'

It was a record that changed everything, a pathway into rock'n'roll that inspired the Quarrymen and a whole new generation of post-war teenagers to thrash out a DIY music style called skiffle, the punk of its day. 'We were a garage band without the garage!' they laughed.

We'd also recorded a long conversation with Cynthia Lennon at her son Julian's home in Chelsea; it was the first time she and Trudie had met. We'd taken Miles, Dylan and Flo with us and it was a wonderful family afternoon, the beginning of a friendship between us all that deepens more and more as time goes by. In recent years we have spent holidays with her at her island home in Mallorca (where some of this book was written) and we love her very much. With her strong connections to Abbey Road, we invited Cyn to Sound and Vision and, as we worked with the CRUK team to draw up a shortlist of favourite artists, I composed a letter to Paul McCartney, asking him if he would also like join us for the show.

A lot of things have to come together for an artist to appear. They've got to want to do it – not a given in this charity-saturated age – and they have to be free to do it. The bigger the stars the more in demand they are, constantly being approached to put their names to all sorts of different projects, so diaries tend to be full as much as eighteen months ahead. If they're not touring, they'll probably have to pull a band together and rehearse. With the show on a Thursday evening and full run-through the day before, it's a big commitment, particularly to create the unique performances the event became known for. It's a charity, so who's going to cover for the time and expenses? There are some very big hitters in the room on the night, paying £200 a ticket to be there – will they all be happy with the bill? There were a lot of things to consider, especially as Paul had replied to say the event was during half-term and he would be away with his daughter, but gradually we settled on one name we all agreed we wanted.

I first met Paul Weller when he appeared on *Whistle Test* with his band The Jam in 1977, and we've remained friends ever since. We'd appeared together at 'Dear Mr Fantasy', a beautiful concert held at the Roundhouse in London in 2007, organized with the help of Trudie by Aninha Capaldi in tribute to her late husband, Jim Capaldi, drummer with the band Traffic. Trudie and I had arrived at the Roundhouse that evening to be greeted by Pete Townshend, who gave me a massive hug. 'I want to apologize for being so rude to you when I was on *Whistle Test* with Ronnie Lane,' he explained. I was struggling to remember. 'I watched the DVD the other day and I was so aggressive,' he went on. 'But I wasn't angry at you. I hope you didn't take it personally. I was just angry!' I laughed and returned his hug and we shook hands as we made our way through to meet the other artists at the gig.

It was an incredible line-up featuring Yusuf Islam, Jon Lord, Joe Walsh, Steve Balsamo and his wonderful band The Storys, Stevie Lange, Bill Wyman, Gary Moore, Dennis Locorriere, Simon Kirke, Margo Buchanan and, of course, Jim's soulmate Steve Winwood. Steve played a heartfelt version of Traffic's signature song 'Dear Mr Fantasy' and a beautiful interpretation of 'Love Will Keep Us Alive', which Jim had co-written with Pete Vale and Paul Carrack for the Eagles album *Hell Freezes Over*. Trudie took an armful of programmes to the dressing rooms for everyone to sign for an online auction, expecting to encounter some crazy backstage madness, but there was none. Everyone was drinking green tea and behaving impeccably, very un-rock'n'roll!

Paul Weller was fantastic. It was clear how much he respected Jim and he put everything he had into the show, as he always does. He performed 'Paper Sun', 'Pearly Queen' and 'Here We Go Round The Mulberry Bush', my favourite moments of the entire evening and I knew he would be exactly right for Sound and Vision. Luckily, the timing of my call to him was perfect: he'd just pulled into an M6 service station and was sitting his car, taking a break. I explained the ethos of Sound and Vision and he bought into it immediately, promising to do the show and create something really special.

The event turned out to be a triumph. Nashville singer-songwriter Diana Jones played a beautiful showcase at the start of the evening and there were brilliant performances from Newton Faulkner and R&B star Lemar. Cynthia Lennon made her emotional return to Abbey Road, joining me onstage with photographer and performance artist Mike McCartney (Paul's younger brother) to conduct the crowd in a rousing version of 'Yellow Submarine' and my great friend Dermot O'Leary hosted the auction. Finally, Paul Weller appeared, joined by Kelly Jones and backed by a string quartet, reimagining some of his biggest hits, all uniquely arranged for that moment. It was absolutely magical and fabulously successful, raising more than £230,000 for CRUK. The challenge now was to top that figure in 2010!

While all of this was going on, a strange but rather wonderful thing had happened. Out of nowhere, a tiny, scruffy stray kitten had arrived at home. His matted fur was mostly black but he had big white patches under his chin and on his stomach and he had the cutest white-shoed feet. He couldn't have been more than five weeks old and he was traumatized, ragged and frightened, taking shelter under the floorboards of our house, gaining access from outside through a gap in the brickwork and meowing constantly. We already had a handsome black cat called Colby, who was fascinated by this noisy newcomer, catching voles and mice in the garden and leaving bits of them next to the gap in the wall to keep him alive. I've always loved cats. I've had them around me all my life and I think I understand them, but this little kitten wouldn't let any of us get anywhere near him. He was so skinny and small I wondered if he would be able to survive and in my mind I began to connect him to Olivia and her battle for life.

We called him Razz and with time on my hands, he became a 'project'. I was determined to gain his trust, so each time I put food out for him I would stand near his saucer, speaking constantly (almost in a Whisper!), encouraging him to come so that he would get used to the sound of my voice and associate it with a meal. First of all he would rush in, hoover up all the food and rush off again in seconds, but very slowly he got used to me being there and began to relax. I had the strongest feeling that if he let me stroke him everything would be OK and when, after weeks and weeks of patient persuasion, he finally let me touch his back, it was like an electric charge. I can't explain it. His body language transformed completely and as he relaxed he looked up at me with love in his eyes, and began rubbing his body around my legs. From that moment on we became almost inseparable. He was still too frightened to come into the house but would wait near the kitchen door, trotting out from his hiding place to join me as I walked over to the studio, where he would sit contentedly for hours watching me as I got on with my work. It was like having a cat-dog. He was healthy, happy and a bundle of love.

Meanwhile, despite everything she had endured, Olivia was at home and making fantastic progress. The trauma she suffered as a newly born baby has left its mark on her but she has overcome her physical limitations through sheer will and determination, helped by the care and love of her big sisters, Marnie and Alana. It is a wonderful miracle.

My own prognosis was also really good and my cancer was now completely under control. I knew that I would have to take medication for the rest of my life and the side effects were still occasionally debilitating and depressing but I was alive and my vitality had returned. My early diagnosis had been absolutely vital and I would urge any male reader over fifty to have a routine PSA check. If you take anything from this book, take that. A blood test is really no big deal but it could literally save your life the way it saved mine. It's quick, almost painless and you don't even have to give an armful!

By the summer of 2009 my visits to the clinic had been reduced from once a month to once every three months and the August test results were the best yet. 'Carry on doing what you're doing', I was told, 'and we'll still be having this conversation in twenty years' time.' It was fantastic news and the following Saturday Aninha Capaldi joined us as we celebrated by visiting Fairport's Cropredy Convention to spend a day in the warm sunshine, listening to the music. It's a safe and welcoming world within a world, almost a throw-back to the hippy festivals I used to go to in the 1960s and I love soaking in the gentle atmosphere there, sipping one of the many real ales available at the beer tent, the focal point of the entire operation!

The lovely vibe at Cropredy reminded me of my favourite festival experience ever – the glorious annual four-day celebration of Bluegrass music known as MerleFest, staged in the dramatic setting of the forested foothills of the Blue Ridge Mountains in North Carolina, one of the most picturesque and beautiful places I have ever visited. I was there in 2002 with Dave Shannon and Sue Welch to record live music and interviews for *Bob Harris Country* and to shine a light on an event that is relatively unknown to British audiences – and I am so glad we made the journey. It turned out to be the definitive outdoor music experience, with no less than fourteen stages scattered across the grounds of the local Wilkes Community College, offering a staggering range of roots music, jam sessions and workshops.

The festival was founded in 1988 to honour local legend Merle Watson, who had been killed in a farming accident three years earlier. What began as an informal gathering of home-grown musicians playing on the back of a flat-bed truck to a small gathering of about three hundred people, has grown organically through the years to become one of America's largest music events and a major fundraiser for the entire area, attracting more than 80,000 fans and pumping more than $9,000,000 into the local economy. Not that the infrastructure is exactly set up to accommodate this huge influx of people. There is only one major hotel within a fifty-mile radius, booked at least a year in advance. Other than that, the options are to pitch a tent in one of the many pop-up campsites or stay, like we did, at a local motel. It was rough-and-ready accommodation but the owner was friendly and obliging when we drew up outside, coming out to greet us carrying a large glass jar full of what looked to me like Calpol, the medicine for children. Wilksboro had been notorious in the past as the 'Moonshine Capital of America', a major distribution point for the sale of illicit whisky throughout the South and this homemade brew was particularly potent. He smiled as he offered us a taste and I could see that there were two peaches floating in the thick, pink liquid. 'Eat them peaches,' he told us, 'and you'll get as drunk as hail!'

The festival had a family atmosphere I found hugely attractive, with all the artists encouraged to mingle with the audience and watch the other acts as they played and with a bill that featured Gillian Welch and David Rawlings, multi-Grammy nominated Bluegrass superstar Sam Bush and the majestic Patty Loveless, the whole experience was an absolute joy. I spent a lot of my time there with Chris Thile, mandolin player with the wonderful Nickel Creek, who provided me with a moment of pure festival magic. As we sat in front of the main stage waiting for the Yonder Mountain String Band to begin their set, a little girl began strumming an out-of-tune guitar just behind us. Chris asked her to pass him the instrument while he tuned it for her, her family looking on amazed. He had his mandolin with him and as we sat there on the grass he began to teach her some basic chords and rhythms. Soon, we were all joining in, her whole family singing, clapping their hands and laughing in the warm sunshine on that lovely April afternoon. It was as spontaneous as it was beautiful.

To my mind, Cropredy is the closest UK equivalent of MerleFest and it is always great to see so many of our friends there. We often meet up with Danny Thompson, who stays with his family in the vast camp site just behind the backstage compound. He is an encyclopaedia of knowledge and I love talking to him about music, reminiscing about the late Alexis Korner or discussing the work he's done with John Martyn and many other great musicians across a broad range of styles. 'It was a musical conversation with John,' he told writer Martin Chilton in a recent interview, 'taking in all strands. I've done a lot of what you might call more commercial music – with Kate Bush, Rod Stewart and the like – and I don't play any different than when I'm down Ronnie Scott's or in a folk club. It's all free form. Someone like Kate is just a fantastic singer and a lovely lady, too, and it's as interesting working with her as with Tubby Hayes.'

As we stood chatting, Richard Thompson and Yusuf Islam joined us just as Ralph McTell went onto the stage to play a brilliant set to the bank of 20,000 people chilling on the grass in the evening sunshine. Life felt good.

Later that evening, Trudie and I talked to organizer Gareth Williams and Stevie Horton and Andy Farquarson from Iconic Media about ways of getting Cropredy across to an even wider audience. I'd established a great working relationship with Sky Arts and had been curator and presenter of programmes on the channel for the previous two years, beginning with a *Bob Harris Night* takeover in 2007 and a concert series called *Centre Stage* the following year, broadcast every weekday evening at nine. It was great fun being at the centre of this vibrant new television channel and I particularly enjoyed working with producer Dan Bougourd, whom I'd met through Celia Quantrill, now a close friend and confidant of Cynthia Lennon. Dan and I worked together on a number of arts shows made at the Serpentine Gallery in Hyde Park and a programme made in tribute to Frank Zappa, filmed at an exhibition and concert held at the Roundhouse to mark what would have been his 70th birthday in 2010. I'd just signed a contract to present a series of *Songbook* programmes with Kelly Jones, KT Tunstall and Diane Warren, so the time seemed right to talk to the channel about the idea of them broadcasting WBBC-produced coverage of the festival the following year. Trudie and I were excited as we discussed the possibilities during the car ride home.

We all had a late start the following morning. The weather was beautiful and I was doing my daily workout on the lawn in the sunshine when Trudie set off to our local shop to buy the ingredients needed for a slap-up Sunday lunch. A few moments later she was running back into the house, screaming that one of our cats had been killed. She thought it was Colby but when I ran to the gate with Miles, Dylan and Flo we discovered it was Razz. He'd been run over and was lying at the side of the road. I was devastated. He'd been my constant companion through my cancer recovery and I was so grateful to him. I couldn't believe he was dead. If he'd run into the road a split second earlier or later the vehicle would have missed him. Miles gently picked him up and we put him into a cardboard box and buried him under the apple tree outside my studio. I still miss him very much and to this day I believe he was sent as some kind of angel to see Olivia and me through the worst times of our fight to get well, and when his job was done he left us.

I felt so sad about Razz but there was little time to dwell on all of this because, as always, we were so busy. I was leaving for Nashville for the Americana Music Awards three weeks later and in the meantime had a WBBC documentary to make, another Colin Hall-inspired programme called *The Songs The Beatles Gave Away*, featuring an interview with

Sir George Martin, which we recorded the following Monday.

If you count 'The Best Things In Life Are Free' by Johnny Gentle, to which John contributed the middle eight in 1960, there are 27 numbers written by either John, Paul or George and that were covered by other artists during the lifetime of the band but never recorded by The Beatles themselves. Running in chronological order from 1960–1970 they are:

1. 'The Best Things In Life Are Free' Johnny Gentle
2. 'I'll Be On My Way' Billy J. Kramer with The Dakotas
3. 'Bad To Me' Billy J. Kramer with The Dakotas
4. 'Tip Of My Tongue' Tommy Quickly
5. 'Hello Little Girl' The Fourmost
6. 'Love Of The Loved' Cilla Black
7. 'I'll Keep You Satisfied' Billy J Kramer with The Dakotas
8. 'I'm In Love' The Fourmost
9. 'A World Without Love' Peter & Gordon
10. 'One And One Is Two' The Strangers with Mike Shannon
11. 'Nobody I Know' Peter & Gordon
12. 'Like Dreamers Do' Applejacks
13. 'From A Window' Billy J. Kramer
14. 'It's For You' Cilla Black
15. 'I Don't Want To See You Again' Peter & Gordon
16. 'That Means A Lot' P. J. Proby
17. 'Woman' Peter & Gordon
18. 'Love In The Open Air' George Martin & His Orchestra
19. 'Cat Call' Chris Barber
20. 'Step Inside Love' Cilla Black
21. 'Thingumybob' John Foster & Sons Ltd. Black Dyke Mills Band
22. 'Goodbye' Mary Hopkin
23. 'Sour Milk Sea' Jackie Lomax
24. 'Badge' Cream
25. 'Penina' Carlos Mendes
26. 'Come and Get It' Badfinger
27. 'Penina' Jotta Herre

It's a fascinating list and much of the material we used in the programme was priceless. It was an absolute delight to talk to Mary Hopkin and reminisce with her about the childhood days we spent together in Pontardawe in South Wales. We never dreamed then that Mary would become the first artist signed to the Beatles' record label, replacing them at the top of the charts with her cover of a Russian gypsy song called 'Those Were The Days' and taking over at No. 1 from 'Hey Jude', the first-ever release on the Apple label in 1968. Paul had seen her on a hugely popular talent show called *Opportunity Knocks*, the *X-Factor* of its day, and Apple sent a telegram inviting her to London to sing for Paul.

'I sang a couple of folk songs and a Donovan song,' she told me. 'Then Paul took my mum and me out to lunch to the Angus Steak House, I think it was ... the one in Oxford Street.' She laughed as she remembered. 'I was in awe of Paul. I'd been a Beatles fan since I was 13, but I didn't feel nervous meeting him.'

As their friendship grew, Paul began to take this sweet, shy girl under his wing and after the huge success of 'Those Were The Days' sent a new song for her to consider.

'I felt privileged that he wrote a song especially for me,' she said. 'Apparently he wrote it in a delightful little Italian restaurant that everyone from Apple used to go to. He was there with some friends one evening, they'd had a meal, he had his guitar with him and came up with this idea. He thought "Mary needs a song", so he wrote "Goodbye" in a matter of minutes, which only he can do – write a great song in minutes.' The single was released as the follow-up to 'Those Were The Days' and took Mary to No. 2 in the UK charts in April 1969.

Billy J. Kramer was not so lucky. Although he'd been the first artist to take a Beatles' song to No.1 with 'Bad To Me' in 1963, he'd then rejected one of the most successful titles in music history. 'I remember going to the ABC in Blackpool and asking Paul for a song. He played me "Yesterday" before anyone else had heard it. I thought it was too mamby-pamby and told him I wanted a rocker. I turned it down.' Ouch!

Olivia Harrison gave us a quite brilliant acoustic demo of 'Sour Milk Sea' for the show that Jackie Lomax had recorded with Olivia's late husband, George, in Esher in 1968 and we discovered some great BBC archive footage of George explaining the reason for the title of the last hit single in the chart career of Cream, the band that featured one of the best guitarists in the world ever – George's best friend Eric Clapton.

'He was round at my house and we'd worked out the chords to

the song,' George explained. 'I was writing down the lyrics on a piece of paper and Eric was sitting opposite me. When it got to the middle part I wrote down "bridge". Well, I think we'd had a few bottles of wine or something and he looked at the paper upside down and just broke up laughing thinking the word was "badge", so he called the song "Badge".'

Alcohol also played an hilarious part in the creation of the accidental hit 'Penina', as Paul told us with some mirth. 'I was on holiday in Portugal and ended up one night at a bar in a golf club. There was a lounge band playing and, not being in full possession of my senses, I got on the drum kit, grabbed a mike and started making up this awful drunken song about the name of the golf club. Someone must've recorded it and passed it on to Carlos Mendes because the next thing I knew it was released as a single!' Unbelievably, there was also a cover version by Dutch band Jotta Herre, released just as The Beatles were breaking up.

Making radio documentaries is a wonderfully enjoyable thing to do. We record all the interviews, usually on location, before taking them back to my studio to be reviewed and edited. I always have a good idea of where I want a programme to go but I like to have enough flexibility to let the interviews guide my direction, so as we assemble the material we look for the most fluent way to tell the story. I source the tracks we need and I script and record the links before the mixing begins. Weaving the threads of a documentary together is my favourite part, a truly creative process; cross-fading the music into a flow and finding exactly the right space for each voice is an instinctive art and I could not have anyone more dedicated by my side than my editor, Neil Myners. We are perfectionists.

The Songs The Beatles Gave Away went out on BBC Radio 2 on 28th November 2009 and was the fifth major documentary to be broadcast on the network made by WBBC. Trudie and I founded the company in 2005 on the advice of the then Radio 2 controller Lesley Douglas and our first commission was a two-part series called The Maple Leaf Revolution, reflecting the history and development of Canadian music, the making of which took Neil Myners and me to another of my favourite cities – Toronto.

ELEVEN

Still Whispering ...

IT WAS HOT AND SUNNY WHEN NEIL MYNERS AND I ARRIVED IN Toronto and we spent a fabulously enjoyable week in this vibrant, multi-cultural metropolis, mostly in the company of Larry LeBlanc, one of the world's greatest music authorities. Described as 'the glue that holds the Canadian music industry together', Larry has been at the centre of the scene in Toronto for almost fifty years, a penetrative, fearless and sometimes bombastic writer and broadcaster with whom I have forged a deep friendship.

He took us to visit Sunrise Records and the Sam The Record Man store in downtown Toronto, where I was recognized by Jann Haust, producer of the recent *Bob Dylan Basement Tapes* box set. He introduced me to Suze Rotolo, Dylan's former girlfriend, who is seen walking with him in the photograph on the cover of *The Freewheelin' Bob Dylan* album, released in 1963. Larry also provided me with my first (and so far only) experience of live, major league baseball, when the Toronto Blue Jays took on the mighty Boston Red Sox at the Rogers Centre stadium, where Alannah Myles sang the National Anthem before the game began. It turned out to be an unexpectedly hilarious evening, as Larry reminded me in a recent email.

I was trying to explain baseball to you, then something I've never seen happen, happened. A player hit a home run but twisted his ankle around second base and couldn't make it home to score. They had to send a cart out to pick him up. I have never ever witnessed that before and I'm not sure you can find another incident of it in baseball.

It was also wonderful to reacquaint with Larry's wife, Anya, who I'd known in the early 70s when she was running the Acme Plug Company, handling press and publicity for Marc Bolan and David Bowie. She moved to Toronto a few years later, heading the promotion team at Cachet Records and working with the great Johnny Cash. Now, she runs her own radio promotion and publicity agency and is, like her husband, a perceptive communicator and commentator on the ways of the music industry.

Larry is currently the senior writer of the weekly American entertainment trade database CelebrityAccess, overseeing the authoritative online profile series 'In The Hot Seat', but at the time of our visit he was Bureau Chief for *Billboard* magazine in Toronto and through his many contacts had organized several days of artist interviews for us, recorded at the headquarters of FACTOR, the Foundation to Assist Canadian Talent on Record.

FACTOR is a non-profit-making organization dedicated to providing assistance towards the growth and development of the music industry in Canada, an enviable initiative that offers programmes of financial support to recording artists, songwriters, managers, labels, publishers, event producers and distributors. It is a wide mandate but the existence of FACTOR and other funding bodies is a constructive force, contributing to the tangible and very attractive sense of community that exists within the culture of the music scene in Canada.

I've always had a strong affinity with Canadian artists, who provided me with two significant firsts – 'Diana' by Paul Anka (born in Ottawa) was the first single I ever bought and 'Cinnamon Girl' by Neil Young (born in Toronto) was the opening track on my debut show on Radio 1 in 1970 – and through the years I have always heavily featured Canadian music on all my programmes, from The Band, Leonard Cohen, Bruce Cockburn and Joni Mitchell in the 1970s through Rush, Bryan Adams and Sarah McLachlan to the new generation of artists who were also represented in the 'Maple Leaf Revolution'.

I was particularly keen to talk to singer/songwriter Kathleen Edwards, described at the time as 'the new "it girl" of alt country', whom I'd discovered through her debut album *Failer* in 2003, a recording made possible through government funding. 'I would not be here talking to you today had it not been for that support,' she told us.

Bright and self-assured, Kathleen is also fiercely patriotic. 'I think people assume that whatever's happening in Canada is just happening off the back of America,' she observed, 'but there is a great sense of community here. There's no New York or LA of Canada, with that whole "I'm gonna make it big" mindset, we don't have that whole pop thing. We have long winters, so we play a lot of music inside and we all face similar challenges, so there's a lot of bonding.'

We also talked to Kathleen's guitarist, Jim Bryson, who had contributed so much to the raw, edgy sound that made *Failer* so striking, and we recorded interviews with Sam Roberts, members of Nickelback, Ron Sexsmith, Gordon Lightfoot, Steven Page from Barenaked Ladies, the Sadies, Michael Timmins from the Cowboy Junkies, the Trews, Sue Foley, producer Colin Linden, Luke Doucet, Todd Clark from emerging band Pilot Speed and Heather Ostertag, the head of FACTOR. It was a packed schedule but all the artists brought a refreshing atmosphere of thoughtful creativity into our makeshift studio and the success of the programmes paved the way for the Radio 2 coverage of the annual North By Northeast Music Festival in Toronto the following year, during which I bumped into Centro-matic, one of my favourite bands. They are from Denton, Texas (home of the also magnificent Midlake) and enthusiastically told me about a fan who had turned up at one of their local gigs a few days earlier, having been introduced to them on my weekend show on Radio 2.

'He only lives about five miles away from where we are in Denton but had never even heard of us before,' they told me. 'He discovered our music listening to your radio show, broadcasting from six thousand miles away!' The power of the internet!

I was particularly pleased to spend time in Toronto with Jim Cuddy, founding member of the multi-Juno award-winning band Blue Rodeo. They are one of the best-loved acts in Canada and had just released their tenth album *Are You Ready*, featuring the track 'Finger Lakes', which was on repeat on my CD player at the time. Like every artist through that whole week, Jim arrived for his interview spot on time, accompanied Susan de Cartier, with whom I struck up an immediate friendship.

Susan is the founder of the artist management company Starfish Entertainment, working with Blue Rodeo, Oh Susanna, the Sadies and the Skydiggers. Sharply intelligent, witty and generous, she has a calm, gentle authority and is much loved by the artists whose careers she helps to shape. She stayed on in the studio to chat after my interview with Jim and we resolved to meet again at the Americana Music Awards in Nashville, where she introduced me to her best friend Shauna de Cartier (no relation), boss of Six Shooter Records in Toronto, whose motto 'life is too short to listen to shitty music', brilliantly encapsulates her strength of spirit, integrity and wonderful sense of humour.

Running an independent record label is a massive challenge, particularly when the music industry is going through an intensive period of rapid change – and, at times, Shauna has had to put her whole life on the line to keep the label afloat – but she believes in her artists, has never compromised her ideals in the name of commercialism and her determination has paid off. Six Shooter has established a peerless reputation with a vibrant catalogue of artists that regularly feed into the playlists on my radio shows including Mary Gauthier, Melissa McClelland, Trampled By Turtles, Amelia Curran and the mournful but beautiful Deep Dark Woods.

Three years ago, with Susan's help, Shauna launched the Interstellar Rodeo, a major three-day summer festival in Edmonton, the success of which has seen her branch out into a new event, staged in Winnipeg for the first time in August 2015 and she richly deserves all the good things that happen. Shauna, Sue and I are very tuned into one another and I am very proud of our friendship. I deeply respect these two amazing women.

My close relationship with Canada has led to me appearing on the prestigious Q radio show on CBC in Toronto (with the Great Lake Swimmers) and at the East Coast Music Awards where, in March 2010, I was the keynote speaker in a two-hour Q&A session with Larry LeBlanc. The event was held in Sydney, Nova Scotia, a small, windswept town situated at the northern tip of Canada on the east coast of Cape Breton Island, which, despite the onset of spring, was without doubt the coldest place I had ever been to. With a temperature of –10 and the island engulfed by an ice storm, it was almost impossible to walk between venues without getting almost sliced in two by the ferocity of the freezing temperature, so most of the musicians and delegates gathered in one of the town's two main hotels for the daily showcases, which began at breakfast time and lasted until the early hours. After the showcases the bands transferred to the rooms and corridors throughout the hotel for the impromptu jam sessions and thrashes that provided a twenty-four hour cacophony of continuous sound, sleep not an option.

Some of the performances were absolutely stunning. It was where I discovered the beautiful and sensitive music of Catherine MacLellan, who is the daughter of Gene MacLellan, writer of the song 'Snowbird', made famous by Ann Murray. I also saw sets from singer/songwriter Dave Gunning, local Indie band The Novaks and a brilliant concert from the sharp and clever Joel Plaskett, who was the big winner at the awards show with six trophies across all categories. The level of musicianship was phenomenal and I felt fortunate to be among such a warm and closely knit musical community.

I have been blessed to meet some truly great characters and personalities through the years but few people have touched our lives as profoundly as the late and much loved Ali Booker.

Trudie met Ali first in 1996, at the playgroup at St James C of E Primary School in Hanney, where our son Miles, her son Douglas and daughter Joanne were pupils. I was introduced to Ali shortly afterwards and as we all stood chatting in the playground it was clear that this wonderful woman was very special. Modest, warm and wickedly funny, she was also one of the brightest people I've ever met. She had a rare and instinctive ability to make everyone around her feel good, fabulous attributes to take into broadcasting. She told us she'd just begun news-reading duties at BBC Radio Oxford, having moved from the West Country, where she'd been working at BBC Radio Devon.

'Oh no, not another DJ!' laughed Trudie.

Within a few months Ali took over the Radio Oxford morning show and I was in awe of her ability to make it all sound so easy. She was sincere, touching and funny and the listeners absolutely loved her. The show was an immediate success and soon she transferred to the early afternoon slot that became her own. I was always on the end of a line if Ali ever needed an emergency interviewee and I loved the times we spent on air together.

In 2002, Ali was diagnosed with breast cancer and had to undergo a double mastectomy and an intensive course of chemotherapy, beginning a fight with cancer that lasted for the rest of her life. She dealt with her illness with astonishing bravery and humour, once joking to a doctor who needed to examine her that she never took her clothes off for anything less than a couple of really good meals and a bunch of flowers! By now she'd met her future husband Andrew (to whom she proposed live on air during the *Children In Need* broadcast in 2005) and he and Trudie formed a strong alliance of support and friendship.

We were thrilled when Ali joined us at WBBC for a while, co-producing a documentary with Trudie for Radio 2 entitled *Who Breaks A Butterfly On A Wheel*, which told the story of The Rolling Stones' traumatic summer of 1967. The programme looked at the events and effects of a highly publicized drugs bust at a party held at Redlands, the Sussex home of the Stones' guitarist Keith Richards, and took its name from the headline of a leading article by William Rees-Mogg, the then-editor of *The Times*, which questioned the outcome of the resulting court case. As a result of the bust, organized by the *News of the World*, Keith Richards was given a twelve-month prison sentence and Mick Jagger was given a jail term of three months, sentences which, Rees-Mogg argued, were more severe than 'any purely anonymous young men' would have received. The culture of pop celebrity had begun.

By the time we began work on the documentary, Ali's cancer had spread to her lungs, forcing her to retire from the BBC. Although increasingly encumbered by the equipment she needed to help her breathing, she 'got bored with sitting around at home and waiting to die' and, following her work on the documentary, had resumed her broadcasting career as a newsreader at Oxfordshire station Jack FM, sounding as bright and articulate as she always did. Before she died she made a series of audio diaries documenting her life with cancer, recordings so moving that they deservedly won her two major radio awards in 2010, a Sony Silver in 'The Best Community Programming' category and a Radio Academy Gold Arqiva, the biggest award in Commercial Radio. The diaries were also featured in *The Sunday Times* and there was even a tribute to Ali in the House of Commons, when Wantage MP Ed Vaisey made a speech in her honour. 'The way she fought cancer,' he said, 'made it seem like she was indestructible.'

At no point during her long ordeal did I once hear Ali complain. Throughout, she was a caring and constant source of inspiration to me in my own battle with cancer and a true and loyal friend to Trudie, who describes her as being her soul sister. Just before she passed away, Ali wrote, 'I have a wobbly moment, silently in my head while no one else notices, and I turn into a frightened little girl who's changed her mind about having terminal cancer now, and would like someone to make it stop.'

Ali Booker died at the Sobell House Hospice in Oxford on 1st July 2010 and we all miss her very much.

Our friendship with Ali and my own health issues had underlined to Trudie and I the importance of the work done by Cancer Research UK, and had focused our minds on our Sound and Vision event, held at Abbey Road a few months before Ali passed away, the planning of which had begun almost two years earlier in Nashville, in the week of the 2008 Americana Music Awards, where Robert Plant and Alison Krauss were the big winners with their Album of the Year Award for *Raising Sand*. I'd spoken to Beth Nielsen Chapman about the possibility of her being involved in the event and we'd been trying to meet up for the entire week to talk about it but I'd been so busy covering the Awards for Radio 2 and compiling material for *Bob Harris Country* that I'd had no free time.

I'd recorded sessions and interviews with country star Suzy Bogguss, John Peel protégé Laura Cantrell, the frightening and intense James McMurtry and Kentucky musician and writer Chris Knight, who had just released his sixth album *Heart Of Stone* produced by Dan Baird of the Georgia Satellites. Chris also works regularly with Ray Kennedy, one of my favourite producers, and is a major talent. Honest, gritty and uncompromising, he should be right up there with Bruce Springsteen and John Mellencamp.

My work schedule had literally filled every minute of the week but finally, on Friday, a window appeared. Beth phoned me to say she was free that afternoon and would collect me at 3 o'clock at the end of my final session and take me for a beer at Bobby's Idle Hour, an old-style drinking house near Music Row, about a block away from the Audio Productions studio.

'The only problem is that I haven't got a lot of time,' she warned. 'I've got a really important meeting with my agent Paul Fenn and whatever happens, I must be away by four.'

A few moments after we finished our conversation my phone rang again. This time it was Robert Plant's manager, Nicola Powell, who had called with a lovely invitation. She and Robert were free that night and would like to take me out to dinner. She was thrilled when I mentioned Beth. 'Robert will love to meet her, he's a big fan.' She told me that Robert had a photoshoot organized for five o'clock at Buddy Miller's house and suggested that we meet up at 4.30 outside a vintage bookshop on the high street at Hillsborough Village, just outside of Nashville, not far from Buddy's house. I agreed, of course, and immediately phoned Beth.

'You're going to have to cancel your meeting,' I told her.

Beth was astonished. 'I can't possibly do that, Bob! It's much too important. We're talking about a UK tour!'

'Beth,' I explained. 'We're having dinner tonight with Robert Plant.'

There was a short pause.

'My dinner is *so* cancelled!' she said.

Beth and I arrived at the bookseller's a few minutes early and sat for a while outside a nearby coffee shop, chatting and chilling in the sunshine as we watched the people go by. Nicola soon joined us and as we sat sipping our coffees we saw Robert pull into the parking lot opposite. He waved as he got out of his car but instead of crossing the street to join us, he turned left and strode up the sidewalk, disappearing into the crowd. We sat waiting for him for ages, to the point where Nicola was getting worried, so I set off to find him, soon discovering him in a little instrument shop about two blocks away. He'd noticed a harmonica in the window as he'd driven past and was playing it as I walked in, lost in the moment.

As we headed back down the high street together, I noticed a couple of boys in baseball caps, probably in their early twenties, skateboarding on the pavement opposite, weaving their way in and out of the pedestrians. At the moment I looked across one of them glanced up and spotted Robert and in a split second an extraordinary thing happened. The boys seemed to lose all sense of reason and control as they sprinted, skateboards flying everywhere, straight into the busy traffic towards us, self-preservation forgotten in the rush. One of them lost his flip-flops in the middle of the road, cars and pick-ups swerved to avoid them, people were pointing and shouting and suddenly it was like being in a slow-motion movie. By the time we joined Beth and Nicola at the coffee shop, we were swamped by a crowd of excited people, all desperate for an autograph or a picture with Robert, exhilarating as well as being a little scary.

'Well,' said Beth to Robert later. 'If you must stride round Nashville looking like a lion, what do you expect?!'

We eventually made it to Buddy Miller's house for the photo session before heading out to dinner at a sweet, quiet Italian restaurant in the centre of downtown Nashville, where we surrendered to a magical evening of good food, red wine, conversation, memories and laughter. I told Robert of the passion I was feeling for the Sound and Vision project and he immediately promised to get involved but only on one condition – that he was given the freedom to create a performance that was absolutely unique. Boy, did he keep his promise.

As we began to formulate the line-up, I called David Gray, who also generously offered his time. I was probably the first person to play him on UK radio and I still have fond memories of the broadcasts we did together when I was at GLR in London in the 90s. David is a big Manchester United fan and one of his first sessions for my show exactly coincided with a Wednesday night Champions League game. For about the only time ever, I'd left the monitor on in the studio and however much we tried we could not help being drawn to the screen. David was about halfway through his first live number when United scored their first goal. Session forgotten, we were both out of our seats, fists pumping, high fiving in the middle of the studio.

His commitment to Sound and Vision 2010 was really appreciated and the event turned out to be an absolute triumph. Newton Faulkner began the evening with a characteristically funky and rhythmic performance and after David had played, Beth performed a truly beautiful set accompanied by multi-instrumentalist Maartin Allcock. But the focus of the night was Robert. I knew he'd put everything he had into the rehearsals for this moment and when I introduced him to the room, the sense of anticipation was awesome. He and hurdy gurdy player Nigel Eaton were surrounded onstage by the seventy-strong London Oriana Choir, performing a set comprising of songs by one of Robert's great heroes – Scott Walker. It was quite simply one of the best musical moments I have ever witnessed, Robert bending and blending his vocals with the voices of the choir, Beth adding her heavenly harmonies. It was beautiful. Not only that, when the auction proceeds and online bids had been totalled up, we had all raised more than £260,000 for Cancer Research UK.

It was hard to imagine that we would ever top that figure but the following year we did. Essential to the success of the 2011 event was the incredible energy of our auctioneer Al Murray who, in his role as pub landlord, was down from the stage, bantering with the crowd and whipping up bids for the money-can't-buy auction items on display. Nicky Campbell and Jon Briggs helped me with the compering duties, Giles Martin addressed the audience on behalf of his father Sir George, and the music was once again amazing, with perfectly pitched sets from Eve Selis, the perennial Newton Faulkner, Liam Bailey and The Feeling, all setting the tone for Tom Jones to take to the stage to deliver a performance of incredible power and professionalism. Between us all, we raised £340,000 at Abbey Road that night, taking the Sound and Vision total to well over £1,000,000. Finally, to complete what was a truly special moment, Robin Gibb appeared onstage from nowhere to present me with a UK Heritage Award. It was an amazing honour but it wasn't the first time that Robin had brought unexpected joy into my life.

Early in 2003, I'd received a call from Phil Hughes, my executive producer at Radio 2. He told me that the network was making a Bee Gees documentary and that he would like me to record a career interview with Robin at Broadcasting House for the programme.

'It's a major project and we'll be filming it too,' he told me.

The idea of having cameras in the studio didn't surprise me. The BBC was in the early stages of developing its digital service BBCi (later rebranded as The Red Button) and had begun to look for ways of visualizing as much of its radio output as possible, an on-going process that now sees multi-camera shoots for *In Concert* programmes, interactive coverage of the *The Chart Show* and *Sounds Of The 80s* and Go Pro-like technology attached to every microphone in every on-air studio at Radio 1.

I was thrilled by the whole idea of the Bee Gees project but amazed by how uncharacteristically flat and disinterested Trudie appeared to be when I told her the news. This was not like her at all and to be truthful, she hadn't seemed herself for several weeks. She seemed to be drifting away from me, becoming distant and disconnected, constantly disappearing to various parts of the house with her mobile phone or standing out by the washing line in the garden (her favourite private spot), to hold furtive conversations I knew she didn't want me to hear. She seemed reluctant to look me in the eye and was dismissive when I asked her if there was anything wrong.

We had been invited to a Radio Academy Awards event at the Shaw Theatre a few days later and I was hoping this would give her a chance to relax and enjoy herself but we hardly spoke as we drove to London as my worries about our relationship intensified. Thankfully, she seemed to unwind as we took our places in the auditorium to settle in for what became an amazing evening.

I was particularly pleased to see Robin Gibb arrive on stage to collect the Scott Piering Award on behalf of the Bee Gees, receiving a standing ovation as he made an impassioned speech extolling the virtues of UK musicianship.

'I'd like to see British music dominate the American charts again,' he said. 'It's very important British songwriters are supported here at home. We can do it. We've got great writers and talent and we've got originality and innovation in this industry.'

I knew that Steve Harley was going to be one of the main presenters and I had with me a valuable white label copy of the first Cockney Rebel album, which I planned to give him later to auction for charity. Steve is a tireless campaigner, raising money for the Mines Advisory Group and working with several schools for disabled children, projects that in recent years have seen him lead two fundraising treks, one in Cambodia and another across the formidable Death Valley in Eastern California. Soon, he took the microphone to hand over the PRS award for Outstanding Contribution to Music Radio, and as he started his introduction I was speculating as to whom the recipient might be.

'This fellow has the right attitude to rock music,' he began. 'He started his career on Radio 1 on *Sounds Of The 70s* in August 1970 ...'

I lost the rest of his speech in the excitement of the moment, engulfed by the realization that the recipient was me! It was a total surprise and as Steve recited a roll call of my career highlights, I turned to look at Trudie.

'Did you know about this?' I asked. As she smiled, I began to feel a whole lot better.

'Of course you did!'

Suddenly, the last few weeks of Trudie's covert conversations and whispered phone calls made some sense and I was as much relieved that this was the explanation for her distant behaviour as I was thrilled to get the award itself. I strode onto the stage clutching my Cockney Rebel white label.

'eBay!' said Steve as I handed him the record.

I felt so happy. I'd been acknowledged by the Radio Academy, everything was good with Trudie and we were celebrating a wonderful evening surrounded by people who were special in our lives. Amanda Beel had booked a table at the Four Lanterns in Cleveland Street, one of her favourite restaurants, where we were joined by Radio 2 controller Lesley Douglas and my producer Phil Swern.

Amanda has been part of our world since my early days back on Radio 1 in the 1990s, when she was part of the promotion team for Sony Records, delivering music to my desk from such as Shawn Colvin, Mary Chapin Carpenter, Bruce Springsteen and Jeff Buckley. She was a colleague of the late and much missed Stuart Emery before founding her own company, All About Promotions, in 2003, representing a roster of artists which currently includes Paul Carrack, Fiona Bevan, Red Sky July, Midge Ure and Callaghan. I love spending time with Amanda. She knows the music industry like the back of her hand and truly cares for the artists she represents. Like Susan de Cartier and Shauna de Cartier in Toronto, she is a dedicated and phenomenal woman surviving and thriving in the male-dominated world of the music business.

The atmosphere on the journey home with Trudie was in total contrast to the silent drive to London earlier that evening and, as we spilled laughing into our house, we were met with a hug from our beautiful friend Marie, who had been babysitting for us. We'd first met Marie, her husband Mark and their boys Toby and Ben in the playground at Hanney School, soon after meeting Ali Booker and our families have been close right through the nearly twenty years that have passed since then.

'How was your evening?' she asked me.

'It was fabulous,' I replied. 'Steve Harley did this whole career retrospective before he gave me the award. It felt a bit like being on *This Is Your Life*!'

She nearly spat out the champagne she was drinking. There was a silent pause before a now flustered Marie unexpectedly explained that Mark and the boys were waiting for her and she really had to get home. Seconds later she'd grabbed her coat, was out of the door and gone.

Trudie and I stayed up celebrating until the early hours and I was so pleased things between us would now settle back to normal. Alarmingly, however, the reassurance did not last long. The furtive phone calls picked up again and I knew she was concealing something. The more it became clear that the Radio Academy evening wasn't the answer after all, the more suspicious I became of these furtive, half-heard conversations.

'Oh, it was the parent/teacher association again,' she would unconvincingly explain.

All these worries were rumbling around in my head as I got to Broadcasting House a few days later for the big recording with Robin Gibb. My friend Roy Webber had called to tell me that he'd be in London that day, so I'd invited him to be there too. I'd built myself up for this moment and when Roy and I arrived to discover a full film crew in the studio and a control room packed with people I realized Phil Hughes was right; this interview really was a very big deal. Robin arrived shortly after and I complimented him on his brilliant Radio Academy speech as he and I took our places under the studio lights. Soon we were reminiscing about the amazing and memorable day we'd spent together twenty-five years earlier at the Criteria Sound Studios in Miami, where he and his brothers Barry and Maurice had given me a private and exclusive live performance of their much anticipated new album *Spirits Having Flown*, months before its release, still one of the absolute highlights of my musical life.

As he always was, Robin was sensitive, enthusiastic and engaging and we were well into a really enjoyable interview when I heard someone push open the big soundproofed door behind me. There is a strict protocol preventing anyone entering a studio when a recording is taking place and it was with some irritation that I turned to see who was interrupting us. The first thing I saw, as I squinted through the haze of the television lights, was a big red book, held by a smiling Michael Aspel who was walking across the studio towards us. I leaned back, expecting him to address Robin but instead, he turned to me.

'Pardon the invasion into your studio, Bob. Robin Gibb, you know that you're not just here to be interviewed by Whispering Bob, because you know I'm here to say ... Bob Harris, This Is Your Life!'

I absolutely could not believe it. I'd been a fan of the programme for many years, going right back to the Eamonn Andrews days of the 50s and 60s but I never dreamed I would ever be the subject. This was a huge honour and I was thrilled and excited, but how naive had I been? All those weeks of suspicion, Trudie's secret phone calls, Marie's reaction, Radio 2's deception and (now I began to think about it) a thousand other little signs ... I looked at Roy and Robin, who burst out laughing as they stepped forward to give me a big hug. More and more people spilled into the studio, slapping my back and shaking me by the hand, Phil Hughes tapping his nose with a knowing look.

Soon, the programme production team were pulling Roy and I away and escorting us out of Broadcasting House and into a waiting Mercedes. Roy explained that he was my designated chaperone and, of course, he was not going to breathe a word of what was about to happen. Months of planning had gone into all of this.

We were whooshed across London to the Thames Television studios, to be met by a welcoming committee that quickly escorted us to the far side of the main building and into a stylish but windowless dressing room.

'We're going to have to lock you in here,' they told us. 'We don't want you to see any of the guests and ruin the surprise.'

If this was going to be our prison for the next few hours it was fine; bright, airy and beautifully furnished, with a table groaning under the weight of sandwiches, crisps, fruit, biscuits, a large and beautiful bunch of flowers and enough alcohol for Roy and I to have got seriously drunk. With several hours to kill, there was a brief temptation to pour ourselves a couple of large glasses of red but I wanted to keep a completely clear head. I didn't want anything to get in the way of total recall.

Shortly before the show, Roy was called to take part in the final rehearsals, leaving me to choose what I was going to wear from the many different options Trudie had left in the wardrobe for me. My favourite jacket was there, a new pair of shoes ... she really had thought of everything.

Alone for the first time that day, I paced around the dressing room in a state of suspended animation, thinking back over my life, trying to anticipate what the evening might bring, until finally came the expected knock on the door and I was led through what seemed like an endless maze of corridors to join Michael Aspel, who was waiting for me in a quiet corner of the studio, out of sight of the audience and guests, ready for the start of the show. My heart was beating so hard I could actually hear it and the feeling of nervous excitement was almost overwhelming as we stood there waiting for our cue, but Michael was calm and kind.

'You don't have to worry about anything,' he smiled. 'It's all been rehearsed and I'll take care of everything. This is your night, Bob, all you have to do is enjoy it!'

I really appreciated the reassurance and his words were ringing in my ears as the familiar theme music struck up and we stepped through the famous doors together.

Trudie gave me a knowing smile as she came forward to hug me and, as the applause died down and we took our seats, I looked around at all the familiar faces. My Mum and Dad were at the front, sitting next to my wonderful and stout-hearted Aunt Margaret, who is still alive today, a proud 100 years old. Sue, Jackie and Val were all there too, introduced by Michael Aspel who noted, 'To prove this is a rock'n'roll show and, I think, for the first time in *This Is Your Life* history, we have a record three ex-wives on the set with us!'

Much was made of the size of my family, as my children Miri, Emily, Charlie, Ben, Jamie (wearing a 'Who's the Daddy?' T-shirt), Miles, Dylan and Flo all burst through the doors, alongside my granddaughters Marnie and Alana and, the youngest of all, little Niamh, her face covered in chocolate, carried by her father John. Trudie's entire family was also in attendance and there were friends and colleagues spanning every era of my life.

My great friend Jeff Griffin, producer of my first-ever radio programmes, talked about the Radio 1 audition he supervised in 1970.

'I liked the sound of his voice,' he said. 'It was a bit unusual, and he was knowledgeable, so we set up a pilot programme a few weeks later and he did that very well. I then put that forward to the audition panel for DJs and he passed that. But of course the trouble was, having told him that he passed it, he then wouldn't stop phoning me to find out when he could get a proper job!'

It's true. I pestered Jeff unmercifully throughout the entire ten months I had to wait before I finally made it on air, Jeff booking me to sit in for my great hero John Peel on *Sounds Of The 70s* in August 1970.

My former Radio 1 controller Johnny Beerling spoke warmly of my return to Radio 1 in 1989, when I took over on Sunday evening from the late Roger Scott – huge boots to fill. There was much laughter as *Whistle Test* producer Mike Appleton told the story of the two of us hobbling off a plane together at JFK airport for the first of our many working trips to New York. Just before leaving Los Angeles earlier in the day, I'd bought a pair of tight brown leather boots which, for comfort's sake, I'd taken off for the duration of the flight, a bad decision as it turned out. As we came into JFK and I tried to put them back on again, I realized that the left boot just wouldn't fit. No matter how hard I tried, I couldn't lever my foot back into it. I had managed to force the other one on but it hurt like hell and was so tight I couldn't get it off again. I know that feet tend to swell when you're flying but I must've bought boots that were at least one size too small. I'm not sure how I got them on in the first place. It was comical. Mike had a bad back and was limping with a walking stick while I was clumping up and down on one Cuban heel, holding my other boot like hand luggage as we disembarked from the plane. It was not, as Mike observed, the coolest way for these two supposed rock'n'roll dudes to arrive in New York!

As the evening went on fellow broadcasters Tony Blackburn, Paul Gambaccini, Dave Lee Travis, Nicky Campbell and John Inverdale all appeared onstage to tell stories of times we spent sharing microphones or at cricket grounds together. Roy Webber reminisced about our recording days with his band Wally at Morgan Studios in London, and George Nicholson described the notorious night at the Speakeasy with the Sex Pistols.

Suzi Quatro told the story of a visit we'd made to her house. 'I invited Bob and Trudie over for Christmas a couple of years ago and we had a nice cheese and wine evening planned. Nice evening. Not only did they arrive about two hours late, but this man arrived in leather trousers. Now, how dare you come to my house wearing leather?' she chuckled.

The warmth of the evening was incredible and it was particularly lovely to hear Judie Tzuke talk with great affection about our long-time friendship. She and I were first introduced by Marc Bolan's wife June at the time that Jude signed to Elton John's Rocket record label in 1977 and we've been close friends ever since. I had no idea, of course, that Elton himself was about to appear onscreen.

As I later learned, the planning of all of this had begun months earlier, when Trudie was putting together a promotion campaign for the release of a forthcoming *Bob Harris Presents* ... compilation. She had asked Amanda Beel for advice as to how to promote the album and, in addition to helping line up some radio and press interviews, Amanda suggested calling her friend Deborah Cohen, one of the *This Is Your Life* producers, who loved the idea of me being a subject for the show. Plans were now underway and gradually, over the next few weeks, Trudie, Amanda, Deborah and her co-producer Sue Green began building the guest list. The first person they approached was Robert Plant, with whom Amanda was working on the extraordinary 'Festival In The Desert' project. He immediately agreed to take part, filming this wonderful message.

'Hi Bob!' he said. 'You are an institution,' [or, as Trudie says, I should be in one!]. Your presentations and interviews on the *Whistle Test* were imaginative, informative and focused, while dealing with so many egos and so many loonies back then. I know because I was one of them! Your consistency down the years is second to none and you, like me, have an insatiable appetite for hunting out beautiful, challenging music way to the left side of that High Street fluff. You bring fresh, alternative music to me, and many like me. So thanks to you, and I'll see you soon.'

As always, Robert's words were thoughtful and considered and I was particularly struck by the word 'consistency', a huge compliment.

David Gray came on screen to thank me for the support I gave him at the beginning of his career (United games notwithstanding!) and Nanci Griffith appeared on film from Nashville, clutching a Ken Bruce-branded radio and suggesting to the BBC that I should have one too! It was an amusing and lovely moment and I was thrilled to be able to reciprocate when I presented Nanci with a Lifetime Achievement Award at the Radio 2 Folk Awards in February 2010.

But perhaps the most touching contribution to the programme came from Elton John who, at the time, was in the middle of a huge 'Face To Face' American tour with Billy Joel. Through a combination of luck and detective work, Trudie had tracked down Elton's manager Frank Presland on a Friday afternoon at the tour hotel in Philadelphia (obviously!) and was delighted to find him friendly and receptive.

'We'll put it to Elton and we'll see what he says,' Frank said. 'Call us again on Monday.'

It was just the reaction Trudie had been hoping for and Deborah Cohen was impressed that contact had been made. 'Tell them we can organize it all,' she told Trudie. 'We'll get a crew out there to film him and provide them with everything they'll need.'

It was a big call for the programme and when Trudie finally got through again on the Monday afternoon, she couldn't wait to explain what the *This Is Your Life* team were offering.

'There's no need for you to do anything,' Frank Presland told her.

'Oh. Does this mean he doesn't want to do it?' asked Trudie.

'No, it means he's already done it. He really wanted to do it for Bob, so he pulled out all the stops, hired a crew over the weekend and filmed it here. I just need to know where to send it!'

The production team were blown away by how generous and accommodating Elton and Frank had been; unprecedented, they said. The tape arrived a few days later and it was a very moving moment when, towards the end of the show, Elton's film came up on the studio monitor screens.

'Why I wanted to do this was to say thank you to you for all the wonderful support you gave me early on in your career. People should never forget who helped them when they first started out and you were such a big supporter of mine. I did many an *Old Grey Whistle Test*. We had a lot of fun in those days. It's still a lot of fun but it's not as nice as it used to be, but you know, there are not people like you around anymore. So I hope you have the best evening. Thank you so much for supporting me early in my career. It meant so much to me and it still does. Thank you.'

It was such a beautiful message. I'm actually feeling quite emotional about it as I type this, but there was still one more fantastic surprise to come on that magical evening, as Michael Aspel explained.

'Finally, Bob, let's rewind to your youth. As a teenager you tuned the family radiogram in to your favourite shows and on Saturday nights the big date for you and millions of other kids was *Pick Of The Pops*. You were such a fan that for your fifteenth birthday your mother wrote in to the show for a dedication.'

As if the evening had not been amazing enough, now here was David Jacobs, my original inspiration. 'I was delighted to give you your first-ever mention on the radio, Bob,' David said as he joined us on the stage, my mother waving from the audience. It was such a huge moment for her and she just could not contain herself in the excitement of it all. As the applause died down, her voice came ringing across the studio like a bell. 'Oh, David, I'm your greatest fan!'

'The Harris's are a bit of an item in your life,' commented Michael Aspel.

'Well, really I know his mother better than I know Bob,' David replied. 'You see, she's been one of my regular correspondents. But it wasn't until you joined Radio 2, Bob, that I realized that your mother was *my* Mrs Harris. I'm sure she is very proud of you, as should all of your family be, because your dedication to music and radio is absolutely incredible. So for heaven's sake just keep on doing what you do so well and always let us have "Whispering Bob" with us.'

After he had read out that first dedication all those years ago my Mum had written to David again, thanking him for mentioning me and complimenting him on the music he was playing on his show. Like the gentleman he was, David wrote back, exchanging thoughts about music and the radio, which my Mum loved so much, and that triggered a correspondence between the two of them that had spanned more than four decades. Yet, despite the longevity of their relationship, this was the first time they had actually met. It was a dream come true and my most vivid memory from that glorious evening is of my Mum looking as happy and animated as she had for years, sitting with my Dad, chatting with David at the after-show party. And what a party it was, lasting way into the early hours, a gathering of all the people who were special in my life. I felt so happy that my parents were able to be there to share the evening with me.

It was particularly poignant for the fact that my Dad's health was beginning to fade. It was, as it turned out, the last major event he was able attend. He died a few months later, at the Queen Elizabeth Hospital in King's Lynn. I was with him when he passed away. It's so hard to think about it now, remembering those final hours as I sat watching him at his bedside, listening to his shallow breathing getting weaker and weaker as life slowly drained from him. We had become very close in his later years and I knew he was very proud of me. I was certainly proud of him. He was a lovely man; contented, relaxed, intelligent and philosophical, with a calm strength and a generosity of spirit I deeply admired.

His death was a devastating blow to my Mum, from which she never really recovered. She had built her whole life around him and she found it almost impossible to cope on her own. She felt so isolated, lonely and unhappy it was heart breaking. I regularly drove from Oxfordshire to Norfolk to see her, staying at the sweet Le Strange Arms Hotel just outside of Hunstanton, overlooking the sand banks on the North Norfolk coastline. I got to know the hotel and the staff there very well and the visits provided me with welcome breaks, suspending me from my always busy schedule. It was lovely to walk with my Mum along the windswept promenade at Hunstanton or sit in her garden and talk but I never felt I was able to be with her for long enough and I hated leaving her alone.

Eventually she, Trudie and I decided it would be best if she came to live with us, and the children were all in agreement, particularly my daughter Emily, who was always very close to her Nana and Papa. The move was a massive upheaval but for a while Mum rallied, enjoying the hustle and bustle of our busy lives. I was installing my new studio at the bottom of the garden with help from my former wife Sue's partner Dixie and Mum would occasionally wander down to see us, sometimes bringing us egg and bacon sandwiches and cups of tea to keep us going as we laid the carpet, put up the shelving and sorted my CD and vinyl collection back into alphabetical order. She even briefly joined Miles, Dylan and Flo one afternoon for a game of tennis on the lawn. But the Indian summer didn't last. She was missing my Dad terribly and, as her health deteriorated, I knew it was the worst possible sign when she stopped listening to her beloved radio. A short time later she was admitted to the John Radcliffe Hospital in Oxford, where she died on 27th September 2005. She was buried next to my Dad in the Northampton cemetery on 11th October, two days before what would have been her ninetieth birthday.

My links with my home town have lessened since my parents passed away and I rarely go back there now (apart from very occasional visits to Sixfields Stadium to watch the Northampton Town football team navigate the ups and downs of Division 2), so imagine my delight and amazement when, out of the blue, I was invited to receive an Honorary Fellowship by the University of Northampton, joining 2,000 students for a week of graduations in the summer of 2007. Trudie, Miles, Dylan and Flo all came with me and the ceremony was also attended by flamboyant fashion designer Zandra Rhodes, who collected an honorary doctorate wearing an outfit of vibrant pink and orange, a glorious distraction as I began my acceptance speech.

'This is somewhat ironic,' I observed as I addressed the students. 'It's a very happy surprise to be here considering I left school under a large cloud. I was spotted by one of my teachers drinking half a lager shandy at a pub during the summer holidays and was sent to see the head teacher. I was seventeen and a half and it felt like I was being unfairly treated. I just handed in my books and stormed out, without really thinking what I was going to do after that. Today is testament to the support I got from my parents, who really backed me when I walked out of school with virtually no qualifications.'

I received the Fellowship in the middle of a run of accolades that has become both mind-blowing and humbling. In 2002 I was awarded a Gold Badge by the British Academy of Composers and Songwriters. Twelve months later, the UK Radio Academy acknowledged my 'outstanding contribution to British radio'. In 2004 I was voted 'International Broadcaster of the Year' by the Country Music Association in Nashville, a massive honour that was repeated when I was presented with the award again in 2013 by the wonderful Little Big Town in the full glare of the television crews lining the red carpet at the CMA Awards. I also received the 'Wesley Rose International Media Achievement Award' from the Country Music Association in 2012, following Taylor Swift onto the podium. I was inducted into the British Country Music Association Hall of Fame in 2012, the Radio Academy Hall of Fame in 2009 and our WBBC documentaries *The Day John Met Paul* and *The Sandy Denny Story* both won Silver at the Sony's, in 2008 and 2009 respectively.

Then, in 2014, I received perhaps the greatest accolade of all when I was chosen to join Kirsty Young as a castaway on *Desert Island Discs* on BBC Radio 4, a major ambition realized. I gave great consideration to my musical choices, eventually settling on a list of tracks that resonated most closely with important moments in my life. The list is as follows.

1. Mark Germino 'Rex Bob Lowenstein' from the album *Caught In The Act Of Being Ourselves*, a brilliant song about a free-form DJ, first played on the radio by the late Roger Scott
2. Robert Plant & Alison Krauss 'Gone Gone Gone' from the *Raising Sand* album, so important in my life
3. Paul Anka 'Diana', my first-time buy
4. Love 'Alone Again' from the *Forever Changes* album, given to me by John Peel
5. Neil Young 'Cinnamon Girl', the first track I played on the radio, on *Sounds Of The 70s* in August 1970
6. Dick Stratton 'Music City USA', the first song on the soundtrack of the film *Bob Harris: My Nashville*
7. Kacey Musgraves 'Merry Go Round' from her album *Same Trailer, Different Park*, chosen to represent the refreshing surge of young energy that has burst into the country music scene
8. Ben E. King 'Stand By Me', my all-time favourite record

For my book choice, I managed to persuade Kirsty and the production team to allow me to take a massive file of cricket statistics onto the island with me and for my luxury item I chose a greenhouse, in which to indulge my passion for gardening, a neglected pursuit I wish I had more time for.

I am a notorious workaholic but I am fortunate in that I absolutely love what I do. My professional world is a very creative place and I am extremely motivated to establish WBBC as a self-sufficient and successful production house able to provide a secure future for Trudie and my family, an ambition that has become a priority and a driving force in my life. Running a family business is not always easy, particularly in the ultra-competitive environments of radio and television. Our schedule is sometimes relentlessly demanding and holidays are a rarity but we are an amazingly productive team, willing to push ourselves to the limit. We set very high standards but I am a great believer that you get back what you put in. 'And in the end, the love you take, is equal to the love you make' as the Beatles put it.

Nevertheless, there are times when even I am amazed at our ability to sustain our high-intensity schedule, as a quick glance at my diary for early 2011 demonstrates; an awesome mix of work and pleasure.

My first studio session of the year was on the 4th January at Western House, pre-recording my Radio 2 weekend show, containing a beautiful, mellow session with a band called The Low Anthem from Providence, Rhode Island, whose album *Oh My God, Charlie Darwin* was one of my favourites at the time. It was the first of fourteen shows I built and broadcast that month. The following morning I was back in London to do some location filming with Sky Arts before returning to Western House to pre-record the first of a new series of programmes for the three-hour Friday night slot I had just inherited from Mark Lamarr. Starting a new series is always a special moment and I'd spent hours crafting a diverse playlist of UK artists with tracks ranging from vintage Pink Floyd and Deep Purple to Kate Rusby, Lonnie Donegan, Cherry Ghost, Paul Weller and The Damned. Once the show was in the can, I walked to Wardour Street where I ended my working day in a voice-over studio recording an ad for Virgin Atlantic.

A couple of days later, Miles and I drove to Manchester to link up with our friend Clive Tyldsley, who was commentating on the United versus Liverpool third round FA Cup tie for ITV. We'd been really looking forward to this and made sure we arrived in time to sit in on a fascinating early morning production meeting before Clive took us backstage at Old Trafford to meet some of the United legends, a very cool experience indeed. It was an absolute pleasure to be introduced to the warm and sincere Paddy Crerand, with whom Miles chatted for maybe fifteen or twenty minutes, and we were briefly in the same room as Sir Bobby Charlton, my all-time sporting hero. We even stood in the tunnel watching Sir Alex Ferguson and Kenny Dalglish give their pre-match television interviews although, judging by the looks he kept giving us, Sir Alex was not best pleased to see us in this hallowed place, particularly when the Liverpool assistant manager Sammy Lee came over to tell me how much he enjoyed my country show!

Then, a few moments later, we were walking in the footsteps of giants, as Clive took us out of the tunnel into the stadium and onto the edge of the pitch, a tingle running down my spine as we took in the awesome pre-match atmosphere generating from the stands all around us. With the fans of both teams in full voice, the decibel level was higher than a rock concert and we were happy to take some sharp, shouted banter as we walked past the managers' dug-out in front of the crowd before climbing the flight of steps that leads into the heart of the South Stand and right up into the roof of the building, where we negotiated our way across the narrow, precarious little walkway that drops down into the television gantry situated high above the 76,000 crowd. The view up there was absolutely incredible, taking in the panorama of the entire ground and beyond, a privileged vantage point from which to watch United's hard fought 1–0 win secured by a third minute Ryan Giggs penalty.

I love watching football and I still enjoy the simple pleasure of kicking a ball around in the garden with Miles and Dylan but cricket is also a major sporting passion and I was honoured to take part in the glorious *Voices Of Summer* programme on BBC Radio 5-Live, celebrating the work of some of the greatest broadcasters of all time, and to be invited to Lords as a lunchtime 'View From The Boundary' guest on *Test Match Special* on the first Saturday of the Test series against the West Indies in May 2012, joining the peerless Jonathan Agnew in the commentary box. Miles was with me there too, and it was a pleasure to introduce him to David Gower, whom I'd not seen for many years. We also bumped into Mark Butcher who, as well as being an outstanding international batsman, is also a fine musician. He's even played a session on my radio show.

Everyone was keen for Miles and I to stay on and join them for lunch – and I couldn't imagine anything more enjoyable – but we had to leave immediately after the broadcast. As coincidence would have it, our friends Sara and Saul were getting married later that same afternoon, way on the other side of Oxfordshire, and Miles was due to be filming the ceremony. We legged it out of Lords, jumped into the car, hurtled down the M40 and somehow made it to the church on time, just as the first guests were beginning to arrive. One or two of the old boys in the congregation were amazed to see me there. 'Didn't we just hear you on *Test Match Special*?' they asked, incredulously.

We'd also had to leave Old Trafford in a hurry too, after our day with Clive Tyldsley. Trudie and I had two important meetings in London early the following morning, the first of which was at Cancer Research UK. Tom Jones had just confirmed his appearance at the 2011 Sound and Vision evening and additionally we were planning a huge Race Day event at Silverstone, working with the endearing and charismatic

Stephanie Moore, widow of the former England football captain Bobby Moore. Bobby died of bowel cancer in 1993 since when Stephanie has tirelessly dedicated her life to the Bobby Moore fund, a charity that has raised nearly £19m and funded more than fifty research programmes into the disease that killed her husband at the age of just fifty-one. I have huge respect for Stephanie and the important work she does. She is a truly special person and it was an honour to become part of her team.

Our second meeting of the day was with my producer Mark Simpson and editor Neil Myners to discuss what proved to be one of the most enjoyable projects I have ever been involved with. Entitled *OGWT 40*, it was a major WBBC series for Radio 2 marking the fortieth anniversary of the *Old Grey Whistle Test*.

The first *Whistle Test* was broadcast on BBC 2 in September 1971, running from then until 1987, and we were working to recreate the ethos of the programme across sixteen one-hour shows, each one celebrating a year of *Whistle Test* history. The organization was a massive undertaking and Trudie and Miles were joined in our WBBC office by the indispensible Steph Punfield and Miles's beautiful girlfriend Catherine Snell, who worked with us through most of the twelve months it took to put it all together.

To help us capture the original atmosphere, we commandeered the famous Maida Vale Studio 3, the BBC equivalent of Abbey Road, where we hosted more than 120 artists and bands. The tone was set at the beginning of the first programme with original archive appearances by David Bowie, who performed 'Five Years', 'Keep On Keeping On' by Curtis Mayfield, introduced by the first *Whistle Test* presenter Richard Williams and 'Under My Wheels' by Alice Cooper, with whom I reminisced about that first-ever UK television performance and our subsequent meeting in LA in 1974, where he took Mike Appleton and I into the weird and rather wonderful world of a private room at the Rainbow Bar and Grill, a notorious late-night hang out on Sunset Strip. Alice was in full make up and garb, the place was absolutely rocking and I couldn't believe the crazy madness of the West Hollywood night-lifers who surrounded him.

'It was the lair of the vampires,' he recalled. 'Bernie Taupin was there that night, Keith Moon also, probably Harry Nilsson. It was a last-man-standing drinking club and you did very well, Bob, as I recall! The first thing I learned when I got to LA was how to drink all night, because when you were out with Jim Morrison and those guys you had to know how to drink! But then Jim, Janis Joplin, Hendrix ... all the guys we used to hang out with were all dying aged 27 years old. What it said to me was if you're going to have an image as strong as Alice Cooper you can't live that image off-stage, because that's what killed all those guys.'

The first *OGWT 40* also featured a beautiful new acoustic session with Yusuf Islam, who played 'Trouble' and 'Road Singer' and a heart-warming interview with Elton John. 'It was the show to do,' he told me. 'The forerunner of *Later ... With Jools Holland* and having looked again at the DVDs it was archive, historic footage. It was part of a pantheon of great television music shows – *Oh Boy!*, *Ready Steady Go!*, *The Old Grey Whistle Test* ... those programmes stand the test of time.'

It was exciting to record new interviews and 'in the round' sessions for the series with a cast-list of artists and friends that reads like a who's who of rock'n'roll history. In addition to Elton and Alice, Brian May, Peter Frampton, Emmylou Harris, Jackson Browne (who bought Dawes and Jonathan Wilson to Maida Vale with him), Roger Daltrey, Rab Noakes, Jim Kerr, Mark Knopfler, Kiki Dee, Joan Armatrading, John Ottway, John Hiatt, Thomas Dolby, Robin Hitchcock, Andy Partridge, Rod Argent, Russ Ballard, Colin Blunstone, Thijs van Leer, Iain Matthews, Andy Roberts, Steve Harley, Greg Allman, Greg Lake, Steve Hackett, Deborah Harry, Chris Difford and Glenn Tilbrook, Gordin Giltrap, Ralph McTell, Randy Newman, Billy Bragg, Hazel O'Connor, Wilko Johnson, Thin Lizzy, Bob Geldof, Judie Tzuke, Ian Anderson, Chuck Prophet, Jack Bruce, Fish, Loudon Wainwright, Gang of Four, Clare Grogan, Roger Hodgson, Paul Rodgers, Paul Young, Nick Lowe, Midge Ure, Chris Rea, Dave Stewart, Robert Plant and many more joined us for this amazing reunion, as did *Whistle Test* producer Mike Appleton, film-maker Ian Emes and almost all of the presenters of the original show – Mark Ellen, David Hepworth, Andy Kershaw, Richard Skinner and Ro Newton. It's a sensational list. Eric Brace recorded a new version of the theme tune 'Stone Fox Chase' for us in East Nashville with his band Last Train Home, featuring the original harmonica player Charlie McCoy, and the announcement of the series even made the front page of *The Times*.

I will always be grateful to *Whistle Test* for catapulting me into the centre of the music world I love and creating a legacy I am proud of to this day. Of the many incredible experiences it brought into my life, perhaps the most exciting of all was the three days Mike Appleton and I spent with John Lennon in New York in 1975 to record an interview for a *Whistle Test* special, for which he filmed exclusive versions of 'Slippin' and Slidin'' and my all-time favourite song 'Stand By Me'. John saw the moment as a way of sending a postcard from America to his estranged young son, who he knew would be watching back home in the UK, so it was an honour to close the series with an emotional full-circle performance of the song by Julian Lennon, particularly poignant for the fact that his mother Cynthia was in the studio with us too, her husband Noel Charles at her side. It was a wonderful and fitting moment, in keeping with the four months we spent at Maida Vale making the *OGWT 40* series, one of the most fulfilling and creative times of my career. But 2011 wasn't over yet.

On 7th May, the postman delivered his usual sack full of post – a handful of letters wrapped with an elastic band among the mountain of parcels and packages that had arrived from across the Globe. I receive approximately 200 CDs every week from artists, managers and record labels and it is a source of stress to me that I receive far more than I have ever got time to listen to. I know that whoever has sent me this latest recording is counting on me to listen to it and maybe play it on the radio, but there are only twenty-four hours in a day and it is literally impossible to keep up with the expectation.

Selecting the music to listen to from the never-ending supply is a tried and trusted mix of intuition and subjectivity. Not surprisingly, I prioritise releases from artists I like and I also look at the sleeve credits to check the names of producers and backing musicians. I'll take more notice of a record sent by someone whose opinion I value and there are certain labels I always trust, like Bella Union, Six Shooter, New West, Nonesuch, Sugar Hill and Rounder. I know that anything on Big Machine is going to have huge mainstream potential, and so it goes on. I'll follow links to downloads too, but that's a much less personal route. It is impossible to replicate the 'feel' of a physical copy and sometimes I just get a vibe from the look of an album, something about the design or the atmosphere that compels me to put it in the machine.

It was with all this in mind that I was sorting through the parcels when one of the small batch of letters caught my eye. It looked official and interesting and when I opened it I could scarcely believe what I was reading.

'The Prime Minister has asked me to inform you, in strict confidence, that he has in mind, on the occasion of the forthcoming list of New Year's honours to submit your name to the Queen with a recommendation that Her Majesty may be graciously pleased to approve that you be appointed an Officer of the Order of the British Empire for services to music broadcasting.'

An OBE! I had to go through the letter again to make sure I hadn't misread it and to say I was flabbergasted is an understatement. To this day I'm still in the process of trying to connect it with me, because I still have a feeling of not being worthy in any way. It is a massive honour, one that came to me as a result of doing something I love.

I replied immediately accepting the invitation and soon received a follow-up letter from St James's Palace which began: 'I am commanded to inform you that an Investiture will be held at Windsor Castle on Thursday 20th October 2011 at which your attendance is requested. You may bring three guests to watch the ceremony.'

Obviously, one of the guests would be Trudie but who else should I take? However much I wished to have all my children there with me, only two could attend. It was a tough call and I didn't want anyone to feel disappointed, so I knew that the selection process had to be totally democratic. After much thought, I decided on an FA Cup-style draw. I typed out the names Miri, Emily, Charlie, Ben, Jamie, Miles, Dylan and Flo in capital letters onto separate squares of identically sized paper, each of which I folded several times out of sight of anyone before putting them all into the large gold Himalayan cowbell (a present from our friend Sara), which I keep in the studio. Before Neil Myners and I began our *OGWT 40* editing that day, I filmed him as he closed his eyes, reached into the bell and pulled out two pieces of paper, which we carefully unfolded on to the mixing desk. The first name we saw was CHARLIE, the second name was MILES.

The lead up to the investiture was busy and exciting. Four days earlier I'd been in Nashville, where I'd become only the third ever recipient (following Nanci Griffith and Lyle Lovett) of the prestigious Trailblazer Award at the Americana Music Awards, presented to me by

Emmylou Harris, an honour that was almost as important to me as my OBE, as I explained in my acceptance speech. 'To get such an award on the stage of the Ryman Auditorium, the Mother Church of Country Music, is amazing,' I said. 'Being accepted and acknowledged by the music community I love and respect so much is very special.'

I'd got back from Nashville absolutely buzzing and had pitched straight back into work. Neil and I were still editing *OGWT 40* programmes the day before the investiture and while we were in the studio, Trudie and our WBBC film director Luke Jeans were attending an important appointment at Sky Arts, a meeting that confirmed our coverage of the Cropredy Festival for the channel the following summer. So I was in celebratory mood, if slightly jet-lagged, when Charlie arrived later that afternoon to prepare for the big day that followed. She was pregnant and I was so happy to see her looking glowing and radiant.

The next morning we were all up at the crack of dawn to get ourselves ready before the arrival of the chauffer-driven car Trudie had organized for the day. The journey along the M4 was mercifully smooth, so we arrived at Windsor in good time to take in the sights. The setting was absolutely perfect: the sky was a cloudless blue and the castle looked imposing and magnificent in the shimmering autumn sunshine as we walked up the long drive and into the quadrangle in front of the state apartments, seeing the Queen's private residence to the right. On entering the castle, I was separated from Trudie, Charlie and Miles, who were taken to the grand Waterloo Chamber to await the ceremony while I was led to a vestry deep in the heart of the building, joining the other recipients to await instructions. The Central Chancery of the Orders of Knighthood, which is a branch of the Lord Chamberlain's Office, is responsible for the staging of each investiture, and the organization was an awesome timetable of pomp and precision.

After a detailed briefing, all the recipients were escorted through the ornate and opulent state rooms to the door of the Waterloo Chamber, where we formed an orderly queue to wait for the ceremony to begin at eleven o'clock sharp. Her Royal Highness the Princess Royal was conducting the Investiture and I felt a huge surge of excitement as the orchestra from the Household Division struck up the National Anthem, announcing her arrival in the Chamber. I'd been playing this scene through in my head for months and the sense of anticipation was almost overwhelming as I stepped forward into the Chamber, trying to remember all the instructions I'd been given. As I approached the dias on which the Princess Royal was standing I stopped and bowed my head then stepped forward and stood in front of her while she put the medal into the clip that had been pinned to my lapel. I'd been told not to speak until spoken to, but as I stepped back she looked at me and smiled.

'I thought you were in Nashville,' she said. I was stunned that she even knew.

'I was, Your Royal Highness,' I replied. 'I've just got back!'

'You were there for the Americana Awards,' she added. I looked at her quizzically, thinking that maybe she'd been briefed. 'I listen to your country show,' she explained.

This was amazing news and as I relaxed, we talked for a few moments about the Tennessee stud, of all things. Then she stood back, shook my hand and the moment was over. I left the Waterloo Chamber almost bursting with pride, imagining what my parents would have thought if they could have been there to witness one of the most beautiful and important events of my life.

I couldn't wait to be reunited with Trudie, Charlie and Miles for the photographs and interviews that followed. Charlie told me afterwards that as Princess Anne presented me with my insignia, she had felt her baby kick for the first time – an amazing moment. I didn't want us to break away from this incredible experience but finally we made our way back to the car and headed to our favourite restaurant, The White Hart in Fyfield in Oxfordshire, where I was engulfed by my family and my friends for one of the best parties ever.

Trudie is probably the greatest party organizer in the world. Three years after the spectacular *This Is Your Life* evening, she had staged a sixtieth birthday bash for me at Lains Barn in the Oxfordshire countryside, a party so enjoyable that it is still talked about and fondly remembered by everyone who attended. Larry LeBlanc had flown over from Toronto, Alan Messer had made the journey from Nashville, as had Tia McGraff and her husband Tommy Parham. Johnnie Beerling was there, sharing memories with Jeff Griffin, his wife Rita and radio producer Kevin Howlett. Miles had his best mates Ben Granville and Doug Booker with him, Dylan and Flo pretended to play giant inflatable guitars, messing around with their friends Toby and Ben Barnard on the lawn outside the venue, while The Storys played an acoustic set for the people who were arriving. The music set the tone perfectly and it was wonderful to see everyone looking so happy.

The party was 60s themed and, with two major exceptions, everybody had come dressed in appropriately fab gear. Trudie and Marie were wearing identical Mary Quant mini-dresses, Trudie sporting a black wig, Marie a blonde wig. There were Mods, Beatle outfits, outrageous leopard skin prints and, notably, a 1966 full England World Cup-winning football strip, worn by Neil Myners. Janice Long, Sally Boazman, PR boss Gabby Green and my friend and agent June Ford-Crush were flower girls, Steve Wright and Johnnie Walker looked like something from the *Sgt. Pepper* album sleeve, songwriter Gary Osborne was wearing a flamboyant silver velvet jacket and Trudie's long-time friend Fiona Ronaldson wore crushed velvet. I went in character as an old hippie. Wearing beads, bells, purple loons and a stupid long blond wig, I looked like a cross between Jerry Garcia and Willie Nelson.

Trudie had commissioned a specially designed cake with an exact reproduction of my original 78 rpm version of 'Diana' by Paul Anka etched into icing that was beginning to melt from the heat of the lighted candles. As I bent over to blow them out, a flame touched my wig, setting it on fire, briefly threatening disaster before a handily placed soda siphon came to my rescue. It was a ridiculous moment, captured brilliantly in a stand-up speech by comic and broadcaster Mark Lamarr: 'I always thought the 60s was the promiscuous decade, the era of free love,' he joked. 'But how any of you ever got a fuck looking like that is beyond me!'

Mark was one of the two people not in fancy dress that night. The other was Robert Plant. It was my fault, I'm afraid. I'd forgotten to tell them! Not that it mattered, as Robert got up onstage to add the sound of his stunning electric guitar playing and vocals to the beat of the massive blues jam session that rounded off the evening with a line-up that additionally featured Steve Balsamo and The Storys, Belfast singer songwriter Brian Houston, Thea Gilmore and her husband Nigel Stonier, the great Bernie Marsden from Whitesnake and Martyn Joseph, who had bought me a beautiful SXI Panther cricket bat as a sixtieth birthday present.

Martyn and I have known each other now for almost a quarter of a century and our friendship continues to grow. He is a true artist, recognized worldwide as a performer of rare talent, courage, warmth and dedication, and I was very proud when he invited me to become Patron of his Let Yourself Trust, a project-based initiative that he founded with his charismatic partner Justine. The Trust is a labour of love, designed to pull together the threads of his humanitarian endeavours, work for which he was given an Amnesty International award in 2002. Martyn is a genuine force for good in the world and the warmth between us somehow sums up my feelings as I come towards the end of writing this book. I have been massively fortunate that my work and my life have taken me to places that most could only dream of, yet, underpinning all of those experiences, has been the sharing of them with the people who made them so special.

Central to so much of what has happened over the past few years has been my country producer Al Booth, now Head of Specialist Music at Radio 2. We began to get to know each other at approximately the same time as the first edition of this book was published, when Dave Shannon took her to Nashville to work with us on the coverage of the CMA Awards in 2001, and she has been one of the most important people in my life ever since. She is strong, funny and incredibly perceptive and I would trust her with my life. She is part of the superb and professional team at Radio 2 that oversee my programmes and I am indebted to Bob Shennan, Mark Simpson, Mark Hagen and Janine Mayer-Smith for the fantastic support they give me and to Maria Byrne for adding to the soundtrack of our lives.

However, although my work is still very important to me, my family is my stability and it is impossible to adequately express the love I have for them.

My son Miles is now twenty-two and I am in awe of him. His drive and work ethic are second to none and he has a skill set I can only envy. We work together in my studio, producing the acoustic *Under The Apple Tree* sessions we post on our website and YouTube channel, and Miles is cameraman, lighting engineer and sound mixer, creating the beautiful films he edits so skilfully. He has recently worked on videos with Mollie Marriott, Deborah Rose and Scott Matthews and is a go-to filmmaker for Cancer Research UK. He was also the editor of the much-praised *Back To Beth's* house concert shown on BBC 4 in November 2014. Miles is still with his beautiful girlfriend, Catherine Snell, who we all adore. She has a warm and happy spirit and brings light and laughter into our lives.

Dylan's three-month stay in America and his exciting multi-country European adventure in 2014 have further fuelled his desire to see as much of the world as possible and he is currently saving for his next major project, an animal conservation trip to South Africa and Botswana in the summer. He is a people person, a knowledgeable and engaging conversationalist, and I love the chats we have together. His warm and sunny disposition is wonderful to behold. 'You have a gift,' Cynthia Lennon told him recently. 'Make sure you use it.' I know he will.

Flo loves her music and has been to more than twenty gigs and festivals in the past year, including The Radio 1 Big Weekend in Glasgow, One Direction at Wembley Stadium (she still hasn't met them yet!), Taylor Swift at O2, Paulo Nutini and Ed Sheeran in the Live Lounge and Justin Timberlake at the BBC Radio Theatre, where I introduced her to Sara Cox and Scott Mills. Flo and I have also forged a great friendship with Radio 1 DJ Greg James, a genuinely lovely person and one of the brightest and most naturally talented broadcasters I've heard for many years. Flo and I are very alike and we always seem to be in sync with one another, a lovely feeling.

Miri and her family are about to move to Brighton, where she will continue her nursing work. Her husband Graeme runs a garden landscaping company, which he plans to transport to East Sussex with them. Marnie is currently pondering the options of University, Alana is approaching her A level exams and Olivia is a bright, thriving, feisty seven-year-old, absolutely doted on by her proud dad.

Emily is the Harris organizer. She is the one everybody in the family calls upon because she is kind, sympathetic and caring. Like her mum, she devotes much of her life to looking after others and is a care worker at a special needs school in Camden. She lives in North London with her husband John and their three daughters Niamh who is now fourteen, Ysobel who is eleven and Eliza who is four.

Charlie followed me into the music industry and after two years at MTV was head hunted across into PR, working with Midas, Omnibus Press and Music Sales, looking after authors and organizing their promotion and publicity schedule, so she knows exactly where I am in my writing process right now. A few months after she came to my Investiture at Windsor Castle she gave birth to a beautiful little girl, the adorable Lola Mae, who is now three years old. So, I have seven grandchildren, all of them girls, and my eldest granddaughter, Marnie, is older than my youngest daughter, Flo, who is her auntie. It's a mind-boggling thought.

Ben also tried the music industry for a while, co-hosting a brilliantly eclectic cutting-edge radio show called *Beltdriven* with Paul McCarthy for Radio Reverb in Brighton, before following his mother Valentina's footsteps and becoming a chef, founding a catering company called 'Bepino's'. Like his mother, Ben can also write and I have a feeling that one day he will make writing his passion. Meanwhile, Jamie is busy working with Miri's husband Graeme, applying his awesome physical strength and natural athleticism to the heavy demands of a landscape gardening business.

I have a close-knit family and Trudie is the foundation of everything, the rock upon which my whole life is built, and I am so fortunate she has chosen to spend her life with me. She is an incredible, dynamic force – a loving, loyal wife, mother, manager, company director ... it's a hell of a lot of relationships to keep together and sometimes I wonder how she does it all but my absolute certainty is that I love her more than words can say. When everything is good with Trudie, everything is good with the world.

The most important thing to me is that everyone is well. I am healthy too and I still maintain the fitness regime that helps me sustain the busy pace of my life. As I write, *Bob Harris Country* has just been nominated in the 'Best Radio Show' category at the *Music Week* Awards and I am just about to launch the digital radio service 'BBC Radio 2 Country', which runs for the four days of the spectacular 'Country 2 Country' Festival at the O2, where I will be multi-tasking. As well as hosting our WBBC *Under The Apple Tree* sessions that will showcase Kimmie Rhodes, Ward Thomas and Katie Armiger, I will be compering on the main stage and joining my Radio 2 colleagues Patrick Kielty, Alex Lester and Jo Whiley to broadcast live backstage interviews and sessions with all the major stars, after which I join Eric Brace and his wife Mary Ann for a seven-day break in North Carolina, which I think I'm going to need!

My brush with cancer has taught me to live in the moment and despite the fact that I am seventy next year I still have the energy to put my heart and soul into everything I do. You can follow my daily life via Twitter, a social medium I have enthusiastically embraced @ WhisperingBob and we also have a WBBC account @WBBCOfficial.

I am still driven by my work, am surrounded by people who care and I love the life I live. I am very lucky and blessed to be still whispering after all these years.

ACKNOWLEDGEMENTS

Heartfelt thanks to Louise Dixon and everyone at Michael O'Mara Books for their fantastic support and belief in me; to Cynthia Lennon, Eric Brace and Mary Ann Werner for allowing me the space to complete some of the writing; to the Nashville music community for the joy you bring; to Radio 2 for giving me the freedom to play the music I love; to my listeners for sharing it all with me; and to my family for being the bedrock of my life. I love you very much.

PICTURE CREDITS

All photographs courtesy of the author, except:

Section 1
Page 3   Above Alan Messer/REX
                Below Dezo Hoffmann/REX
Page 4   Both Alan Messer/REX
Page 5   Above Alan Messer/REX

Section 2
Pages 2–3   All photographs Miles Myerscough-Harris
Page 8   Bottom Chris Ison/WPA Pool/Getty Images

INDEX

Unattributed subheadings refer to Bob Harris

Fleetwood Mac 188
Fogerty, John 211
'Fooled Around And Fell In Love' (Elvin Bishop) 96
Ford, Gerald 94
Forever Changes (Love) 28
Forte Di Marmi, Italy 131
Foster, Charles 143, 151, 157, 179
Fowler, Bill 75, 82
Fox, Barry 147
Fox, Samantha 142
Fox, Tony 146, 160, 179
'Frankenstein' (Edgar Winter) 59
Franklin, Aretha 82
Free (band) 72, 133
Freed, Audley 173, 218
Freeman, Alan 54, 165
Freeman, David 137
Friends (magazine) 35
'From Me To You' (Lennon and McCartney) 16
Fulham FC 185

Garden Cricket Club 134, 136
Garland, Judy 71
Geffen, David 48
Geldof, Bob 142
Gentry, Bobby 213
Germino, Mark 116, 175
Gerry House Show 195
'Get Together' (Jesse Colin Young) 80
Gibb brothers 113, 252, 254 *see also* Bee Gees, The
Gibraltar 154, 157
Gillett, Charlie 181
Gilmour, Dave 161
Glasgow Herald 50
Glass, Dave 127
Gleason scale 222
Godard, Jean-Luc 15
Godspell 139
'Going Down' (Don Nix) 189
Golding, John 68
Good, Jack 11–12
'Good Time' (The Beach Boys) 62
'Goodnight My Love' (Jessie Belvin) 127
Gorton, Ted 134, 137
Gotch, Tarquin 107, 133
Gough Square 145
Gower, David 140–1, 265
Graceland 111
Gracey, Joe 207
Grand Ole Opry 202, 209, 215
Grant, Peter 84
Gray, David 250
Great Ormond Street Hospital 148, 229

Great Western Valkyrie (The Rival Sons) 201
Greater London Radio (GLR) 180–4, 189, 190, 250
Green, Derek 102
Green, Jonathan 35
Green, Peter 188–9
'Green Manalishi' (Fleetwood Mac) 189
Greenwich Village 209
Greyhound pub, Fulham 66
Griffin, Jeff 35–40, 42, 53, 72, 75, 78, 81, 82, 84, 89, 153, 159, 166, 256
Grossman, Albert 97
Grundig tape machines 18
Grundy, Stuart 154, 158, 163
Guardian 171
Guildford Festival 188
Gulf War 163
GWR (commercial radio station) 141–2, 180

Haddon Hall 64
Hagen, Mark 201, 210, 215
Hall, Colin 230, 238
Hall, John 40, 41
Hall, Tom T. 210
Hammersmith Hospital 102
Hammersmith Odeon 91, 93, 137
Hampstead 13–15, 20, 48
Hancock, Butch 207–8
Hands Across The Water 63
Hangtown Dancehall (Eric Brace) 209–10
Harley, Steve 252–3
Harley Davidsons 148–9, 175
Harper, Roy 52–3
Harriman, Ed 147
Harrington, Dee 71
Harris, Ben (son) 136, 139, 140, 153, 190, 275
Harris, Bob *see also* Myerscough-Harris, Trudie (wife), plus children
   EARLY YEARS: buying records 16, 18–20; cinema visits 15; John Peel interview 25–6; listening to the radio 17, 20–1; music clubs 21–5; parents 9–13, 16–18, 25, 51–2; 119, 129, 135–6, 152, 256, 260–1; Police Cadets 10–11; Radio London 27; school 9–10; *Time Out* 30–1, 33–4; Tiranti's 29, 30; writing for magazines 23–5
   ESTABLISHING HIMSELF: disc jockeying 41–2; filming 52–3; first radio programme 43–4; Marquee 49; *Melody Maker* article 54–5; *Monday Programme* 46; playlist 38; Radio 1 research project 35; recording for the first time 39–40; *Roundtable* 54
   FAMILY: *see* individual family members
   HEALTH: legionnaire's disease 117–22; prostate cancer 220–30, 235, 275